Dedicated
to the American spirit,
which has invented
this most courageous,
complex and creative
game to reflect and
to challenge itself.

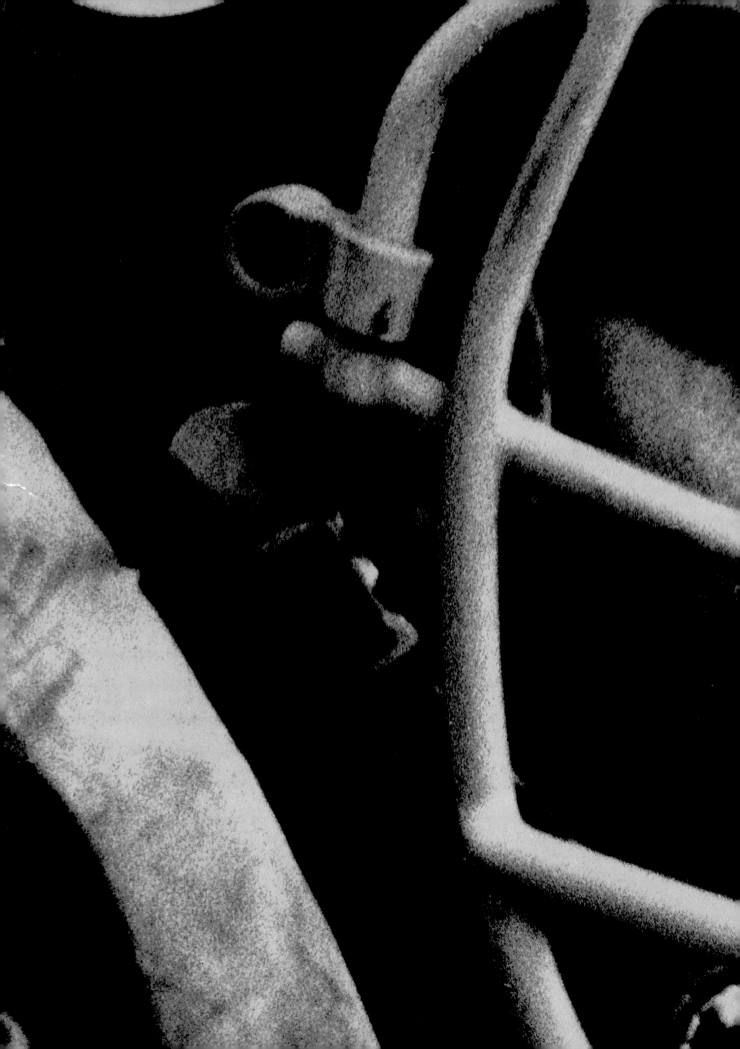

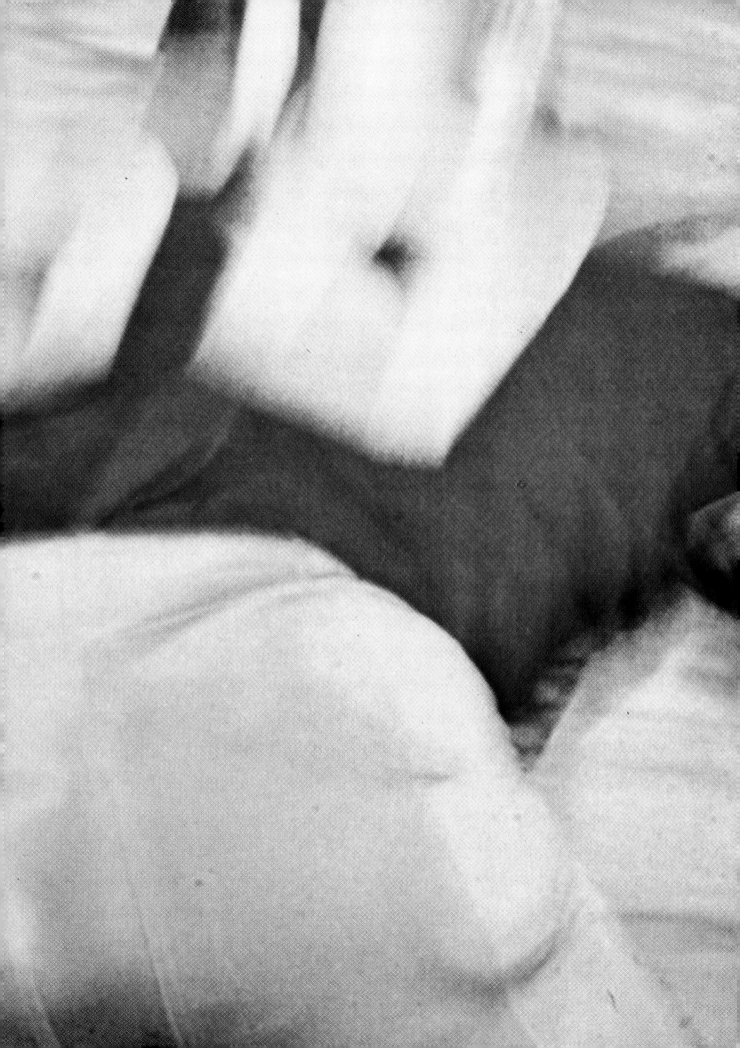

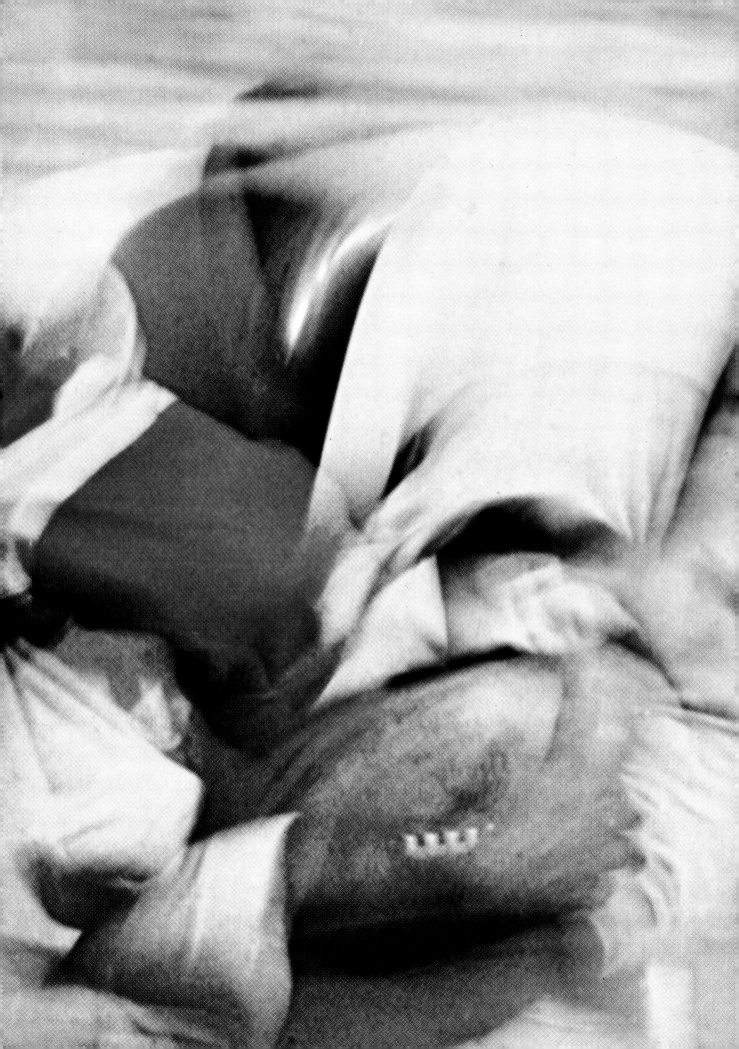

THE FIRST FIFTY YEARS

Prepared and Produced
by the Creative Services Division of
National Football League Properties, Inc.

THE FIRST FIFTY YEARS

A Celebration
of the National Football League
in its Fifty-Sixth Season

A Ridge Press/Benjamin Company Book
Distributed by Simon and Schuster, Inc.

THE FIRST FIFTY YEARS   A Celebration of the National Football League in its Fifty-Sixth Season

Produced by the Creative Services Division
of National Football League Properties, Inc.
Creative Director: David Boss
Editor: Bob Oates, Jr.
Designer: Deanna Glad
Researcher: Steve Taylor
Production: Earl Metter, Tor Benson

Quotation on pages 82-83 from *The Sane Society* by Erich Fromm. © 1955 by Erich Fromm. Reprinted by permission of Holt, Rinehart & Winston, Inc. All rights reserved.

Quotations on pages 66-67 and 80-81 from *The Territorial Imperative* by Robert Ardrey. © 1966 by Robert Ardrey. Reprinted by permission of Atheneum Publishers. All rights reserved.

Quotations on pages 64-65 and 70-71 from *War and Peace in the Global Village* by Marshall McLuhan and Quentin Fiore. © 1968 by Marshall McLuhan, Quentin Fiore and Jerome Agel. By permission of Bantam Books, Inc. All rights reserved.

Quotation on pages 62-63 from *On Aggression* by Konrad Lorenz. © 1966 by Konrad Lorenz. Reprinted by permission of Harcourt, Brace & World. All rights reserved.

Prepared and produced by
National Football League Properties, Inc., 410 Park Avenue, New York, N.Y. 10022
Library of Congress Catalog Card Number 74-77093
ISBN: 671-22189-2
Printed in Italy by Mondadori, Verona

Artists
George Bartell, pages *96-99, 101-131*; Merv Corning, pages *197-208*; Don Weller, pages *33-36*.

Photographers
Vernon Biever *57, 76-77, 148, 149, 181, 182, 183, 185, 187, 242, 243, 245, 248, 249*; Dave Boss *8, 58-59, 60, 61, 65, 72, 73, 76-77, 79, 141, 147, 151, 177, 188, 191, 239, 241, 244, 255*; Malcom Emmons *43, 60, 62-63, 68, 72, 149, 153, 180, 244, 248, 250, 253*; Nate Fine *139, 147*; Paul Fine *10, 42, 44, 46, 49, 50, 74-75, 82-83, 251*; George Gellatley *2, 43, 48*; Ken Hardin *152*; Hall of Fame *1, 134, 135, 136, 137, 139, 141, 142, 145, 161, 166, 212, 213, 216, 217, 218, 219, 223, 224, 227, 232, 234, 236, 240*; Miami Herald *29*; Marvin Newman *237*; Darryl Norenberg *188*; Philadelphia Enquirer *168*; Frank Rippon *146*; Fred Roe *142, 174, 183, 188, 189, 190, 235, 238, 239, 252*; Russ Russell *6, 16, 26, 46, 47, 57, 157, 184, 187, 250, 255*; San Francisco Examiner *179*; Vic Stein *142, 143, 232, 251, 252*; Tony Tomsic *12, 64, 241,* UPI *162, 164, 165, 170, 223*; Bob Verlin *70-71*; Herb Weitman *3, 14, 25, 31, 38, 39, 40, 41, 45, 52, 53, 57, 60, 67, 72, 80-81, 153, 154, 155, 156*; Wide World *138, 140, 144, 167, 175, 178, 224*

CONTENTS

A Game For Our Time

The field is an artificial plain, flat and spare, the focal point of a monumental stadium of concrete and steel. It is an area for war, with the rules and unwritten ethics of classic warring places, and on any autumn Sunday, the field is occupied by two dedicated and disciplined armies. Outfitted in the distinctive armor of the gladiator, twenty-two athletes, eleven to a side, cross the boundaries to test one another in the most primordial manner — hand to hand combat.

Other societies have had their symbolic wars. The gladiator in the arena, the knight at the joust, provided entertainment while performing the skills of battle. In her turn, America has created her own vicarious warfare, nurtured by the technology which is this land's hallmark and tuned to the needs of this people's spirit.

Professional football is basically a physical assault by one team upon another in a desperate fight for land. Most people see themselves as the sum of their possessions — I am what I own. The most basic possession, land, is the issue in football and the most basic weapon, the body, is the means of acquiring it. It is a game of physical dominance; the weak are punished unmercifully and the unskilled are run off the field. So much of a man's personality is at stake that the game becomes a fanatical crusade.

It is a sport which demands unusual dedication. The many men who have tried it and failed have found unmistakably that it takes more than the promise of a pay check to encourage participation. The game challenges a man to discover the very source of his competitive spirit, forcing him through pain, adversity and the despair of defeat. The very difficulty of the game is a call to excellence, an invitation for a man to express himself violently and powerfully while achieving the acclaim of victory.

The professional football player uses the gridiron as a stage, performing with a courage and skill raised above savagery only by the meaningful purpose and inner discipline of civilized man. His is a spectacle of flashing, brutal magnificence and the great stadiums that dot this nation fill with resounding congregations of the American people who create the ebbing, flowing masses of sound through which the game is played.

For the spectators, it is an exhilarating experience. They raise the players into celebrities of the political community, famous leaders who carry the team against the artificial enemy of the city-state. There are marching bands, flags, posters, cheerleaders and community excitement. Victory is the goal, an identification of community excellence. Defeat is gray but temporary, vulnerable to the effort of the succeeding season.

To the winners, the nation is grateful in the ways it knows how. A victorious player attains the success of the American dream: money, recognition, glory, status, acceptance. This gratitude is lavish because the professional athletes occupy an important position in the psyche of an unsettled and generous nation.

A game of varied but elemental excitement, pro football rose to dominance in the 1960s, at a time when the United States experienced a social-political crisis unparalleled in its history. Crowded into increasingly unmanageable cities, governed by a seemingly unreachable bureaucracy, given an unwanted war in Asia and the upheavals of racial and educational

factions at home, distraught by continuing violence and tragedy, the nation fell into a period of introspection its leaders could not assuage. In such a mood, the people turned gratefully to a sport whose driving excitement not only filled certain needs more felt than acknowledged, but did so in patterns well suited to this complex, scientific society.

An examination of the basic factors behind the unrest of the Sixties would yield many answers. But three which are directly relevant to the role of athletics as entertainment can be summed up as loneliness, the lack of challenge, and the revolutionary impact of pop culture.

Loneliness has been partly a paradoxical result of the crowding of people into big urban complexes. The new America of monster cities and exploding technology has cracked society into millions of tiny parts, each man alienated from most others. The human race came from the simple oneness of tribes through the close community of small towns. Now people are almost alone, cut off from their kind by cell-like apartments and insular automobiles. Neighbors are more annoyances than friends' and even the structure of the family has crumbled under the impact of easy travel, easy money, wide education and a swiftly changing society.

From this empty isolation, hundreds of thousands of people escape to the mass fraternity and emotional involvement of a Sunday at a pro football game. Millions more tune in on television, establishing unity with their fellows through common experience and joint hero-worship. A big televised football game is a cross-country talking point, connecting millions the way news of a young boy's first deer used to connect tribal members.

For the players themselves, football is an even more intense solution to loneliness; few human endeavors demand as much cooperation from fifty people. The job is extremely challenging to the individual player, yet his work has an importance which exceeds his own personal drives and desires. He has people who need him and people who help him. The best football teams are the closest teams.

Beyond the sense of unity it provides, professional football also presents exciting challenges to people living routinized lives. Modern man has difficulty finding his meaning and goals because he is cut off from the basics of his own existence. A farmer or hunter, on the other hand, is in touch with his own life. His need for food, water, shelter, and defense are matters of continual concern and personal accomplishment. But in the big city, someone else packages the food, pipes the water and builds the houses. Man is left to search for challenges in a Saran-Wrapped existence.

He finds them on the football field. A football player has but split seconds to solve problems that develop with quick and sudden truthfulness and then he must sacrifice his body to make the solutions work. No one else protects him or does his job. The crisis is immediate and the outcome clear. As the player fights for supremacy, the spectators live through him, forgetting their confusion and boredom in the spectacle of the complex, thrilling and elemental battle.

Professional football, despite these contributions to the sense of community and of challenge, could still not have risen as sharply as it did in the Sixties had it not been in tune with the nation's development of pop culture. Out of semi-commercialized art forms, America discovered a new sense of style, which is to say, America discovered herself. The young market generated its own ideas of taste, structured upon irreverance of established ideas. Nothing had traditional significance. In this ever-widening celebration of discovery, politicians were suddenly confronted with people trying to live in the manner they had always been told was their birthright. These political leaders grew rigid and unyielding, shutting off dialog with their own youth. American business also shrank back, bemused, and then, realizing a bonanza was to be made, reversed its field to cash in on the trend. Money has always been the main motivator in this country but, due to the mass market's new eye for quality, the quest for the dollar has incongruously become a test of sensitivity and integrity.

Art, music and theatre are now commercially plausible cultural forms. The value of today's art lies in the aptitude of its creator and/or performer. Only the artist can raise a given experience to a level of meaningfulness that transcends financial reward for art performed. Culture in the world today is commercial art forms developed by genius. It is this which excites and stimulates a people force-fed a constant diet of merchandised entertainment and draws the line between legitimacy and promotion. It is this which makes the Beatles accredited and Truffaut, Mailer and Dylan the interpreters of our life style.

As America's creators exercised their art forms, an urban population experienced new ways to acknowledge its status as history's best-educated people. Like a kid in a fun house, a 1960s man is either appalled or delighted but always moved by the distortions found in the mirror images artists give him. In the competition with movies, museums, concert halls and stages for the public's attention, professional sport has raced headlong into the problems that result when a nation is emotionally motivated by new and exciting stimuli.

The qualities that had driven sport forward in the Golden Twenties and sustained it over the next three decades were found to be obsolete in the Sixties. Many sports attempted to expand, creating new teams in new cities, but they found that a discriminating public rejected losing teams created from expansion drafts. Only one sport, professional football, grew continuously and soundly, building on the values inherent in the game.

For professional football is an art of its own, a thrilling art, an art against odds. The game is full of opportunities that showcase human daring and accomplishment, the powerful grace of modern dance put to a purpose against a background of impending pain. Accidents happen — a play goes wrong — developing combustible improvisations that galvanize the crowd and create instantaneous heroes. Art is developed from an atavistic spectacle and creates an experience that lures the spectator again and again.

Through the Fifties, Americans were made aware of the pros, but it was in the Sixties that they discovered football as another art form. Despite the fact that it takes money and effort to attend, season ticket buyers made it possible for teams in New York, Baltimore, Washington, Philadelphia, Chicago and Green Bay to hang up sold-out signs before the season began. Other teams in other cities played before capacity and near-capacity houses each week. At the half-century mark of professional football over twelve million people annually — plus other millions on television — watch the ballplayers in the twenty-six cities of professional football tell them something important about man in America.

Pro football's popularity, then, can be accounted for partly because it fills the needs for group involvement and for basic challenges and also because it satisfies the public's newly-awakened sense of honest style. Yet this is not all. Football fits because, in a highly complex and scientifically oriented society, it is a fitting condensation and model. "Technologyland," Norman Mailer calls America; and football is a sport uniquely compatible to the products and organization of our proud technological capabilities. One could shorthand modern America as plastics, film, computers and television. All four are integral parts of a sport which grows and changes with every new device it confronts.

Plastics have been used in football because

the player puts such extreme demands upon his body that his uniform is more an aid and protection than it is an identifying symbol. In his desperate need to squeeze every bit of performance from his body, the player has demanded better and better equipment. America's answer has been plastics and synthetics—for the helmets, pads, cloth, cleats and even the field. And with the players' bodies on the line, football will continue to adapt each new technique available.

Film has been used not only to produce beautiful essays on the sport, fast- and slow-motion tributes to the art and courage of the ballplayers, but also as an indispensable strategic device. In a sport so complicated that not even coaches can tell what happens in person, the camera becomes a recording observer, preserving for long hours of analysis the dancing patterns of the field. Film gives coaches a standpoint for viewing a sport which is otherwise past control. Through its careful use, professional coaches have been able to get a full perspective on the game and organize it with all the varying detail which twenty-two men are capable of executing.

As film has aided the powers of observation, increasing the amount of facts available, computers have been called in to remember and collate those facts. Computers are used in scouting, where many reports on hundreds of players are fed into the machines and a list rank-ordering the players is produced. They are also fed great amounts of film-bred information on rival teams which they read out into "tendency charts", charts which give probabilities on what any team is most likely to do in any situation.

But if modern America is built of plastics, enjoys films and organizes on computers, it feeds on television. Television is the electronic

core of the nation and football is the television sport. It was during the early Fifties, in a union of near perfection, that television and pro football conspired to develop a viewer's medium that was unexcelled for excitement, clarity and sustained interest.

Football is a complex, patterned sport, a visual image well-suited to the changing glow of a television screen. In football, the action happens all at once. The television, which is boring if the camera focuses on only one thing at a time, jumps with the simultaneous movements of many men during a football telecast; and the viewer is personally involved in the process. He makes sense of the action faster than the announcer can describe it.

Football's television adaptability was enhanced by technical innovations developed in the Sixties which greatly added to the visual appeal. Instant replay, slow motion and isolated camera shots provided a review of the spectacular action that, in many respects, created an art form, inducing a brand new appreciation for the talents of the athletes. These innovations also widened the appeal of the game, allowing viewers time to savor a play from several angles.

Football is not merely the sport best suited to the screen. Judging by ratings and viewer responses, it is one of the most important aspects of America's television culture. This is easily understood by comparing the entertainment of a football game with the normal television fare. Any good game, and the pros rarely play poor ones, has more excitement than most full weeks of prime time fare. The action, moreover, isn't faked or scripted. On live television, football players act out the crucial moments in their lives. In situations of potential triumph and tragedy, the men reach down to come up with their best — and it just happens to be highly photogenic.

Small wonder, then, that in 1968, when NBC pre-empted the last minute of a free-scoring game between the New York Jets and Oakland Raiders to air a network special of Heidi, a furor was developed across the land that touched the industry at its highest levels. A month later, during the Western Conference playoff between Minnesota and Baltimore, the last few moments of the first half of a tense ball game were cut off and replaced by shots from Apollo Eight on its historic moon mission. Despite live coverage of man's most incredible moment, many a viewer was distressed by this decision of CBS to deprive him of key moments from an important game. Only the fact that the game action was taped and re-played at halftime saved another explosion of viewer discontent.

The marriage of television and football is so perfect that in some ways a television viewer has a more accurate perspective than an in-person spectator. From the vantage point of the stadium wall, the game is seen as a swift, pre-cisely executed series of maneuvers beyond the reaches of hearing. The prompt movement of the players is a smooth, efficient pattern devoid of the association of pain and violence. There is only the tense action of the run, pass and kick. Thus, from fifty yards away, the game comes across as if in another time field, a vigorous ballet that moves to the thunderous musical accompaniment of seventy thousand sets of lungs and vocal cords, a giant organ pumping out huge chords of oohs and ahhs in rhythm with the action.

In contrast, television conveys a truer sense of the ferocity developed within the momen-tary sieges of the scrimmage. Telephoto lenses make it possible to pull in tight on the action and study the exertions of the players as they grasp and claw for the man with the ball.

Nonetheless, no non-participant can partake of the true experience on the field. Football may be the most honest excitement available on television, but still the camera is a false eye, guilty of creating a two-dimensional per-spective that only alludes to realism. And no microphone accurately transmits the sounds of big men laboring heavily against one another. Slow motion replay makes art of effort, isolat-ing human skill into dramatic beauty, but depriving the viewer of the borderline fear known by the ballplayer as he careens along the thin edge of bodily control, balancing pre-cariously between failure and success.

Down on the field, along the sideline, real people replace the puppet figures known to the spectators. Numbered jerseys, easily identi-fiable from the stands and on television, take on the faces, voices and emotions of men. There is no sense of fun evident in the serious faces. Furrowed brows, dark eyes and graying temples give thirty-year-old athletes the look of men half again that age. The weight of the contest is a burden that makes it apparent that this is not a game at all.

On the field, the linemen labor in a brutal obscurity. A special breed, they are saved from total anonymity only by the numbers on their backs which occasionally stand out in the action of the scrimmage, reminding people they are there. Football is, ultimately, a test of a man's willingness to endure difficulty in an effort to achieve success. It is the yardstick for judging a lineman. Money cannot buy his devotion to the game; there are easier ways to make a living.

For the quarterback and his receivers and runners, every play is like a run down a dark alley at midnight. They never know where the hit is coming from, only that it will. Sometimes the fear in the mind is greater than the reality. Resisting fear is as important as overcoming pain, and a man who courts panic does not spend many moments on the live side of football's boundary line.

When the ball is snapped, the trappings of the game disappear from the player's consciousness. The design of equipment, the computer-complex strategy, have become a part of sub-conscious environment, necessary but taken for granted. The circles and crosses of the game plan become walls of flesh, padding and obstinacy. The options from the computer are no longer IBM cards but parts of a split-second action decision. All the technology comes down to the explosion of bodies hurled against one another in primal confrontation.

The involvement and emotion of the contest usually provide anesthesia to the inevitable pain. Caught up in the fierce intensity of the game, players are unaware of the results of high-speed collisions that will make getting out of bed the next morning an agonizing ordeal. Because of their ability to play with pain, the players are often discussed as unfeeling brutes, hardened to the sensitivities that grace less courageous men. The truth is something else. They have faced the reality of pain and relegated it to its place—one element to be balanced against others in the quest for excellence.

As these modern warriors flash through their patterned movements, with high-speed precision and a fierceness borne of the near perfection of the human physique, it is hard to connect them with the beleaguered men who pioneered their game fifty years ago. The men in the NFL today are well equipped, well paid and well known. Yet, they are tied by inheritance and spirit to the obscure men of the Twenties who played this game before small crowds on primitive fields for meager pay. The players today live well and their predecessors did not, but that is due to the public acceptance which has been generated by a half-century of effort. The pioneers worked and played hard to build a dream which has manifested in the last third of the twentieth century.

The men are larger now, stronger, faster and more capable athletes. But the fire that burns inside them is no hotter than the flame that inspired the rugged little men a half century ago. It is a rare game, a unique game. The men have made it so.

Their efforts have had a meaning beyond themselves. Through their devotion to their sport, America discovers a portion of herself and, in the delight of recognition, responds with a roar of approval.

Familia

For the first thirty years after the NFL was formed, professional football labored in the shadows of other major sports, primarily baseball, college football and prize fighting.

Pro football was small time by comparison, a little game struggling for existence and borne on the shoulders of a few dedicated men in the major cities of the nation. While George Halas, Tim Mara, George Marshall, Art Rooney, Bert Bell and Charles Bidwill sustained the growing pains of teams in the league's prestige cities, numerous smaller towns tried their luck with the professional sport.

The earliest professional football was played by teams in small midwestern towns, often supported by companies as a promotional venture. Players were offered salaried jobs and allowed to practice and play football and other sports on company time. Twenty-two-year-old George Halas, athletic director and player-coach for the Staley Starch Company of Decatur, Illinois, began his pro sports career in this environment. A member of the APFA in its first season, the Decatur Staleys netted $1,800 after expenses and the 22 players shared in it. "The players voted me, as coach and player, two full shares," reminisces Halas. "We practiced every afternoon, six days a week on a very well kept baseball field owned by the Staley Company."

Throughout the Twenties a number of cities established franchises, many folding the same year they were brought into existence. Their names ring with a particular American quality: The Akron Pros, Buffalo All Americans, Columbus Panhandles, Dayton Triangles, Rock Island Independents, Evansville Crimson Giants, Muncie Flyers, Oorang Indians and Pottsville Maroons.

The NFL hit a high point in 1926 with 22 teams from coast to coast, but such expansion was premature. Nearly half of the teams closed their box offices for the 1927 season and when the Great Depression struck in the Thirties, the league had already winnowed down to around ten teams and most of those were solid enough to last out the difficult decade. In 1933 the league broke into two five-team divisions and although there were a few franchise changes and division switches the basic structure remained unaltered until the Sixties. The only major alteration was in 1950 when three teams, Cleveland, San Francisco and Baltimore, came into the NFL as the last remains of the All-America Football Conference which had existed from 1946 to 1949.

By the end of the Fifties, the sport had matured. No longer dependent on the strength of a few men, the NFL was on the verge of booming success.

(continued on page 37)

From the optimistic proliferation of the Twenties through the solid structure of the Sixties, the National Football League has had a varied and colorful history. The following four pages detail the league's ancestral background.

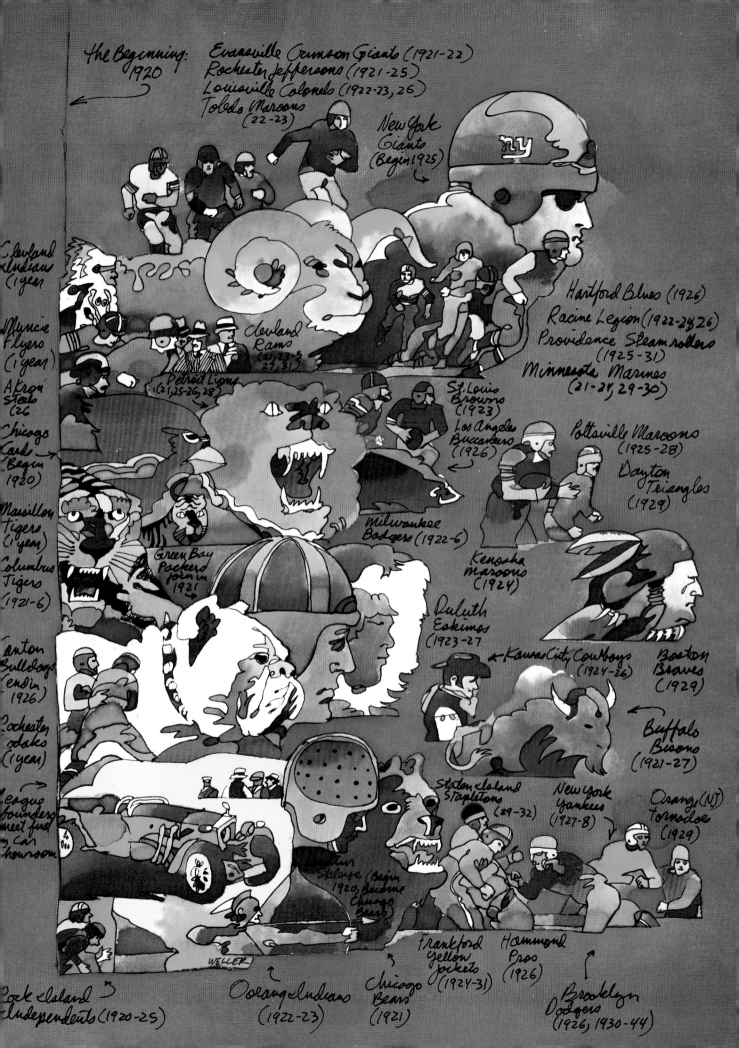

the Beginning: Evansville Crimson Giants (1921-22)
1920 Rochester Jeffersons (1921-25)
Louisville Colonels (1922-23, 26)
Toledo Maroons (22-23)

New York Giants (Begin 1925)

Cleveland Indians (1 year)

Muncie Flyers (1 year)

Akron Steels (26

Chicago Cards (Begin 1920)

Massillon Tigers (1 year)

Columbus Tigers (1921-6)

Canton Bulldogs (end in 1926)

Rochester Jakes (1 year)

League founders meet first in Car showroom

Cleveland Rams (21, 23-5, 27, 31)

Detroit Lions (21, 25-26, 28)

St. Louis Browns (1923)

Los Angeles Buccaneers (1926)

Milwaukee Badgers (1922-6)

Green Bay Packers join in 1921

Kenosha Maroons (1924)

Duluth Eskimos (1923-27

Hartford Blues (1926)
Racine Legion (1922-24, 26)
Providence Steamrollers (1925-31)
Minnesota Marines (21-24, 29-30)

Pottsville Maroons (1925-28)

Dayton Triangles (1929)

Kansas City Cowboys (1924-26)

Boston Braves (1929)

Buffalo Bisons (1921-27)

Staten Island Stapletons (29-32)

New York Yankees (1927-8)

Orange (NJ) Tornadoes (1929)

Decatur Staleys (Begin 1920, Become Chicago Bears)

WELLER

Frankford Yellow Jackets (1924-31)

Hammond Pros (1926)

Rock Island Independents (1920-25)

Oorang Indians (1922-23)

Chicago Bears (1921)

Brooklyn Dodgers (1926, 1930-44)

Pittsburgh Pirates (1933-40)

Pittsburgh Steelers (begin 1940)

Philadelphia Eagles (begin 1933). In 1940 the Philadelphia and Pittsburgh franchises exchange cities. Pirates become Eagles. Eagles become Steelers

Newark Tornadoes (1930)

Portsmouth Spartans (1930-33)

St. Louis Gunners (1934)

New York Bulldogs (1949)

Detroit Lions (Begin 1934)

Cincinnati Reds (1933-4)

Boston Yanks (1948)

Boston Redskins (1932-36)

Redskins move to Washington (1937)

After 56 years, six divisions are needed to organize the 26 teams of a vigorously growing NFL.

THE NFL IN 1975

AMERICAN CONFERENCE
Eastern Division
BALTIMORE COLTS
BUFFALO BILLS
MIAMI DOLPHINS
NEW ENGLAND PATRIOTS
NEW YORK JETS

Central Division
CINCINNATI BENGALS
CLEVELAND BROWNS
HOUSTON OILERS
PITTSBURGH STEELERS

Western Division
DENVER BRONCOS
KANSAS CITY CHIEFS
OAKLAND RAIDERS
SAN DIEGO CHARGERS

NATIONAL CONFERENCE
Eastern Division
DALLAS COWBOYS
NEW YORK GIANTS
PHILADELPHIA EAGLES
ST. LOUIS CARDINALS
WASHINGTON REDSKINS

Central Division
CHICAGO BEARS
DETROIT LIONS
GREEN BAY PACKERS
MINNESOTA VIKINGS

Western Division
ATLANTA FALCONS
LOS ANGELES RAMS
NEW ORLEANS SAINTS
SAN FRANCISCO 49ERS

In the Sixties, the twelve-team nucleus of professional football exploded into a twenty-six team national profusion. It was a decade of spectacular growth, rooted in the country-wide appeal of televised football.

The growth appeared in two branches. First, the NFL nurtured four expansion franchises in Dallas, Minnesota, Atlanta and New Orleans. Second, a rival league, the American Football League, sprouted in 1960 and matured to ten members before the two leagues signed a merger agreement in 1966.

With all the new teams, the old two-conference structure became obsolete. In 1967, the NFL adjusted to its four new franchises by breaking each of its two conferences into two divisions, resulting in four groupings of four teams each. In the old two-conference system there would have been eight teams in each title race; that is, seven losers for each winner. A ratio like that is unappealing to players and fans alike. Under the four-four system, exactly half the teams were either winners or runners-up each year. Despite expansion, this spread title-race excitement to a greater percentage of NFL cities than ever before.

When the original merger agreement was signed in 1966, the integration of the two leagues was postponed. But for 1970, the first year of the NFL's second half-century, all twenty-six teams were put into one organization. The combined league retained the National Football League name and was split into two thirteen-team conferences. Three of the old NFL teams, Baltimore, Cleveland and Pittsburgh, joined the old AFL teams in the new American Conference. The remaining thirteen teams formed the National Conference. The two Conferences, in turn, were divided into three divisions. Two divisions in each Conference were assigned four members and the other division received five.

To settle the championship, a three-week round of playoffs was instituted. In the first round, the six divisional winners will be entered, along with one second-place team from each Conference, chosen on the basis of best won-lost percentage. The four winners of the first weekend's games fight for their conference championships on the second weekend. The two conference champions enter the Super Bowl.

Under this sytem, although the total number of teams is large, each team has a fighting chance at the Super Bowl. Only three or four teams must be beaten during the regular season to gain entry to the playoffs, and once in the playoffs, an inspired team can go all the way.

Exactly fifty-six years after its inception, the National Football League has been born anew. And if in the future the thrills won't be any greater, there are at least more of them per week — six title races full of that special excitement which is professional football.

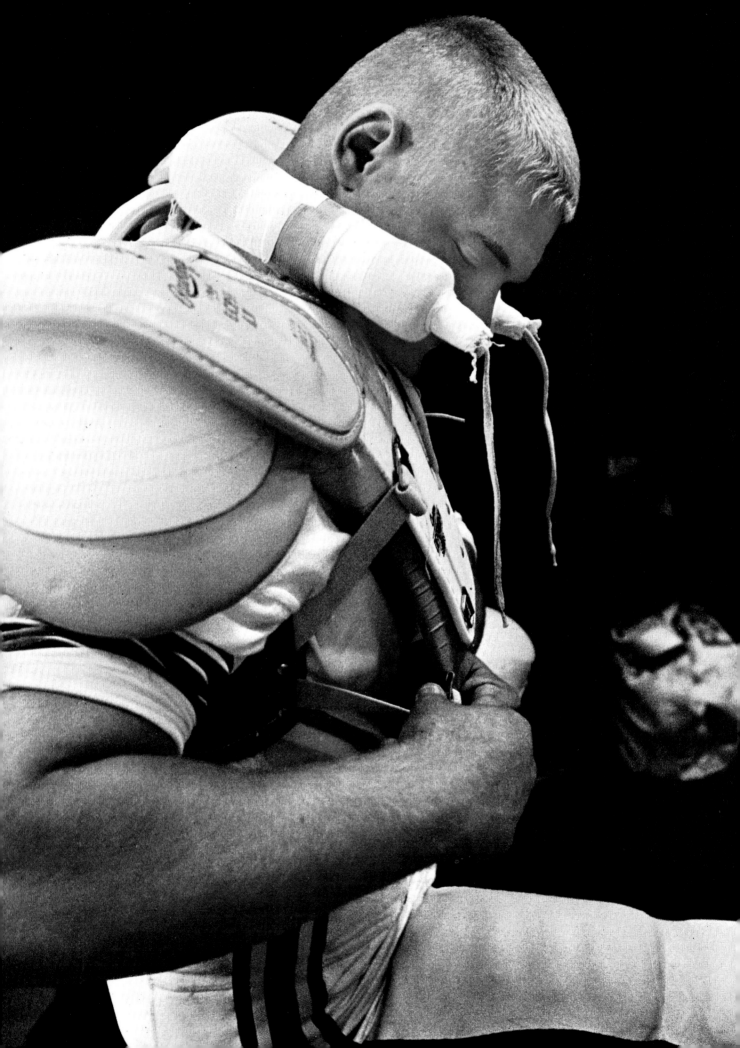

The Planned Collision

The conflict is imminent. Vast resources have been applied to bring it to this. Thousands, perhaps millions, are anticipating the outcome. For the individual player there is a sense of impasse. He occupies himself with the ritual of final locker room preparations. They serve both physical and mental needs. Elaborate pads and harnesses and yards of tape and elastic are fitted for violent collisions. And all the time, the mind is harnessed and uniformed, too, and made taut and ready.

Pain is a part of the game and a player learns to live with it and play with it, but serious injury is something else. It is the dread and constant menace of his profession, for it could mean the end of a career. Every player knows this, and his knowledge nourishes the roots of the peculiar fear that is felt before every game and heightens the sense of impasse. Always, it has to be faced—out the door, through the dark tunnel, and into the bright arena.

All of your knowledge is in order. All plans are made. Your forces are arranged for battle. Now reach out for other allies. Invoke every power. Summon up the emotions and set the blood astir. Bring everything to a focus of controlled fury. Then depend, significantly, on the flip of a coin to begin. Send the football soaring and feel your expectations hang in the violated air by sounds breaking overhead and fresh forces sweeping over the green toward the first collision of hopes.

The prelude to conflict is ordered and disciplined. Taut lines of suspended violence break to cadenced commands. And even in the maelstrom that follows, there are pockets of quiet grace, as if another game were being played.

The fundamentalists like to say that to
win you have to establish a ground
game. You do this with the enforcers—
the men who carry the ball. They build
a respect that keeps opposing linemen
from homing recklessly on the quarterback. You run so that you can pass, for
most of the plays on which the game
swings are made by the men who throw
and the men who catch the ball. You aim
for that moment when a gazelle-like
receiver, by speed and artifice, has made
an empty place in hostile country thick
with enemies, and, solitary, takes the
ball on stretching fingers from the
friendly air and is running free.

47

The best way to watch the game is to follow the ball. To do this, you keep your eyes on the quarterback, for he is the man who has it most of the time. The defenders, too, focus upon him. His job is unlike any other. The physical requirements are rare enough: the strength, quickness, size, coordination, the unique ability to throw the ball. The mental and emotional qualities are something else: intelligence, good judgment, reflexes, toughness, courage, the ability to lead. But these are not all. There is another aspect that distinguishes him. He must perform despite the attrition of continuous punishment, in the face of a constant threat of violence. Where else can you find a job like this?

You never ask the price of victory. The heart has no truck with cost. There is only one absolute—a total commitment. And when it is made, and the victory you aimed for is achieved, there is a reaffirmation of old values, and sweet serenity.

The Football Experie

Football players function on the outer edge of man's emotional and physical capabilities. A man performing in the swarming, hostile environment of a football field is forced to expand the limits of his physical skill, his endurance, his courage, his concentration. He is alive at an intensity most people never reach.

Under such pressure, the normal needs and drives and desires of the human being become clearly visible. While people in more normal existences can slide from day to day controlled by the routines of job and home, rarely conscious of their own motivations or abilities, football players are allowed no such deadened life. In an immediate and visceral way they are forced to confront their own makeup. Their own self-image is continually tested: their pride, their courage, the meaning of their pain, the reality of their hostility, their need for group affection, the level of their ability, their worth to other people.

Their problems are not different in kind from those of any other human, just more immediately and basically apparent. A linebacker's fear of missing a tackle is a condensed and explicit form of the nagging and formless fear of failure in all people. But football players cannot deny their fears or needs. They must deal with them. And as they do, they can show us. They *are* us, in a concentrated stress situation, and their reactions are ours lived through them.

This section is an attempt to suggest the variety and depth of their experience. Some of the needs and motivations of the ball players are presented in the words of the players themselves or as seen in the words of doctors, psychologists and anthropologists not directly concerned with football. It is not possible to present a simple and complete picture because the reality is complex, contradictory and without end. Life has so many sides that it is hard to keep them all in mind at once. And pro football, with its many different positions and demands, allows many sides of life to exist and be tested at the same time. If this section opens some of these areas and suggests certain lines of thought, it will have reached its goal. It has no final answers. There are none.

In a middle class society, inhibitions and controls on one's emotional and physical expression are a problem. Delayed gratification of these emotional and physical needs can cause tensions and anxieties. In contrast, it seems likely that the spontaneity and release experienced by the football player is enjoyable and satisfying.

Dr. Seymour Feshback, professor of psychology, University of California at Los Angeles

As a youngster I was very shy. I was scared to death of people. But football gave me an outlet for my emotions. You get the chance to go man-to-man and see if you can stand up against the best they can throw at you. On a football field I was just a different person.

Ernie Nevers, Hall of Fame tailback

In this century people in ordinary jobs are cut off from what they are doing. They sit behind their desks and don't have any real relationship to what else is going on. They are struggling against things they can't see. There is a day-to-day routine but never any crisis situation. But in football it all builds up to a peak performance for two-and-a-half hours on Sunday. There is a clearly defined objective, an obvious opponent. You have to be emotionally and physically and psychologically ready for that two-and-a-half hour crisis. And if you triumph in that two-and-a-half hour crisis. Football is so exciting because it's clear right away. Football is an intensified slice of life.

Bill Glass, defensive end, Cleveland Browns

I have worked for a savings and loan in the off-season and I may be working on a loan for a month or six weeks before I feel the accomplishment of closing it. But on the football field I experience accomplishment of bang, right there.

Larry Wilson, safety, St. Louis Cardinals

THE WHOLE POINT TO YOUR EMOTIONAL INC

I thought back on a pretty good catch I made one day and the thrill of it was the feeling of extreme power. I felt I could have jumped 18 feet in the air if I tried. Getting that ball and going is a tremendous physical thrill, an ego thrill, a personal power satisfaction.

Johnny Blood, Hall of Fame halfback

The beauty of the game of football is that so often you are called upon to do something beyond your capabilities — and you do it.

Dub Jones, All-Pro halfback, 1946-55

During the game, I get caught up in the feeling of action, in the intensity and movement and being a part of what's happening on that field. As soon as I walk off the field I have this tremendous letdown, this tremendous emotional relapse, just like coming down off the clouds.

Merlin Olsen, defensive tackle, Los Angeles Rams

The most important thing is that you feel like you are ready to go every minute of your life. We endure hard training for it but we get superb physical condition. It's nice just to feel well every morning. It is the most contented life that a man is ever engaged in. I must admit that I dream of coming back, whatever dreams are worth, and I think about playing and running and trying to make a team good.
Russ Craft, All-Pro defensive back, 1946-54

LIFE IS TO MAXIMIZE
ME.

Much of the excitement of football is due to the risk involved. After a game of tennis or golf, you are just tired. But in risk exercise there is a consuming feeling of exhilaration bordering on euphoria that one doesn't get any other time of his life. The thesis of risk exercise is that calculated risk on a physical or mental basis is necessary for our daily well being. Man has evolved through action and risk. Thus, complacency for any period of time leads to emotional and mental staleness or deterioration. A professional football head coach told me that after a game the players are not tired. They feel exhilarated. They feel so great they want to go out and do something.
Dr. Sol Roy Rosenthal, Professor of Preventive Medicine, Illinois University, School of medicine.

The fear of football players is not the fear of pain, but the fear that an injury will keep them from doing their job. In this business, you can be dedicated, work hard, prepare yourself physically and mentally, and in most fields you would succeed because of your attitude. In football all that can be wiped out in one second and no matter what your attitude is, you just can't do your job.
Andy Russell, linebacker, Pittsburgh Steelers

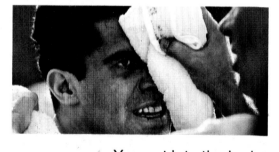

The running back always has a little fear in him. You know that you've got that ball and wherever the ball is, that's where the crowd is going to be. And getting tackled is a thing that hurts. You know, nobody in his right mind wants to go ramming head on into someone else. But when you get out on the football field, I think you tend to go out of your right mind. And then that fear just makes you run faster and try harder.
Mel Farr, halfback, Detroit Lions

You get into the locker room and sit for that minute just realizing that the contest is over. It was like a fear experience and you think of what the consequences might have been, and you tend to relive it. It's like driving an automobile and coming close to having a wreck and there's that fear for a moment, and then you drive along a few miles and think back over what might have happened.
Willie Davis, defensive end, Green Bay Packers

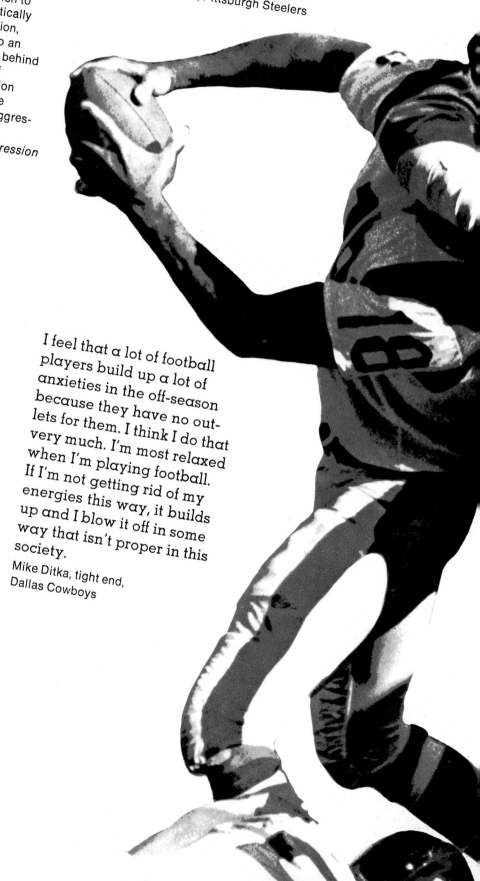

There is, in the modern community, no legitimate outlet for aggressive behavior. To keep the peace is the first of civic duties, and the hostile neighboring tribe, once the target at which to discharge phylogenetically programmed aggression, has now withdrawn to an ideal distance, hidden behind a curtain, if possible of iron. . . . The main function of sport today lies in the cathartic discharge of aggressive urge.

Konrad Lorentz, *On Aggression*

It's a feeling of exhilaration. Boy, you really knocked the hell out of that guy. You just feel great because you hit somebody.
Ernie Stautner, tackle, Pittsburgh Steelers

I feel that a lot of football players build up a lot of anxieties in the off-season because they have no outlets for them. I think I do that very much. I'm most relaxed when I'm playing football. If I'm not getting rid of my energies this way, it builds up and I blow it off in some way that isn't proper in this society.

Mike Ditka, tight end, Dallas Cowboys

I can only speak from my own standpoint, but I think that to some degree I'm a masochist about it. I almost enjoy hitting someone and at the same time maybe hurting myself a little bit. Maybe I have tremendous guilt feelings about something. I'm not sure. But I think a number of football players are the same way.
Paul Martha, safety, Pittsburgh Steelers

Football is a violent game. You are physically attacking another person. To do this, you almost have to change your personality, to break down some of the things taught you, because this is not accepted in our society.
Howard Mudd, guard, San Francisco 49ers

I never will forget a game in 1952 in Cleveland and I
had my first chance to tackle Marion Motley. He looked
like a big tank rolling down on me. But you got to take
him on. I hit him with my head in the knees and he came
down. I saw a few stars but I felt good, because I
tackled Marion Motley.
Night Train Lane, defensive back with Rams, Cardinals and Lions

On most defenses the middle linebacker keys the fullback. If I get a hole in the line then
it's the linebacker and me in a one-on-one tackling situation. If that linebacker is
defeating me 8 out of 10 times, then I'd better worry about my abilities. But if I am
defeating him, then I know I am doing my job. That's the game — defeating your man.
Jim Taylor, fullback, Packers and Saints

Anybody who says this game is beastly, brutal and nasty,
he's right. You are out there to inflict punishment, but not to take
it. You want to be the hitter not the hittee. It's a great personal
satisfaction when you get a good hit on someone. You know you
have done a good job. And you know that the other guy is
wondering what the hell happened, and who the hell are you
and now he's got to respect you a little bit.
Wayne Walker, linebacker, Detroit Lions

Violence, in its many
forms, [is] an involuntary
quest for identity.
When our identity is in
danger, we feel certain
that we have a mandate
for war.
Marshall McLuhan,
*War and Peace in the
Global Village*

Ethics and aggression have been the heads and tails of sport. The respectability of rivalry has in a sense generated and compelled the morality — the ritualization — of rivalry's rules and regulations.
Robert Ardrey,
The Territorial Imperative

This is one place you can get away with it. You go out in the street and start knocking people around and you are going to end up in jail. A big man, he needs this physical contact, he needs to get beat up once in a while and the football field is one place that he can go and do it. On the other hand, you don't get a lot of dirty play. Each of us has taken fifteen or twenty years to develop the skills for this job, and we respect each other for it. I don't think anybody is out there to put somebody in a hospital or end his career.
Chuck Howley, linebacker, Dallas Cowboys

I think the nature of man is to be aggressive and football is a violent game. But I think the very violence is one of the great things about the game, because a man has to learn control. He is going to go in to knock somebody's block off, and yet he must keep a rein on it. I can't think of any other place that demands such discipline.
Vince Lombardi, coach, Green Bay Packers, Washington Redskins

I'm sure that I take out many of my personal aggressions on the field, but I don't play football for that reason. I don't feel any hatred on the field. Usually the guys I'm playing right opposite are my best friends around the league because we get to respect each other. My roughness and aggressiveness at certain times are prompted by my desire to be a better football player. I don't enjoy contact.
Merlin Olsen, tackle, Los Angeles Rams

I've known women who thought football was worthless and brutal. But they just don't understand the sport and they don't understand the nature of the male. Most of those big collisions don't really hurt. The players are dressed and protected. They are young and strong. Anyway, the fact is that young men enjoy it. Nothing is going to stop it. If we could just have a Super Bowl between Russia and the United States, instead of all those tanks and ballistic missiles, things would be a lot better.
Paul Brown, coach, Cleveland Browns, Cincinnati Bengals

On the field, first of all, you are quite reserved. You have to have fantastic concentration. You must be aggressive, but you can't go completely nuts because you will just make a lot of mistakes. It's a difficult balance.
Bob Lilly, tackle, Dallas Cowboys

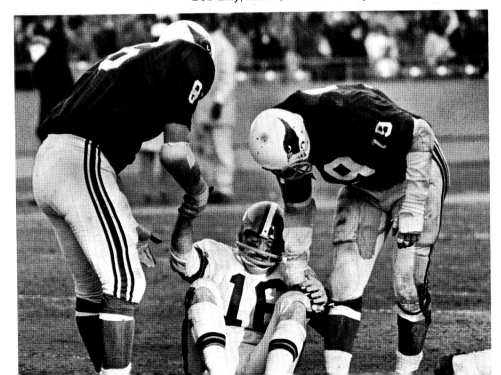

From a psychological journal of 1903:
    The game acts as a sort of Aristotelian catharsis, purging our pent-up feelings and enabling us to return more placidly to the slow upward toiling.
    By inner imitation the spectators themselves participate in the game and at the same time give an unrestrained expression to their emotions. If at a great football game any one will watch the spectators instead of the players, he will see at once that the people before him are not his associates of the school, the library, the office, the shop, the street or the factory. The spectators at an exciting football game no longer attempt to restrain emotional expression. They shout and yell, blow horns and dance, swing their arms about and stamp, throw their hats in air and snatch off their neighbors' hats, howl and gesticulate, little realizing how foreign this is to their wonted behavior or how odd it would look at their places of work.
Professor G.T.W. Patrick, "The American Journal of Psychology," Vol. 14

This is one way for people to release their aggressions. I see them coming out of the stands, they are wringing wet with sweat, they are mad, they have played a football game and they look as beat up as the football players on the field.
Larry Wilson, safety, St. Louis Cardinals

Let's face it, most of the people in our society enjoy watching one guy knock down another one.
John Niland, tackle, Dallas Cowboys

The fans wouldn't like football without the hitting. They appreciate the long run or big pass because they know how hard it is to do. They know that one step out of line and someone is going to really nail the guy. If you take away the contact, you take away the danger and the discipline. It would be all fancy guys.
Andy Russell, linebacker, Pittsburgh Steelers

You see a tremendous block from the blind side and you can hear 50,000 "oooh's" all at once. So they must like it.
Elroy Hirsch, Hall of Fame flanker

The fans pay our way and they have a certain proprietorship over us. If they want to boo us, that's fine and if they want to cheer, that's their prerogative. The game changes all the time and the fans react. That's the beauty of it—you can't control it. A man in an eight-to-five job has to control himself, or get fired or hated. But when that man gets to the football game he could care less. He yells and screams and boos and cries. He can do it because everybody else is doing it. The only thing he cares about is sharing emotions with everyone else. The whole crowd gets to live vicariously through us.
Howard Mudd, guard, San Francisco 49ers

The role of sport [is that of] a sort of capsule or live paradigm of any society. Games are fashions in the same way as clothes because they involve the sensory life of a society in a mocking and fictitious way. To simulate one situation by means of another one, to turn the whole working environment into a small model, is a means of perception and control by means of public ritual. The audience as participants is indispensable to most games. The greatest contest in the world in which only the players are present would have no game character whatever.
Marshall McLuhan,
*War and Peace
in the Global Village*

I've always considered myself a group therapist for 60,000 people. Every Sunday I hold group therapy and the people come and take out their frustrations on me. If I fail, it magnifies their failures, and if I succeed it minimizes them. The fans actually add to the game itself, because if you are playing at home, they are pulling for you, and if you are on the road, you are fighting 60,000 people.
Sonny Jurgensen, quarterback,
Washington Redskins.

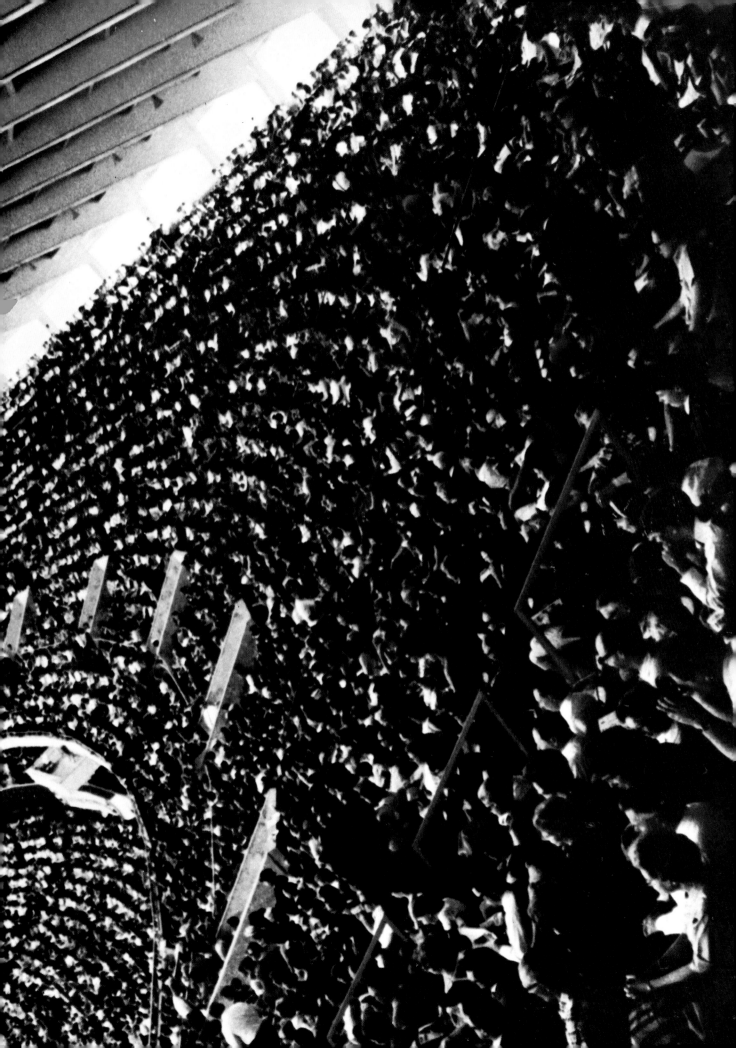

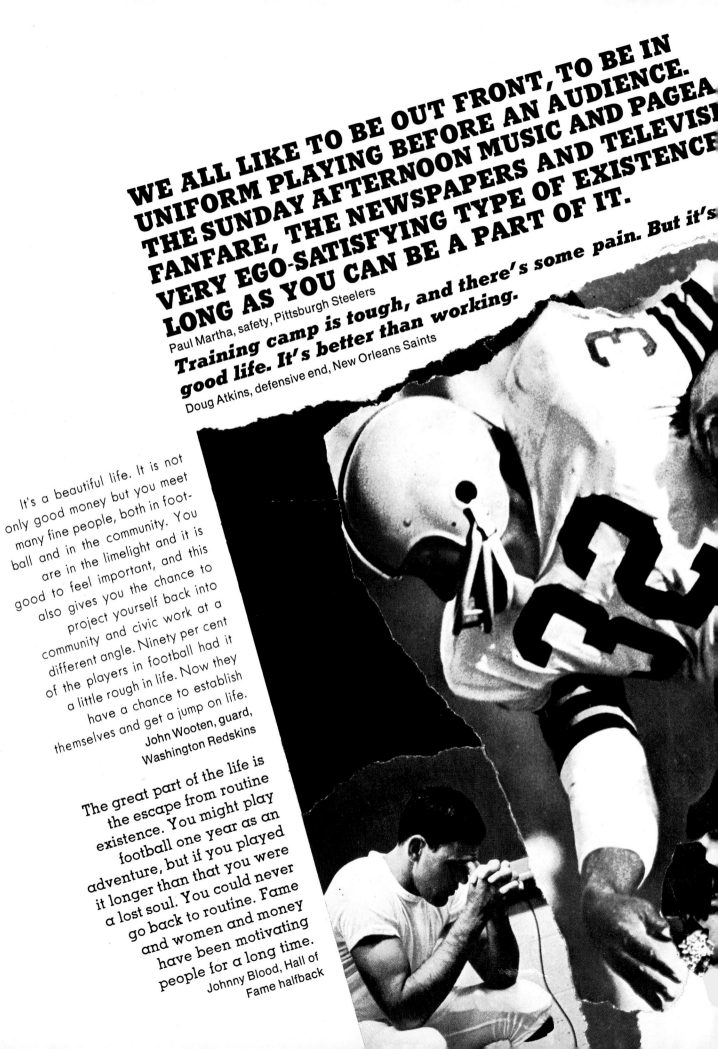

WE ALL LIKE TO BE OUT FRONT, TO BE IN UNIFORM PLAYING BEFORE AN AUDIENCE. THE SUNDAY AFTERNOON MUSIC AND PAGEA FANFARE, THE NEWSPAPERS AND TELEVISI VERY EGO-SATISFYING TYPE OF EXISTENCE LONG AS YOU CAN BE A PART OF IT.

Paul Martha, safety, Pittsburgh Steelers

Training camp is tough, and there's some pain. But it's good life. It's better than working.

Doug Atkins, defensive end, New Orleans Saints

It's a beautiful life. It is not only good money but you meet many fine people, both in football and in the community. You are in the limelight and it is good to feel important, and this also gives you the chance to project yourself back into community and civic work at a different angle. Ninety per cent of the players in football had it a little rough in life. Now they have a chance to establish themselves and get a jump on life.
John Wooten, guard, Washington Redskins

The great part of the life is the escape from routine existence. You might play football one year as an adventure, but if you played it longer than that you were a lost soul. You could never go back to routine. Fame and women and money have been motivating people for a long time.
Johnny Blood, Hall of Fame halfback

AND
IT'S A
R AS

Glory is a part of it. If you are recognized wherever you go, if you score and get your name in the paper or in a newsreel, that's important to your ego. If a man doesn't have some level of ego he shouldn't be playing football.

Elroy Hirsch, Hall of Fame flanker

We live in a materialistic society and let's face it— it's economics that count. Football opens a lot of doors for you.

Clifton McNeil, flanker,
San Francisco 49ers

It's not a glorified life. You hit every Sunday, practice every day. Most guys have some other business so it winds up a 13 or 14 hour day. The traveling wears you out. It's a good life and good money, don't get me wrong, but you pay for it.

Cornell Green, defensive back,
Dallas Cowboys

I've played sports all my life, because I liked them. But by now football is a profession to me like any other. My best moment is getting open and catching the ball, but it's no big thrill. I'm just thankful I didn't drop it.

Carroll Dale, flanker,
Green Bay Packers

he winner.

to match it for closeness.
per charge.

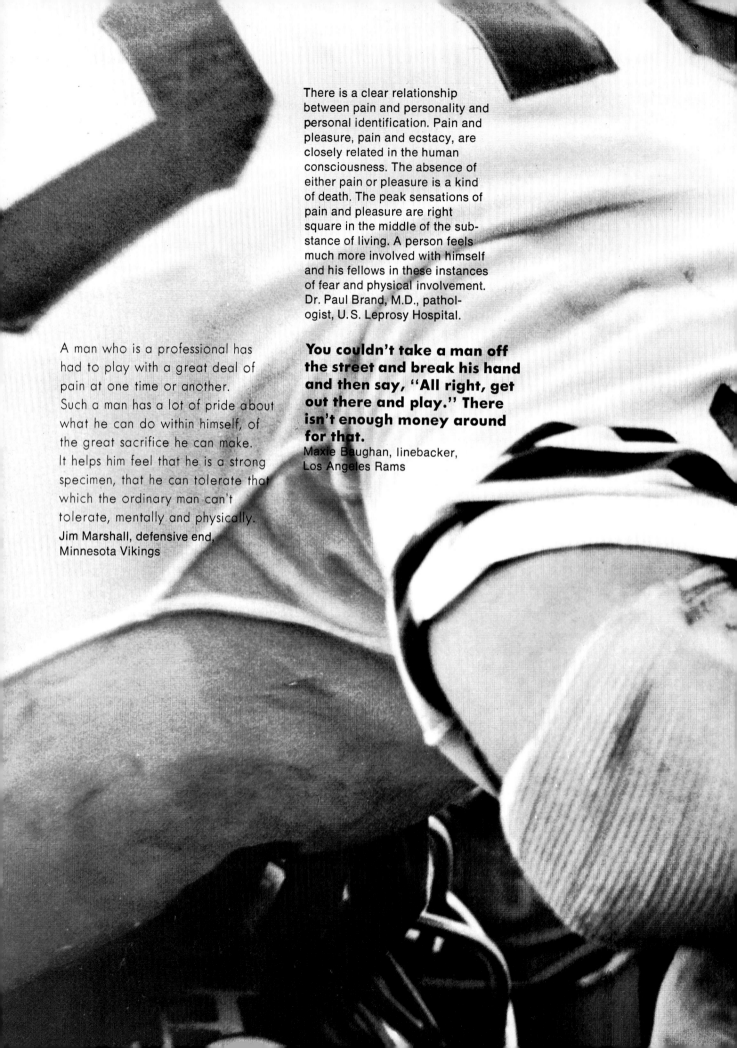

There is a clear relationship between pain and personality and personal identification. Pain and pleasure, pain and ecstacy, are closely related in the human consciousness. The absence of either pain or pleasure is a kind of death. The peak sensations of pain and pleasure are right square in the middle of the substance of living. A person feels much more involved with himself and his fellows in these instances of fear and physical involvement. Dr. Paul Brand, M.D., pathologist, U.S. Leprosy Hospital.

A man who is a professional has had to play with a great deal of pain at one time or another. Such a man has a lot of pride about what he can do within himself, of the great sacrifice he can make. It helps him feel that he is a strong specimen, that he can tolerate that which the ordinary man can't tolerate, mentally and physically. Jim Marshall, defensive end, Minnesota Vikings

You couldn't take a man off the street and break his hand and then say, "All right, get out there and play." There isn't enough money around for that. Maxie Baughan, linebacker, Los Angeles Rams

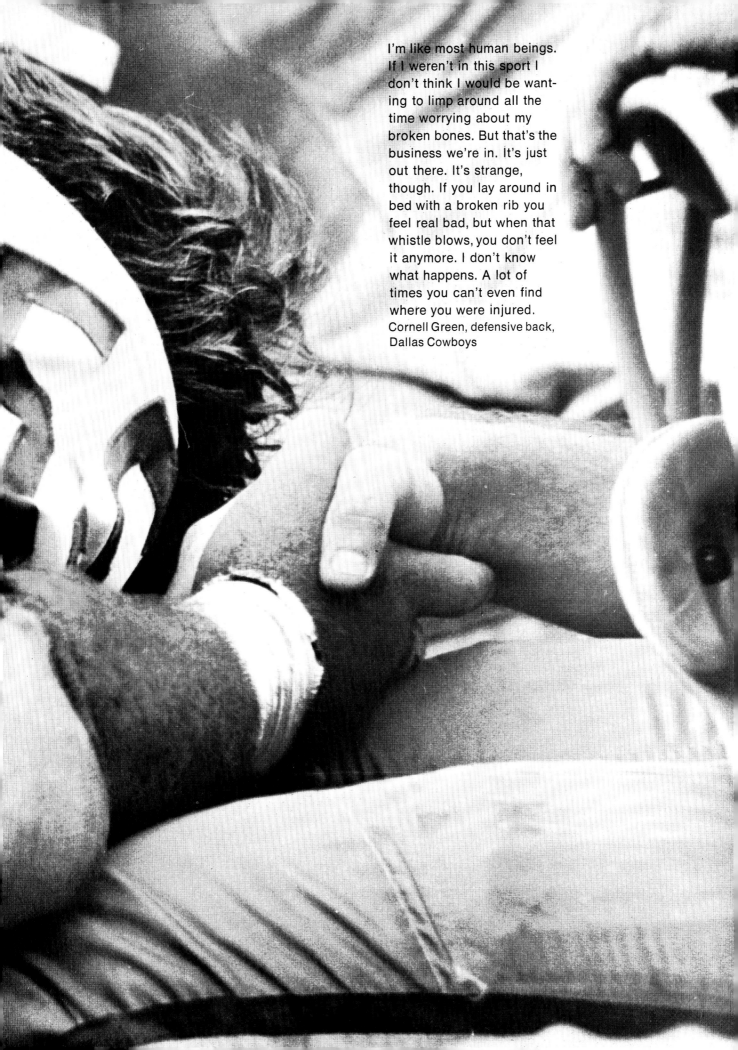

I'm like most human beings. If I weren't in this sport I don't think I would be wanting to limp around all the time worrying about my broken bones. But that's the business we're in. It's just out there. It's strange, though. If you lay around in bed with a broken rib you feel real bad, but when that whistle blows, you don't feel it anymore. I don't know what happens. A lot of times you can't even find where you were injured.
Cornell Green, defensive back, Dallas Cowboys

One of the great satisfactions of this game is when you are coming up to an important game and you are hurt. You know the guys need you. And you think, "Well, heck, I'm going to get in there and see if I can't gut it out for them." And you do. You shouldn't be out there, but you get the job done. They don't have to come out and tell you they are grateful for what you did. You can just feel it.
Wayne Walker, linebacker, Detroit Lions

By mid-season, everybody's hurting all the time. But the training room can be a cruel place. Athletes are very hard. They are all in pain and if you miss games, you are damaging the team. If you are out a couple of games with a bad leg, they'll come in and say, "How long you going to ride that horse? You're going to wear that horse out."
George Menefee, trainer, Los Angeles Rams

A football player must learn to accept pain. It is a very competitive life and you are judged solely on performance. I believe that through discipline and mental conditioning, a man can learn to accept pain as part of his endeavor. In fact, I think each man needs pain, because if he hasn't the discipline to endure pain and continue, something is lacking in his emotional make-up. That's not to say you should go out and get hit by a car. But every man must find his appropriate pain.
Bernie Casey, flanker, Los Angeles Rams

Pain and injuries are in the contract. John Niland, tackle, Dallas Cowboys

Enmity is the biological condition of cross-purposes. It is the innate response of any organism to any and all members of its own species, and enmity will be suspended, totally or partially, only for such period of time as two or more individuals are embraced by a single, more powerful purpose which inhibits all or part of their mutual animosities and channels the inhibited energy into a joint drive to achieve the joint purpose.
— Robert Ardrey
The Territorial Imperative

The most thrilling thing in football to me is for the team to execute a play perfectly. The coaches design the play and then we practice it for hours. But in the game so many things can happen that it almost never works out right. So when that time comes, and all eleven men do their job just right, it's a beautiful moment.
Ernie Green, halfback, Cleveland Browns

The important thing is that all members of the team be at the same level of consciousness — an awareness of his individual role and the place of that role in the whole team endeavor. Individual emotions don't matter. I may be hurting, some other guy may be scared or angry. But when we go, each man must be ready. You are intensely involved in your own personal part of the game, yet there is a great feeling of unity and mutual respect. Your emotions have all risen together during the week's work. And then, say, I hold my man out and John Brodie puts it out there and Clifton McNeil makes a fantastic catch — you just feel happy for everybody. You are all jumping up and down. You get chills and all that corny stuff.
Howard Mudd, guard,
San Francisco 49ers

I think defensive football players get a lot of satisfaction out of just playing together. Just having a good, sound, successful, respected, defensive unit. The whole unit, the lineman, linebackers and defensive backs. It just feels good, working together.
Paul Martha, safety, Pittsburgh Steelers

I'd much rather miss the All-Pro team and have the team win. When you win, the whole club is happy. There's a feeling that you've really accomplished something both as a person and as a team. It's a whole lot better than any individual reward that you might get.
Bob Lilly, tackle, Dallas Cowboys

There is only one passion which satisfies man's need to unite himself with the world, and to acquire at the same time a sense of integrity and individuality, and this is love. Love is union with somebody, or something, outside oneself, *under the condition of retaining the separateness and integrity of one's own self.* —Erich Fromm, The Sane Society

You have to have love for your teammate. I'm talking about respect, not physical love, but respect and loyalty, which are the greatest of loves really. This is what you've got to get across to your own team, the love and respect for the dignity of another man. There's got to be a great deal of charity. This is what brings your own men together as a team. Love is teamwork. And when you play an opponent, you've got to feel that that man on the other side is your enemy — and he is. Vince Lombardi, coach, Green Bay Packers, Washington Redskins

You go with pain because you know you have a job to do. It's going to hurt you but you know your playing can help the team, and you find yourself in there doing what you are supposed to do. As football players, we have something more important to us than our own selves.

Carl Lockhart, safety, New York Giants

I love the guys. The camaraderie and the friendship that we have, the togetherness and closeness—to me this is the greatest thing in the world. A month after the season is over, I'm really missing the guys. You know, it's almost like war on a football field, like being in a foxhole with a guy. Say you've got a three-point lead and something happens, a fumble or something and the defense has to go in there and save the game. That's crucial, it's critical, and you know it, and you've all got to get in there as a team. And when you do get it done it's a great feeling. You know that you've all done it together.

Wayne Walker, linebacker, Detroit Lions

The All Pros: Five Squads

Introduction

In its first fifty years, the National Football League fielded many great stars. From the legendary greats of the Twenties through the violent craftsmen of the Sixties, these players have progressively created a game which reflects, and excites, the American mind. These are the men who have made the big plays, the men whose skill and daring have expanded the game and drawn the crowds. They have come in many sizes, from many backgrounds, but they are unified by the successful quest of a common goal — stardom in a demanding sport.

Each of pro football's five decades had its own style and stars, and it is difficult to compare athletes accurately across the years. If it be true that the great linemen of the early years would be too small today, it is equally true that the finely trained specialists of modern football would find hard going in the sixty-minute endurance grind of the older game.

With this in mind, Pro Football's Hall of Fame has commemorated the first half-century of pro football by selecting five All-NFL squads, one for each decade of the sport's history. The size of the all-star squad in each decade was determined by the average size of an NFL squad during that period. Thus, the size of the all-star squad for the Twenties is 18, for the Thirties 25, for the Forties 33,

for the Fifties 35 and for the Sixties 40. In addition, each squad has been broken down by position in the manner of the successful teams of each era.

The official selectors of the Hall of Fame made their selections from nominations submitted by each of the teams in the National Football League. Their choices are informed and impartial but, of course, no endeavor of this nature can be considered definitive. As with fine wines, the choice of great football players is finally a matter of opinion.

Two special difficulties should be noted. Although each decade has had its own style, the use of fixed dates for a period obviously creates problems for those players whose careers reach deeply into two decades. In such cases (Raymond Berry is one example) an attempt has been made to place the player in the decade when he and his team had the maximum impact, consistent with the inclusions of the highest-rated ballplayers of both decades. Also, several great players who played only a few years in the NFL spent most of their years in the All-America Football Conference, which existed from 1946 to 1949 before merging into the NFL. In most of those cases, the players have been placed on the Forties squad.

Football fans come to see great players. Five squads of them are listed on the following pages. Computers could perhaps detail the results if the various squads were matched against one another, but that would be less fun than playing the

Position
End
Tackle
Guard
Center
Backs

	Ht.	Wt.	Years in League	Teams
Chamberlin, Guy	6-2	210	1920-27	Chicago Bears, Canton Bulldogs, Frankford Yellowjackets, Chicago Cardinals, Cleveland Bulldogs
Dilweg, Lavern	6-3	203	1926-34	Green Bay Packers, Milwaukee Badgers
Halas, George	6-1	180	1920-29	Chicago Bears
Healey, Ed	6-3	196	1920-27	Rock Island Independents, Chicago Bears
Henry, Pete (Fats)	6-0	250	1920-23, 1925-28	Canton Bulldogs, Akron Steels, New York Giants, Pottsville Maroons
Hubbard, Cal	6-5	250	1927-33, 1935-36	New York Giants, Green Bay Packers, Pittsburgh Pirates
Owen, Steve	6-2	235	1924-31, 1933	Kansas City Cowboys, New York Giants
Anderson, Heartley (Hunk)	5-11	195	1922-25	Chicago Bears
Kiesling, Walt	6-2	245	1926-38	Duluth Eskimos, Pottsville Maroons, Chicago Cardinals, Chicago Bears, Green Bay Packers, Pittsburgh Pirates
Michalske, Mike	6-0	210	1927-35, 1937	New York Yankees, Green Bay Packers
Trafton, George	6-2	235	1920-32	Chicago Bears
Conzelman, Jimmy	6-0	180	1920-29	Decatur Staleys, Rock Island Independents, Milwaukee Badgers, Detroit Panthers, Providence Steamrollers
Driscoll, John (Paddy)	5-11	170	1920-29	Chicago Cardinals, Chicago Bears
Grange, Harold (Red)	6-1	190	1925-27, 1929-34	Chicago Bears, New York Yankees
Guyon, Joe	6-1	180	1920-27	Canton Bulldogs, Cleveland Indians, Oorang Indians, Rock Island Independents, New York Giants, Kansas City Cowboys
Lambeau, Earl (Curly)	6-0	195	1921-29	Green Bay Packers
Nevers, Ernie	6-1	205	1926-27, 1929-31	Duluth Eskimos, Chicago Cardinals
Thorpe, Jim	6-1	190	1920-26, 1929	Canton Bulldogs, Cleveland Indians, Oorang Indians, Rock-Island Independents, New York Giants, Toledo Maroons, Chicago Cardinals

(Story on 1920s squad appears on page 86)

1930s
A Struggle For Existence

In its first two decades, pro football went from a glorified hobby to an established sport. In the early days, the playing grounds could be anything from a high school stadium to a deserted field. The rosters were fluid and the schedules haphazard. Pro football stayed afloat on love and improvisation.

But by the end of the Thirties, as the nation emerged from the Depression, the National Football League had steadied into a functional organization. All the teams had usable stadiums, rosters were stable and filled with quality ballplayers and league scheduling was firmly structured around a two-division concept. By then the pros had adopted rules which made for fan excitement, spreading the game out so that skills became visible and speeding it up to allow more happenings per minute. The sport was on the edge of emergence as a dominant force in American athletics.

The all-star roster of the Twenties is a doorway to legend. Seen from pro football's second half-century, these players seem to float through daring deeds in a luminous gray haze. There were no films, there are few pictures and newspaper clippings. All that is left is memory and it is hard to know if the memories are bigger than the men were or if the men were too big for memory.

Jim Thorpe stands out, the gypsy genius who played out his last years skipping from one NFL team to another. George Halas, Curly Lambeau, Steve Owen, Jimmy Conzelman, Ernie Nevers — these were the player-coaches, the men who loved to play so much that they made it happen, men who could lead the practices because they led on the field. And Red Grange, the ghost who streaked through pro football, pointed the way to league acceptance.

The roster of all-stars for the Thirties seems more real. By then there were statistics, all-pro teams chosen every year, still pictures, even movies of most of the players. There is less of myth to these men. They are remembered because, in an organized and competitive league, they did their job the best. It was a rough game then, mostly single wing, mostly running; and rough-hewn, two-way ball players stand out on the all-star roster — Nagurski, Strong, Hinkle, Fortmann, Edwards, Hein, Hewitt — men of endurance and desire. Only here and there, with a receiver like Hutson or a passer like Herber or Isbell, is there a hint of the technical specialization in the modern professional game. In the Depression decade, men were stripped down to a struggle for existence, and football reflected that feeling. Football is basically a game of physical man-to-man competition, and in the Thirties, very little interfered with the basis.

Position
End

Tackle

Guard

Center

Backs

	Ht.	Wt.	Years in League	Teams
Hewitt, Bill	5-11	195	1932-39, 1943	Chicago Bears, Philadelphia Eagles
Hutson, Don	6-1	180	1935-45	Green Bay Packers
Millner, Wayne	6-0	190	1936-41, 1945	Washington Redskins
Tinsley, Gaynell	6-1	200	1937-38, 1940	Chicago Cardinals
Christensen, George	6-2	238	1931-38	Portsmouth Spartans, Detroit Lions
Cope, Frank	6-3	234	1938-47	New York Giants
Edwards, Albert (Turk)	6-2	256	1932-40	Washington Redskins
Lee, Bill	6-2	235	1935-42, 1946	Brooklyn Dodgers, Green Bay Packers
Stydahar, Joe	6-4	230	1936-42, 1945-46	Chicago Bears
Emerson, Grover (Ox)	6-0	190	1931-38	Portsmouth Spartans, Detroit Lions, Brooklyn Dodgers
Fortmann, Danny	6-0	207	1936-43	Chicago Bears
Goldenberg, Charles (Buckets)	5-10	222	1933-45	Green Bay Packers
Letlow, Russ	6-0	212	1936-42, 1946	Green Bay Packers
Hein, Mel	6-3	230	1931-45	New York Giants
Svendsen, George	6-4	240	1935-37, 1940-41	Green Bay Packers
Battles, Cliff	6-1	185	1932-37	Washington Redskins
Clark, Earl (Dutch)	6-1	185	1931-32, 1934-38	Portsmouth Spartans, Detroit Lions
Feathers, Beattie	5-11	177	1934-40	Chicago Bears, Brooklyn Dodgers, Green Bay Packers
Herber, Arnie	6-1	200	1930-40, 1944-45	Green Bay Packers, New York Giants
Hinkle, Clarke	5-11	201	1932-1941	Green Bay Packers
Isbell, Cecil	6-0	190	1938-42	Green Bay Packers
Leemans, Alphonse (Tuffy)	6-0	200	1936-43	New York Giants
McNally, John (Johnny Blood)	6-1	190	1925-39,	Milwaukee Badgers, Duluth Eskimos, Pottsville Maroons, Green Bay Packers, Pittsburgh Pirates, Pittsburgh Steelers
Nagurski, Bronislaw (Bronko)	6-2	230	1930-37, 1943	Chicago Bears
Strong, Ken	5-11	210	1929-35, 1939, 1944-47	Staten Island Stapletons, New York Giants

1940s
Warfare Of Some Kind

The Forties opened with the Chicago Bears' 73-0 championship barrage and, for professional football as for the nation, the rest of the decade was warfare of some kind or another. Over 600 men went from service in the National Football League to service for their country in mankind's most desperate war. Many men had their pro careers cut off in their prime and many more went straight from school to war. Yet the NFL kept up a remarkably high quality of play despite the loss of executive leaders like George Halas of the Bears and Dan Reeves of the Rams and many of the league's top players.

The appeal and the promise of the professional sport was so strong that as soon as World War II ended, a new pro league was formed, the All-America Football Conference, and pro football broke out in its own war which lasted the rest of the decade. This war was insupportably costly to the owners, but it did gain publicity for the game and the salary struggles for young talent raised the level of pay so much that nearly every athlete who could make it began to turn pro. This, together with the men returning from the war, made the late Forties a period rich in fresh talent.

On the field, the game was transformed during the decade by the T-formation. After the Bear explosion in 1940, team after team changed over to the T. By the end of the decade, the old assortment of formations — the single wing, double wing, A-formation, short punt and all the rest — were mostly memories.

The T brought many changes on the field. It emphasized speed and quickness rather than strength and endurance. It allowed for specialization. Instead of one man running inside and outside and throwing, three different men took on these chores. These factors, along with the deception possible as the backs criss-crossed in the backfield, resulted in more explosive offenses. Big-yardage plays became more common and the offense no longer had a defeatist attitude if it were far from the opponent's goal.

In the war decade, then, the quality of play advanced markedly as linemen became more mobile, backs quicker, passers more accurate and receivers more certain. Yet the T-formation seemed to allow even more specialization and skill development if an athlete had the time to work on his best attributes. Two-platoon football — free substitution — was needed. In 1949, the rule was adopted. That same year, the two rival leagues merged under the name National Football League. Pro football was ready for its burst to acceptance.

Position
End

Tackle

Guard

Center

Quarterback

Halfback

Fullback

	Ht.	Wt.	Years in League	Teams
Benton, Jim	6-3	210	1938-1940, 1942-47	Cleveland Rams, Chicago Bears, Los Angeles Rams
Ferrante, Jack	6-1	205	1941, 1944-50	Philadelphia Eagles
Kavanaugh, Ken	6-3	205	1940-41, 1945-50	Chicago Bears
Lavelli, Dante	6-0	192	1946-56	Cleveland Browns
Pihos, Pete	6-1	215	1947-55	Philadelphia Eagles
Speedie, Mac	6-3	205	1946-52	Cleveland Browns
Sprinkle, Ed	6-1	207	1944-55	Chicago Bears
Blozis, Al	6-7	250	1942-44	New York Giants
Connor, George	6-3	240	1948-55	Chicago Bears
Kilroy, Frank	6-2	244	1943-55	Philadelphia Eagles
Ray, Buford (Baby)	6-6	250	1938-48	Green Bay Packers
Sears, Vic	6-3	236	1941-42, 1945-53	Philadelphia Eagles
Wistert, Al	6-1	214	1943-51	Philadelphia Eagles
Banducci, Bruno	5-11	220	1944-54	Philadelphia Eagles, San Francisco 49ers
Edwards, Bill	6-3	218	1940-42, 1946	New York Giants
Ramsey, Garrard (Buster)	6-1	220	1946-51	Chicago Cardinals
Willis, Bill	6-2	215	1946-53	Cleveland Browns
Younce, Len	6-1	210	1941, 1943-44, 1946-48	New York Giants
Brock, Charles	6-2	210	1939-47	Green Bay Packers
Turner, Clyde (Bulldog)	6-2	240	1940-52	Chicago Bears
Wojciechowicz, Alex	6-0	235	1938-50	Detroit Lions, Philadelphia Eagles
Baugh, Sammy	6-2	185	1937-52	Washington Redskins
Luckman, Sid	6-0	195	1939-50	Chicago Bears
Waterfield, Bob	6-2	200	1945-52	Cleveland Rams, Los Angeles Rams
Canadeo, Tony	5-11	190	1941-44, 1946-52	Green Bay Packers
Dudley, Bill	5-10	175	1942, 1945-51, 1953	Pittsburgh Steelers, Detroit Lions, Washington Redskins
McAfee, George	6-0	180	1940-41, 1945-50	Chicago Bears
Trippi, Charles	6-0	185	1947-55	Chicago Cardinals
Van Buren, Steve	6-0	205	1944-51	Philadelphia Eagles
White, Byron (Whizzer)	6-1	188	1938, 1940-41	Pittsburgh Pirates, Detroit Lions
Harder, Marlin (Pat)	5-11	205	1946-53	Chicago Cardinals, Detroit Lions
Motley, Marion	6-1	238	1946-53, 1955	Cleveland Browns, Pittsburgh Steelers
Osmanski, Bill	5-11	200	1939-43, 1946-47	Chicago Bears

1950s

A Wide Open Showcase

Mid-century brought a sharp dividing line in the nature of professional football. Free substitution allowed a new generation of players—who had come up practicing the skills of such as Hutson, Baugh and McAfee and drilling on the intricacies of the T—to develop their specialties to a fine point. The game exploded with revolutionary talent and a sport which had once seemed muscle-bound and confined was now a wide-open showcase for brilliant and effective gyrations.

The necessities of offense were understood the best, and, at first, the defense was overwhelmed by point-scoring machines. In their time Red Grange and Don Hutson stood out as anachronisms, but in the Fifties, Hugh McElhenny and Elroy Hirsch were only the best of many men who were breaking games with the weaving run or long bomb. Football in this manner is not necessarily better than the earlier game, but it is easier to see from the stands—and the stands began to fill.

As the points rained down in the early years of the decade, defensive football was force-fed by coaches and soon specialization began to have its effect here also. Many of the best athletes were put on defense and new theories were developed to try to slow the offense down. Soon defensive people began to lose their status as faceless obstacles and assumed starring roles alongside the point-scorers.

In Detroit "Chris's Crew," the great defensive backfield led by Jack Christiansen and featuring Yale Lary and Jim David, began to draw crowds on its own. By mid-decade, the New York Giants had put together a defense around Andy Robustelli at end, Sam Huff at linebacker and Emlen Tunnell in the backfield, which became a virtual symbol of NFL football.

In 1958, this Giant defense went up against the many-tonged Baltimore Colts' attack in the sudden-death game which made NFL football a television staple. Television had risen in the same decade that pro football opened up and by the end of the period, the new medium was firmly wedded to the photogenic sport. Pro football became the sport of the electronic generation.

OFFENSE

End

Tackle

Guard

Quarterback

Center

Flanker

Halfback

Fullback

Kicker

DEFENSE

End

Tackle

Linebackers

Halfback

Safety

	Ht.	Wt.	Years in League	Teams
Berry, Raymond	6-2	190	1955-67	Baltimore Colts
Fears, Tom	6-2	215	1948-56	Los Angeles Rams
Walston, Bobby	6-0	195	1951-62	Philadelphia Eagles
Brown, Roosevelt	6-3	255	1953-65	New York Giants
St. Clair, Bob	6-9	265	1953-63	San Francisco 49ers
Barwegan, Richard	6-1	228	1947-54	New York Yankees, Baltimore Colts, Chicago Bears
Parker, Jim	6-3	275	1957-67	Baltimore Colts
Stanfel, Dick	6-3	240	1952-58	Detroit Lions, Washington Redskins
Graham, Otto	6-1	195	1946-55	Cleveland Browns
Layne, Bobby	6-2	210	1948-62	Chicago Bears, New York Bulldogs, Detroit Lions, Pittsburgh Steelers
Van Brocklin, Norm	6-1	202	1949-60	Los Angeles Rams, Philadelphia Eagles
Bednarik, Chuck	6-3	235	1949-62	Philadelphia Eagles
Moore, Lenny	6-1	190	1956-67	Baltimore Colts
Hirsch, Elroy (Crazy Legs)	6-2	190	1946-57	Chicago Rockets, Los Angeles Rams
Gifford, Frank	6-1	200	1952-60, 1962-64	New York Giants
Matson, Ollie	6-2	215	1952, 1954-66	Chicago Cardinals, Los Angeles Rams, Detroit Lions, Philadelphia Eagles
McElhenny, Hugh	6-1	190	1952-64	San Francisco 49ers, Minnesota Vikings, New York Giants, Detroit Lions
Ameche, Alan	6-1	220	1955-60	Baltimore Colts
Perry, Fletcher (Joe)	6-0	200	1948-62	San Francisco 49ers, Baltimore Colts
Groza, Lou	6-3	250	1946-59, 1961-67	Cleveland Browns
Marchetti, Gino	6-4	245	1952-64, 1966	Dallas Texans, Baltimore Colts
Ford, Leonard	6-5	258	1948-58	Los Angeles Dons, Cleveland Browns, Green Bay Packers
Donovan, Art	6-3	270	1950-61	Baltimore Colts, New York Yankees, Dallas Texans
Nomellini, Leo	6-3	262	1950-63	San Francisco 49ers
Stautner, Ernie	6-2	230	1950-63	Pittsburgh Steelers
Fortunato, Joe	6-1	225	1955-66	Chicago Bears
George, Bill	6-2	235	1952-66	Chicago Bears, Los Angeles Rams
Huff, Sam	6-1	230	1956-67	New York Giants, Washington Redskins
Schmidt, Joe	6-0	220	1953-65	Detroit Lions
Butler, Jack	6-1	193	1951-59	Pittsburgh Steelers
Lane, Dick (Night Train)	6-2	200	1952-65	Los Angeles Rams, Chicago Cardinals, Detroit Lions
Christiansen, Jack	6-1	180	1951-58	Detroit Lions
Lary, Yale	5-11	190	1952-53 1956-64	Detroit Lions
Tunnell, Emlen	6-1	210	1948-61	New York Giants, Green Bay Packers

1960s
The Electronic Generation

Television ratings attest that pro football has become a major part of America's leisure and in the Sixties, the sport developed an outlook and a structure which fit such a stature. With the sandlots far behind, the game grew into a professionally organized business. Players were no longer on a youthful lark, but were instead professionals, building a future on their earnings and prominence.

The game grew tremendously, doubling the number of teams in less than ten years. Another new league was formed, the American Football League, and before the merger, in 1966, salary wars seemed likely to bankrupt some franchises. When peace was declared, however, the growth was found to be solid and all the teams from both leagues remained in business. The reason for this was to be found on the field.

Despite the new professionalism, the brute vitality of the game had, if anything, increased. As pro football approached its fiftieth year, it outgrew the fast-and-loose flamboyance of the Fifties. Big, fast men were all over the field and it was no longer possible for a halfback to outrun the defense around end or a passer to throw easy bombs at will. As these avenues were closed the players were turned back upon themselves with a new intensity born of greater strength and better equipment. End runs became power plays and the passing attack was predicted on a successful fight to hold out the mobile monsters in the defensive lines.

At the start of the decade, a new tone was set by Vince Lombardi in Green Bay, a style based on power

and emotional commitment. In other NFL centers, coaches like Tom Landry and Blanton Collier were inventing a football game so subtle and complex that players were likened to human computers, programmed to instantly handle any situation which confronted them. It was a demanding sport, physically, mentally and emotionally, and the best of the men playing it were very good indeed.

The brilliance of the players drew the allegiance of fans of all ages, and one result was that pro football paved the way for its own transcendence. All over the country young athletes practiced the maneuvers created by the Sixties pros in the necessity of the moment. These athletes will arrive in the league, as have other football generations before them, ready to do routinely what only the best of their predecessors could manage.

The All-Pro teams of the National Football League's second half-century will surely be something to see.

OFFENSE

End

Tackle

Guard

Center

Quarterback

Flanker

Tight End

Halfback

Fullback

Field Goal Kicker

Punter

DEFENSE

End

Tackle

Linebacker

Halfback

Safety

	Ht.	Wt.	Years in League	Teams
Shofner, Del	6-3	190	1957-67	Los Angeles Rams, New York Giants
Taylor, Charley	6-3	210	1964-	Washington Redskins
Brown, Bob	6-4	295	1964-73	Philadelphia Eagles, Los Angeles Rams, Oakland Raiders
Gregg, Forrest	6-4	250	1956, 1958-71	Green Bay Packers, Dallas Cowboys
Neely, Ralph	6-6	265	1965-	Dallas Cowboys
Hickerson, Gene	6-3	260	1958-60, 1962-73	Cleveland Browns
Kramer, Jerry	6-3	254	1958-68	Green Bay Packers
Mudd, Howard	6-2	254	1964-70	San Francisco 49ers, Chicago Bears
Ringo, Jim	6-2	230	1953-67	Green Bay Packers, Philadelphia Eagles
Jurgensen, Sonny	6-0	203	1957-74	Philadelphia Eagles, Washington Redskins
Starr, Bart	6-1	190	1956-71	Green Bay Packers
Unitas, John	6-1	196	1956-73	Baltimore Colts, San Diego Chargers
Collins, Gary	6-4	215	1962-71	Cleveland Browns
Dowler, Boyd	6-5	225	1959-69, 1971	Green Bay Packers, Washington Redskins
Mackey, John	6-2	224	1963-72	Baltimore Colts, San Diego Chargers
Crow, John David	6-2	224	1958-68	Chicago Cardinals, St. Louis Cardinals, San Francisco 49ers
Hornung, Paul	6-2	215	1957-62, 1964-66	Green Bay Packers
Kelly, Leroy	6-0	200	1964-73	Cleveland Browns
Sayers, Gale	6-0	198	1965-71	Chicago Bears
Brown, Jim	6-2	232	1957-65	Cleveland Browns
Taylor, Jim	6-0	215	1958-67	Green Bay Packers, New Orleans Saints
Bakken, Jim	6-0	200	1962-	St. Louis Cardinals
Chandler, Don	6-2	210	1956-67	New York Giants, Green Bay Packers
Atkins, Doug	6-8	270	1953-69	Cleveland Browns, Chicago Bears, New Orleans Saints
Davis, Willie	6-3	245	1958-69	Cleveland Browns, Green Bay Packers
Jones, David (Deacon)	6-5	260	1961-74	Los Angeles Rams, San Diego Chargers, Washington Redskins
Karras, Alex	6-2	245	1958-62, 1964-70	Detroit Lions
Lilly, Bob	6-5	260	1961-	Dallas Cowboys
Olsen, Merlin	6-5	276	1962-	Los Angeles Rams
Butkus, Dick	6-3	245	1965-73	Chicago Bears
Morris, Larry	6-2	220	1955-57, 1959-66	Los Angeles Rams, Chicago Bears, Atlanta Falcons
Nitschke, Ray	6-3	240	1958-72	Green Bay Packers
Nobis, Tommy	6-2	235	1966-	Atlanta Falcons
Robinson, Dave	6-3	240	1963-	Green Bay Packers, Washington Redskins
Adderley, Herb	6-0	200	1961-72	Green Bay Packers, Dallas Cowboys
Barney, Lem	6-0	202	1967-	Detroit Lions
Boyd, Bob	5-10	192	1960-68	Baltimore Colts
Meador, Ed	5-11	199	1959-70	Los Angeles Rams
Wilson, Larry	6-0	190	1960-72	St. Louis Cardinals
Wood, Willie	5-10	160	1960-71	Green Bay Packers

The All Pros: Sixteen Men

Introduction

The choice of all-star squads for each decade serves to sharpen another, and yet more contentious, series of questions. Who, finally, has been the greatest all-time quarterback? Who has been the most dangerous flanker? Who has been the most reliable safetyman?

It is as though a coach were sent to a mythical draft meeting and told to select from fifty years of professionals his first choice at every position. Even compared to the annual draft of college talent, a difficult task in itself, this seems a nearly impossible problem. But it is irresistably fascinating.

The men involved have had magic names, names which generate an aura of excitement and fame. Their abilities have been genuine and undeniable, yet comparison is as much a function of the man doing the comparing as the men being compared. There would be as many different mythical "draft lists" as there would be "coaches" who selected them.

From the bias of the present day, current players loom larger than those who played ten or fifteen years ago. The game has grown more difficult and it is natural to feel that the stars of today would be superior to the stars of the earlier game. Against these modern stars, only the storied greats of the founding time seem to maintain a stature that holds substance in the minds of those who would concoct all-time teams. Remembered glories sustain a story-book quality that rivals the actions of today's athletes.

In an effort to create a legitimate all-time selection, the Pro Football Hall of Fame was called upon to compile a list of the NFL's greatest players, by positions. The choice of positions was based upon the arrangement of a modern pro team. Given the all-decade teams, the choice was made by the Hall of Fame selectors, sixteen distinguished journalists in the NFL cities who spend part of each year pondering the merits of all the NFL greats, past and present.

Out of their poll developed the forty-six men found on the following pages. There are two runners-up for each position and fifteen winners. In a special category, Jim Thorpe was singled out as the star that never diminishes, the ideal of the athlete incorporated in a body made inhuman by legend.

These are the men who have been chosen as pro football's best. They have brought to the game skill and strength, courage and perseverance, pride and devotion. They have stirred us to excitement, admiration, respect and affection. These are the enduring pros, the tradition makers upon whom the game was built.

The Players

A Portfolio

QUARTERBACK
Sammy Baugh
Washington Redskins
1937-52

Norm Van Brocklin
Los Angeles Rams
Philadelphia Eagles
1949-60

FULLBACK
Bronko Nagurski
Chicago Bears
1932-37, 1943

Joe Perry
San Francisco 49ers
Baltimore Colts
1948-63

HALFBACK
Harold "Red" Grange
Chicago Bears
New York Yankees
1925-27, 1929-34

Hugh McElhenny
San Francisco 49ers
Minnesota Vikings
New York Giants
Detroit Lions
1952-1964

96

SPLIT END

Raymond Berry
Baltimore Colts
1955-67

Dante Lavelli
Cleveland Browns
1946-56

TIGHT END

Mike Ditka
Chicago Bears
Philadelphia Eagles
Dallas Cowboys
1961-72

Ron Kramer
Green Bay Packers
Detroit Lions
1957, 1959-67

FLANKER

Boyd Dowler
Green Bay Packers
Washington Redskins
1959-69, 71

Lenny Moore
Baltimore Colts
1956-67

KICKER

Ernie Nevers
Duluth Eskimos
Chicago Cardinals
1926-27, 1929-31

Ken Strong
Staten Island Stapletons
New York Giants
New York Yanks
1929-47

OFFENSIVE TACKLE
Forrest Gregg
Green Bay Packers
Dallas Cowboys
1956, 1958-71

Joe Stydahar
Chicago Bears
1936-42, 1945-46

GUARD
Danny Fortmann
Chicago Bears
1936-43

Jim Parker
Baltimore Colts
1957-67

CENTER
Mel Hein
New York Giants
1931-45

Alex Wojciechowicz
Detroit Lions
Philadelphia Eagles
1938-50

LINEBACKER
Joe Schmidt
Detroit Lions
1953-65

Clyde "Bulldog" Turner
Chicago Bears
1940-52

DEFENSIVE END

Len Ford
Los Angeles Dons
Cleveland Browns
Green Bay Packers
1948-58

David "Deacon" Jones
Los Angeles Rams
San Diego Chargers
Washington Redskins
1961-74

DEFENSIVE TACKLE

Art Donovan
Baltimore Colts
New York Yanks
Dallas Texans
1950-61

Ernie Stautner
Pittsburgh Steelers
1950-63

DEFENSIVE HALFBACK

Herb Adderley
Green Bay Packers
Dallas Cowboys
1961-72

Jack Butler
Pittsburgh Steelers
1951-59

SAFETY

Jack Christiansen
Detroit Lions
1951-58

Larry Wilson
St. Louis Cardinals
1960-72

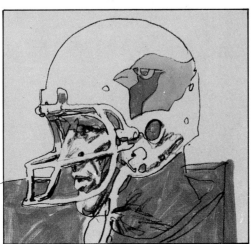

He came out of the flat, featureless land of Oklahoma, a rugged and impassionate Sac and Fox Indian, to strike with legendary greatness through the sports annals of the early twentieth century. He became the acknowledged folk hero of America's athletes, living a factual lore which is now reckoned with the fictional deeds of Paul Bunyan, John Henry and Johnny Appleseed.

Jim Thorpe was without equal on a playing field. In the 1912 Olympics he proved to be the finest all-around track and field athlete in the world, winning both the decathlon and pentathlon with record-breaking performances. The 1913 World Series with the New York Giants highlighted his eight-year baseball career.

But football was his sport, and it is in that game his athletic genius was most vividly expressed. Big Jim could do everything required — run, pass, punt, block, drop kick, place kick, tackle. Thorpe was an uneven and moody competitor. There were periods when it was impossible to get him to rise to a challenge. When he was charged and ready to go, there was no stopping him, and he played with a savage fervor that few men could match. Thorpe was famous and feared for his violence on the playing field.

Thorpe burned his quality years playing on the harvest fields and high-school gridirons of pro football's town-team era. When a team was organized in Canton in 1915, his name insured gate receipts. When pro football organized in 1920, his name gave the president's office instant prestige.

An impartial man, he played for a number of teams in the early years of the NFL, finally ending his career ingloriously sitting on the Giants' bench, a sad caricature of himself. In 1925, he left the game for good, his exit smothered under the avalanche of publicity for Red Grange, football's newest hero. The ironic crossing of their paths was portentous for that year marked the end of a primitive and somewhat innocent era and the beginning of a new, more enlightened one for professional football.

A sullen, almost childlike man, Thorpe was unable to adjust to life away from sport. Off the field he was just another big Indian, ignored by society. He went to Hollywood with promises of fame and, instead, ended up working as a laborer through the Depression. Always fond of alcohol, he turned to it as his only solace. In 1953, he died a stricken and forgotten man.

His Sac and Fox name was Wa-Tho-Huck — Bright Path. He followed it out of Oklahoma to a place in history that cannot be diminished. Thorpe, the man, is remembered as a symbol of much that is good and much that is bad in this land of wide, but finite, opportunity.

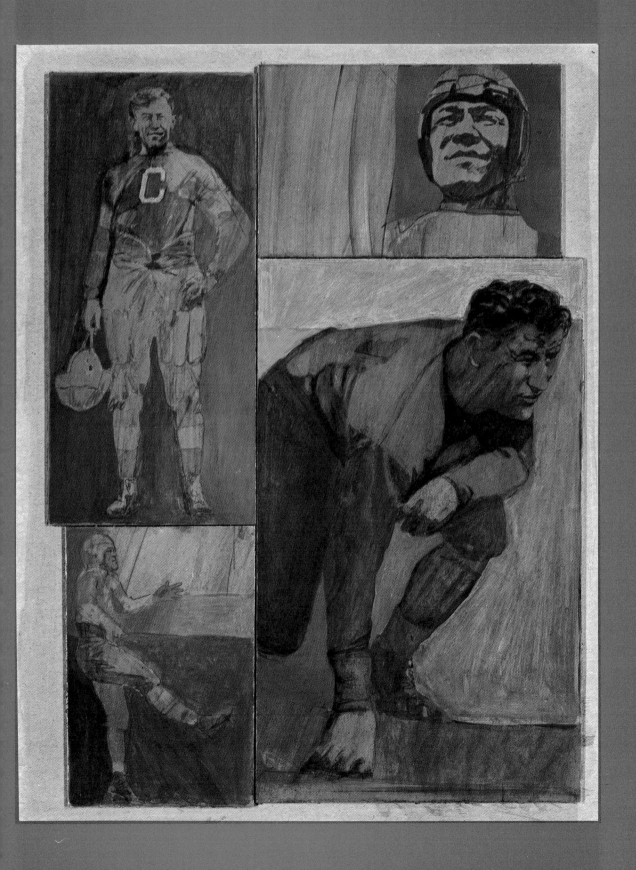

QUARTERBACK
Johnny Unitas
1956-73

He did not look right. An inch over six feet, he appeared shorter because of his stooped shoulders. His arms dangled loosely from the sockets, apparently out of rhythm with his body. His feet toed in and he wore the high-topped black shoes of the lineman, giving his thin legs a heavy, weighted appearance.

But the physical sketch does not sum to the truth of professional football's greatest quarterback, Johnny Unitas of the Baltimore Colts, and, for the final year of his career, the San Diego Chargers. For Unitas, the inner man, was a perfect match for his position in his sport and, by pro football's mid-century mark, the quarterback spot was usually defined by the way Unitas played it. His emotional, mental, and physical qualities were such that when he was on the field, a game often seemed to be merely an extension of his own creative tension. All the independent variables—his teammates, his opponents, the wind, the field, the flight of the ball—appeared to be encompassed and controlled by his own expanded consciousness. A Unitas play or drive had an inexorable rightness, a cohesion, emanating from his mastery of all details of the game.

From this mastery stemmed the pure confidence that Unitas felt even when he was released to the sandlots of Louisville after his first training camp. His confidence allowed him to become most valuable player in only his second year and to perform with taut beauty at the age of 25 in the potentially suffocating pressure of pro football's first sudden-death championship. During his career, and contending against the Lombardi era in Green Bay, the Colts won 212, lost 68, and tied 5, while winning five conference titles and four league championships, including Super Bowl V. Unitas rewrote the passing records. In his tenth season after the sudden-death game, in 1967, Unitas had perhaps his greatest season, earning the most valuable player award for a second time.

As John Unitas moved with professional football into its second half century, his arm wearied. But Unitas was one with football. He played, as he said he would, as long as someone needed him.

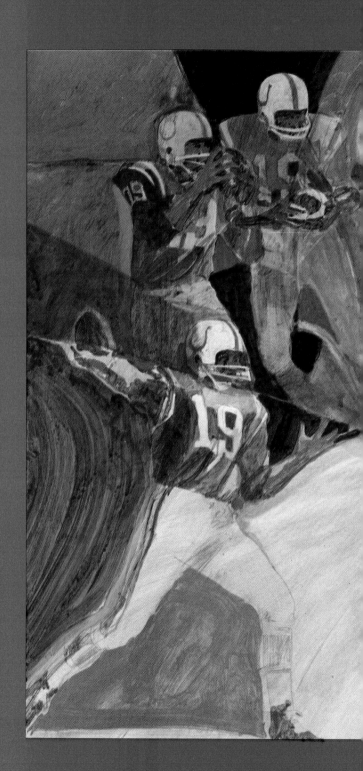

FULLBACK
Jim Brown
1957-1965

Jim Brown was a phenomenon. He was seemingly invincible, a man gifted with the grace, speed, intelligence and strength of a fictional hero. In the wild war on the field, he moved serenely, impervious to the dangers around him. Through a nine-year career as the NFL's marked man, he never missed a game.

Brown carried 232 pounds like a halfback, with a loose, shuffling gait that belied his sprinters' speed. He was content to run by opponents, but cornered, he used his forearm as a bludgeon to knock tacklers aside with a power that Marciano must have envied.

His unique skill invented an offensive style. He would take the ball and then, with his individual loping style, glide into and through the meshing lines, often breaking a certain short gain for a long, ground-eating run. Paul Brown, his coach, invented option blocking to accommodate Jim's fluid style. He told the offensive linemen to push their defensive counterparts the way the defenders chose to go, and let Brown pick his own spot to charge through.

In the small type of statistics, genius is often lost, and Brown's records on the page are almost past comprehension. In 1963, he set a single-season record with 1,863 yards rushing. His nine-year total of 12,312 yards is nearly 4,000 yards more than his closest pursuer. He led the NFL in rushing in eight of his nine seasons, and for five consecutive years, 1957-61. He rushed for more than 200 yards in a game on four occasions and he exceeded the 100-yard mark in each of 58 games. As a parlay, he holds the record for carries, 2,359, and average, 5.22 yards.

He left the game in 1965 to go into motion pictures. No matter what he accomplishes in his new field, it is unlikely he will match his performance on the playing field. He did implausible things in a sport that recognizes greatness by physically testing and punishing it. And today, that memory is more significant than his two-dimensional image on the world's theatre screens.

It is the difference between real and make-believe.

HALFBACK
Gale Sayers
1965-71

The halfback is the consummate athlete. He is to football what El Cordobes was to the bulls and Jimi Hendrix was to rock—an improvisation on a classic theme, maneuvering on the edge of spectacular failure.

The skill that belonged to Gale Sayers could not be taught. His was a rare gift that made him unique in his profession. Others before him, Red Grange, George McAfee, Hugh McElhenny, have moved freely in the open field, but Sayers' elusive, angular grace put him in a one-man category.

Formations and plays could be predetermined for Sayers, but he relied more upon the truth of his instincts to break free than the meticulous blueprint of the play. A blocking failure did not bind him, but freed him from the rigid rule of the team.

It was at this point that Sayers began to function fully. With the instincts of an artist and the discipline of an athlete, he pitted himself against the defense as man against environment. He weighed all probabilities—the angle of approaching tacklers, the ratio of his speed to theirs, the distance from each sideline, the number of opponents left, the vectors of his own blockers, and the texture of the field. In an instant, these facts were programmed into motion. His art, as all art, flowed from being, not thinking.

A daring, wide-open runner, Sayers was the ultimate competitor, constantly challenging the forces that sought to restrain him. When a crowd of tacklers began to converge, most runners would decelerate in order to make quick changes of direction or to prepare for sudden heavy blows. But Sayers slammed on, slashing past startled opponents and jamming through turns with a stiff-legged, heel-first ferocity. This was his unique talent, one that sprung him from seemingly impenetrable congestion into the open field, which he devoured with a wide, galloping stride.

In action, Gale Sayers was an intuitive, sensitive instrument working with incomprehensible decisiveness and truth. The fact that his genius was released on a professional football field brought people to the stadium, for he was the fruition of an idea that began when man first tucked a ball under his arm and started to run.

107

FLANKER
Elroy "Crazy Legs" Hirsch
1946-1957

Elroy Hirsch was always a star. He lived a career that Hollywood made a movie about, from shining success through tragedy and back to the top again, but the movie missed the essence. Elroy Hirsch was not a star by circumstance but by his own skill and very special exuberance.

He was All-Big Ten at 17, as a Wisconsin sophomore, and when he moved to Michigan during World War II he continued his Big Ten dominance as the last of that school's four-sport lettermen. They called him "Crazy Legs," for the wild way his feet splayed behind him when he ran, and those legs carried him through stardom with the College All-Stars in 1946, and on to the Chicago Rockets of the newly formed AAFC.

But in 1948 the good times ran out on Elroy Hirsch. A collision severely fractured his skull and left him with transitory loss of bodily coordination. Doctors told him he was through.

"Crazy Legs, All American" was a movie made about a man who fought his way back. Hirsch discarded the new plastic helmet in which he had been injured, sent to Michigan for his old leather hat, and went to Los Angeles to play halfback for the Los Angeles Rams in 1949. The Rams, in transition to the modern passing game, often split Hirsch wide and finally moved him permanently to end. He became the game's first flanker and helped revolutionize the sport with his high-speed artistry. In 1951 he went wild, outrunning defenders to 17 touchdown passes, tying Don Hutson's record, and totaling 1,495 yards, a record which still stands. He is best remembered running at full tilt, his head back, arms outstretched to stop a flying football with the tips of his fingers. It was a play of such simplistic beauty that it has never been matched.

When he finally retired in 1957, the scene in Los Angeles' Memorial Coliseum was an emotional one. In a town used to everyday association with the world's most famous faces, his fans acted like thrill-crazed teeny boppers. They tore his uniform from his back, leaving only his sweat socks, tape and, modestly, his supporter.

"Crazy Legs" Hirsch was a celebrity.

DON HUTSON
100 T.D. CAREER
RECEPTIONS

SPLIT END
Don Hutson
1935-1945

Don Hutson made it look easy.

In 1935, during the age of ponderous and abrasive ground attacks, he brought the art of receiving to its full flower, striding through opponents with a swiftness and grace that changed the game. Although he played both ways, as rules required, he was truly a specialist in a genre he invented.

He was a slim man, 180 lbs. strung on a 6'1" frame, but looked even smaller since tiny shoulder pads were his only concession to protective equipment other than his helmet. Occasionally he would daub black shoe polish on his cheeks, making his face appear macabre, although the purpose was to cut the glare of the afternoon sun as he looked up for the ball.

This innovation, though functional, was minor compared to his development of the individual pass route. Hutson was the first man to cultivate a full repertoire of fakes. Receivers before him had merely run to their assigned area as directly as possible. But Hutson saw that a devious route was often best, because it would confuse the defenders. His precise effectiveness and brilliant speed allowed his passers, first Arnie Herber and then Cecil Isbell, to lay the ball on predesignated spots, confident that Hutson would arrive there alone.

He was so far beyond his contemporaries that he led the league in pass receiving eight of his eleven seasons, once for five successive years. His record of catching passes in 95 consecutive games was finally broken in 1969. One afternoon in 1945, against Detroit, he caught four touchdowns in one quarter and kicked five extra points to set another record—a brilliant 29 points in one period of play. His 17 touchdown catches in 1942 have been matched only by the Rams' Elroy Hirsch.

No one has personified the professional receiver as Hutson did: a detached member of the offense who passed through the violence suffered by the other members of his team and, in a moment of pure athletic beauty, raced free and effortlessly to unity with the arching football.

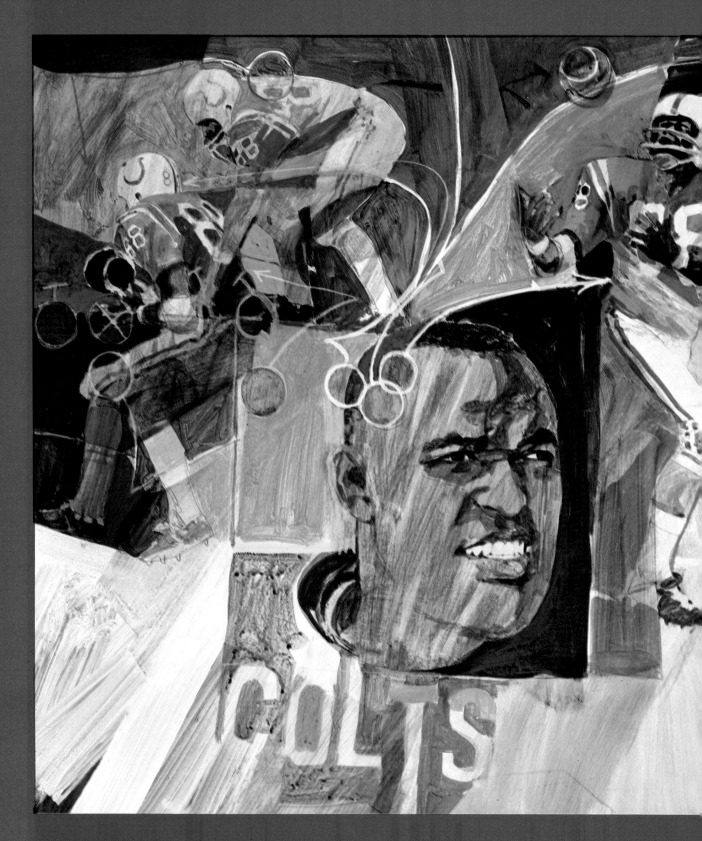

TIGHT END
John Mackey
1963-72

On the playing fields of the NFL, dressed in the celebrated blue and white uniform of the Baltimore Colts, John Mackey was a man apart, separated by an endowment that was unique in a game built upon the integration of individual talents.

His position is a relatively new one in football, an outgrowth of the specialization that has made professional football an unprecedented success. Tight end was created fifteen years ago in an attempt to bring added strength to the offense and is such a difficult position that few men qualify. Mackey fit the position perfectly, filling it with eminent qualities of a prodigy.

Tight end requires a man to participate in the grueling tedium of the blocking game, meshing with the members of the offensive line in breaking holes in the defense for runners to advance through. On the next play, he may be the primary receiver, asked to bring the precise skill of a pass catcher to immediate action. Always he is within easy distance of the thumping forearm shots of defensive ends or linebackers, a punishing confrontation that not only robs strength from a man but weighs heavily on his concentration and involvement with the game. As a runner, once he has caught the ball, the tight end is supposed to get the short, hard yards that provide first downs for his team.

Mackey did all of this with a sure excellence that was not only incredibly consistent but seemingly easy. At 6 feet 2 inches and 225 pounds, he was distinguished by large, muscular thighs that made him look like one of the strongest runners football has ever seen. At full speed he was almost impossible to knock down. His forte was catching the quick pass and breaking it for long, romping gains through the opposition.

The true test of the tight end is his ability to maintain an emotional balance. Because of the demands of the position, the personality of the player can easily be influenced, if not distorted. Spread-eagled between the poles of finesse and savagery, Mackey met the challenge better than anyone in the game, remaining a sensitive, positive, and productive human being while he dispatched his assignment with professional elan.

In an unyielding environment, Mackey displayed the grace of a man larger than his job.

TACKLE
Cal Hubbard
1927-1936

After more than 50 years, the NFL isn't awed by the presence of a big man on the playing field. In the mid-twenties, giants were uncommon. Most linemen weighed in the area of 200 pounds. Heavier men could be found, but the only adjectives that described them were fat and slow.

In 1927, the Giants signed a young man who transfixed opponents with awe, followed immediately by fear. Cal Hubbard, a storied end and tackle from little Centenary College in Louisiana, stood 6-5 and weighed a rock-hard 250 lbs. He could run 100 yards in 11 seconds and excelled as a blocker on running plays. In the heyday of the single wing, tackle was the pivotal position on both offense and defense. Hubbard gloried in the job, destroying opposing lines with a singular savagery that would be remembered into pro football's second half-century.

Despite his immense size and strength, he was so mobile that on offense he was often used as the target of a special tackle eligible pass play and on defense he was given the lateral pursuit responsibilities of a linebacker.

In New York, Hubbard joined forces with another great tackle of the period, Steve Owen, who, at 240 lbs., was famous for his strength. The two of them were indomitable, bringing a 1960s look to the club, and its first championship.

Hubbard moved to the Green Bay Packers in 1929. With the big man contributing his strength and speed to a team already loaded with people like Johnny Blood, Lavern Dilweg, and Mike Michalske, the Packers won three consecutive NFL championships for coach Curly Lambeau.

While in Green Bay, Hubbard began umpiring baseball games during spring and summer, a job which cut short his football career in 1936 and led him, in 1952, to an appointment as umpire-in-chief of the American League.

Awkward size can be a handicap to a man, building an outcast mentality. In Cal Hubbard, great size was managed, creating a man of majestic dominance. He was the first of the line of pro football's mobile giants who have expanded our conception of man's capabilities.

GUARD
Jerry Kramer
1958-1968

Jerry Kramer's effusive personality belies his fierce dedication and discipline as a competitor. From the outset of Vince Lombardi's reign in Green Bay in 1959, Kramer was the Packers' right guard. A poised second year man, No. 64 began to attract attention early, leading the Green Bay runners, Jim Taylor and Paul Hornung, on the play that became a pro football staple in the '60s, the Packer Power Sweep.

An emotionally strong man, he often played with pain, seemingly impervious to the psychological and physiological drain it imposes. To achieve distinction as football's finest guard he overcame the effects of numerous injuries that would have finished the careers of other men. As a schoolboy, he severely wounded himself in the right arm with a shotgun blast, leaving a partially paralyzed hand. At the age of 17, he stepped on a rotting plank which shot large splinters into his groin, requiring surgery for removal. Football gave him a chipped vertebra requiring surgery in 1956, a detached retina in 1960 and a severe leg fracture in 1961. In 1964, after a series of eight exploratory operations, several splinters from the boyhood accident were discovered lodged in his intestines, creating internal disorders and a disease that almost took his life.

In between hospital visits, Kramer played all-pro guard for Green Bay. He was especially effective in terribly cold championship games. He kicked three field goals through bitter wind to beat the Giants in 1962, and made the touchdown block for the decisive score in the icy mud against Cleveland in 1965 and in the sub-zero histrionics against Dallas in 1967.

All through the Lombardi era at Green Bay, it seemed Kramer was always in the forefront, a big smile on his face, doing his manly thing with a little boy's enthusiasm. During the sometimes ebullient, sometimes tragic '60s, Jerry Kramer seemed to fit perfectly, bringing a spontaneous personality to a game that is often known only for its muscular ferocity.

CENTER
Chuck Bednarik
1949-1962

Chuck Bednarik was a pro's pro, a rugged, mashed-nosed warrior who delighted in the crashing wars of the front line. His violence won respect from opponents and an unhappy, if revealing, notoriety among fans.

Everything he ever did was weighted with a heavy masculinity. He flew 30 combat missions as a World War II waist gunner. As a 235-pound lineman for Pennsylvania University after the war, he battered his way to All-America prominence. In 1949, the Philadelphia Eagles made him their first draft choice.

The Eagles were a world championship team, built of hardened pros in their finest hours—men like Steve Van Buren, Pete Pihos and Bucko Kilroy. Bednarik became a regular in mid-season and stayed for 13 years. Although free substitution was adopted in his rookie year, he played both center and linebacker much of his career. At the end, in 1960, he gritted through 394½ minutes playing time to help drive the Eagles back to a championship.

But this, his greatest year, backfired into public disapproval. Late in an important game with the Giants that year, one in which he played 51 minutes, the big linebacker caught Frank Gifford with a legal but crunching blind-side tackle that knocked the ball loose and stretched the popular all-pro halfback unconscious on the ground. In a momentary wave of exuberance, knowing only that the recovered fumble meant his team was going to win that day, Bednarik did a war dance over his fallen foe, a Tarzan-like rage of joy that stunned, and then reviled the fans in Yankee Stadium. Moments later, the unmoving Gifford was carried from the field, with a concussion that took a season from his career.

Even a 58-minute performance and a last-second, game-saving tackle of Jim Taylor in the Eagles' 17-13 championship victory over Green Bay would not blot out the demonic image of that nightmarish moment in New York.

A year later, Philadelphia's iron-man retired, certain of his place in his game's history. He knew the way the game is played. He had no apologies and his fellows demanded none.

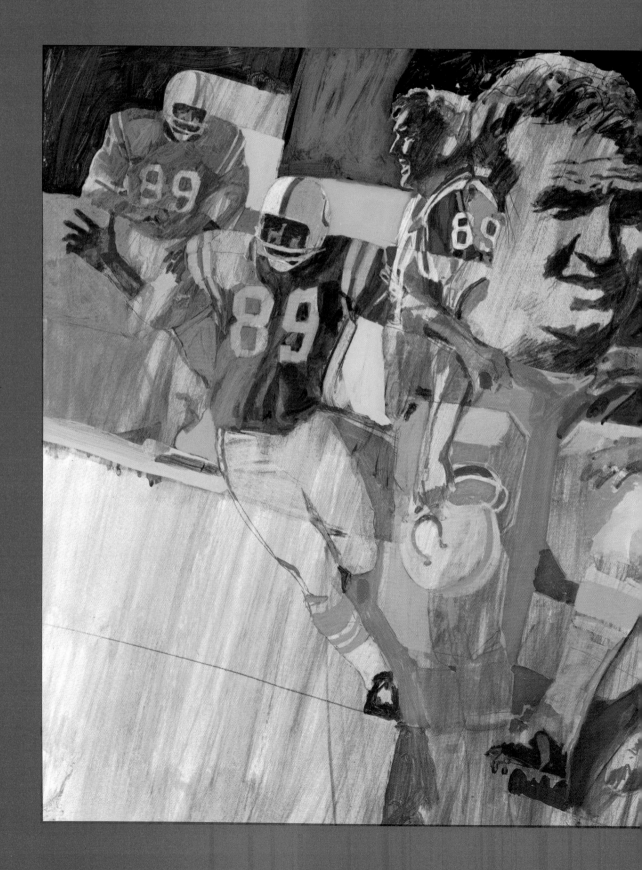

DEFENSIVE END
Gino Marchetti
1953-1964

Baltimore's Gino Marchetti did not get to see the finish of the spectacular sudden-death championship game of 1958. He had been carried off, with little more than a minute to play, after breaking his ankle while tackling New York's Frank Gifford on a crucial third down. As Marchetti fought his pain in the dressing room, John Unitas drove the Colts to the sudden-death victory which the big defensive end had made possible. In a career full of spectacular achievements, this was the only one Marchetti took lying down.

Gino Marchetti created modern defensive end play. He had strength and the meanness necessary to give and take the pounding of interior line play. He used his hands and weight well, pushing and throwing and clubbing offensive linemen.

But his major contribution was not to increase punishment but to add finesse, and it was this element of his ability that raised him above his peers to become the league's greatest defensive end. His fierce battles with offensive tackles were classic, and over the years were as much a part of watching the Colts as seeing Unitas, Moore and Berry. His style set the trend for the quick, mobile defensive ends of the 1960s, men like David Jones and Willie Davis.

Marchetti's imminent challenge was getting the quarterback, the first job of the defensive end. He did it regularly and with the deadliness of a missile homing in on its target. He was as tough against the run, crushing plays inside of him and slicing through plays wide of him. In time, he won the greatest distinction a player can be paid — many teams ran away from Marchetti, choosing to forgo their right-handed running strength rather than face him.

Marchetti brought a desire and a dedication to the game that marks all great players. He played much longer than he had to, retiring when he was 39. Off the field he was a successful businessman. But professional football is not played for money by the great competitors. It is played for pride.

Gino Marchetti had it in abundance.

DEFENSIVE TACKLE
Leo Nomellini
1950-1963

Leo Nomellini was indeed a lion. His habitat was the line of scrimmage, an area he patrolled with authority for thirteen seasons as a 49er. In an area where toughness is a requisite, Leo brought a special kind of fierceness and dedication.

At 6'3", 262, he was big enough to intimidate most people with his size and strength alone. But Leo was a sort of lay psychologist, a knowledge he developed as one of the Bay Area's more successful professional wrestlers in the off-season. He picked up a few tricks while working the mats and brought them down to the playing fields.

Nomellini had a square-cut, meaty face that he learned to twist into grotesque masques. He helped this act along by taking out his two front teeth, creating a black hole through which he emitted explosive wheezes and grunts that sent shivers down spines of opponents and teammates alike. He carefully taped the fingers of each hand between the knuckles and the first two joints and when he grabbed at people, he looked like some iron-clawed super villain out of a Captain America comic book.

Courage was not a press agent's word to Nomellini. As a Marine, he learned all about its meaning participating in the Pacific invasion forces that took Saipan and Okinawa in 1944-45. An Italian-born son of an immigrant family, football allowed him to escape the poverty of Chicago's Northwest side and attain unaccustomed luxuries and success. He fought for them each Sunday with an appreciative ferocity.

One of the first versatile defensive linemen, his quick moves and balance were unsuspected in a man of his size. Most linemen of the Fifties lived anonymous careers, but No. 73 challenged the popularity of his team's great offensive stars, Tittle, Perry, McElhenny and Wilson. Seemingly impervious to injury, Nomellini never missed a game.

In 1962, he set a League record for consecutive games played, 159, and when he retired in 1963 at age 39, he had extended his record to a total of 174 contests, plus 77 pre-season and 10 Pro Bowl games.

LINEBACKER
Ray Nitschke
1958-72

Ray Nitschke was an internal contradiction, the kind of split personality that could be found only in a sport like professional football.

Off the field, away from the game, Nitschke, in his dark horn-rimmed glasses and traditional suits, looked like a tall, balding, mild-mannered professor, the essence of urbane man. A thoughtful, intelligent individual, he reposed easily in conversation, discussing subjects with a quiet, articulate manner.

On the field he was transposed. The glasses came off, causing a dark squint. His teeth came out, bringing a cruel curve to his mouth. The balding head was covered by a helmet that was distinguished by the scars of violent collisions. In the heavy and grotesque pads of the linebacker and the deep forest green and bright gold of Green Bay, he stalked the field like a man possessed of demons.

As the field leader of one of football's greatest defensive units, Nitschke suffered the problems of recognition that frequently befall men on a team loaded with all-pro performers. Often he was bypassed by the selectors who found that in an age of the Packers' dominance, it was impossible to give them all credit.

But in the era of the middle linebacker, Nitschke developed his reputation as the best. As if on an evolutionary table, the great linebackers of the age of specialization can be traced, starting with Joe Schmidt, Les Richter, Bill George, and Sam Huff to Nitschke, Dick Butkus, and Tommy Nobis.

And when the ideal linebacker is discussed by football men, Nitschke is the man who enlivens the conversation—a savage on the field, wrapped in tape, his uniform spotted with blood, pushing through a cordon of blockers to find the ball carrier and take him in an all-out, incredibly intense explosion of flesh.

In the emotional cauldron of professional football, the big linebacker from Green Bay brought the game down to its most elemental form—man against man. In the final analysis, this is football's criterion of excellence.

CORNER BACK
Dick "Night Train" Lane
1952-1965

Dick Lane danced to his own compulsive rhythms on the playing field. In the era of the greatest change in pro defenses, he was instrumental in developing the daring and complicated style of the cornerback, playing the game with the premeditated coolness of an executioner.

For Night Train Lane, football was more than a game; it was his profession and salvation. Though gifted naturally, he dedicated himself to the construction of skills which would maintain his position in the sport. He saw his opponents as vindictive enemies, out to embarrass and defeat him, and none would escape him if he could find a way to handle them. After receipting for numerous headaches, he stopped hitting power runners in the knees, and instead developed the necktie tackle, a high-speed hammer-lock which avoided the punishing knees and also neutralized the elusive legs of runners like Hugh McElhenny and Jon Arnett.

On pass defense he played an equally distinctive game, finding special rewards in his personal vendetta against the offense. An eager ball hawk, he played with a daring that seemed to have a touch of the occult about it.

As a Ram rookie in 1952, in an early version of the zone defense, he intercepted 14 passes, setting a league record. In his career, which eventually took him to the Cardinals and Lions, he captured a total of 68 interceptions, placing him second only to Emlen Tunnell.

Sunday after Sunday he put his career and livelihood on the line, meeting the challenge of the NFL's finest runners and receivers. He did it for 14 years and came away the winner, holding two distinctive marks in the record book and the acclaim of his contemporaries.

When his age finally negated his expertise, Lane retired in 1965, leaving two versions of Night Train in the nation's memory—the big band arrangement of Buddy Morrow and the playing field personification of the music's driving rhythm, Dick Lane, pro football's finest cornerback.

SAFETY
Emlen Tunnell
1948-1961

For Emlen Tunnell, football was a stage for self-expression, a life style allowing him to create an individuality that separated him from his peers. He played the game with a zeal that went beyond fun. As a youth at Toledo U., he had suffered a broken neck, something that doesn't happen in "fun" games. He played past that injury, and others, for the Coast Guard, Iowa and through a 14-year professional career.

He came to the New York Giants in 1948 with wonderful speed, slashing self-assurance and the firm goal of playing offensive tailback. But Giant coach Steve Owen was a defensive genius. He was just developing his famous "umbrella" defense, with four defensive backs and two floating ends fanning out in the shape of an open umbrella.

The defense was designed to stop the explosive new passing attacks and Owen thought that Tunnell was just the man to play safety. With the change to free substitution and specialization at mid-century, Tunnell became a regular at the deep position and Owen's feelings were justified. In a spectacularly effective defensive career, Tunnell set the NFL lifetime mark for interceptions with 79.

Happily, he did not have to give up his dream of carrying the ball, either, because he proved to be the best punt returner in NFL history. Running a punt is the most dangerous moment in football. For Tunnell, with the broken neck a reminder of his vulnerability, it was a crisis moment. But he disdained the fair catch and ran every kick he could, 258 lifetime, well over a hundred more than anyone else. His total yardage, 2,209, is another record and in 1952 he returned kicks 924 yards in the name of defense while the Rams' Dan Towler gained 890 yards in the traditional manner to lead the league in rushing.

Tunnell played his last two seasons for his old friend, Vince Lombardi at Green Bay, retiring in 1961 at age 35, following the Packers' 37-0 championship victory over the Giants.

He left behind a consensus reputation as pro football's finest safety.

KICKER
Lou Groza
1946-1967

School children born and raised in the '30s and '40s thought Franklin Delano Roosevelt was one of only three U.S. Presidents, the other two being George Washington, who chopped down a cherry tree, and Abraham Lincoln, who grew up learning to read by firelight. Many were in their teens before they realized the presidency was an elected office, not a permanent position.

To the kids of the '50s and '60s, Lou Groza brought the same aura of immortality to professional football. A generation which thought TV had always been around learned to love old number 76, a sort of athletic Santa Claus, who brought something warm and dependable to a game of constant change.

He was a man whose whole life was football, the man whom his coach, Paul Brown, will single out if asked to name the player with the perfect attitude for the game. He enjoyed everything about the sport —the meetings and practices, the individual challenge and the teamwork, the tension of a game and the tingling quiet of the aftermath. He went off to the training grind every year like a boy leaves for summer camp.

Groza became a charter member of the Cleveland Browns in 1946 and his fame developed through the accurate distance of his prodigious toe, although he translated his love for the game into effective play at offensive tackle. In the early years, he used a length of tape to measure his step and direction as he brought his foot into the ball. That innovation, and his cardinal rule—keep the head down throughout the follow-through—were adopted by aspiring kicking specialists across the nation.

Groza's perfection led to the feeling that Cleveland could score anytime the team crossed the 50-yard line. His skill affected the game, to the despair of philosophers who derided "easy" points. The drama of his winning field goal in the last minute of the 1950 title game began an era of final-second NFL fireworks. In his career he set the imposing record of 1,349 points, scoring all but six with his toe.

At age 42, after 21 professional seasons, 17 in the NFL, Groza retired. His longevity record attested to his love for the game.

A Physical Science

Pro football is simultaneously the most complicated and the most brutally fundamental game man has ever played. It is strategically so difficult that it is very hard for a man to play unless he has been brought up in it, as he has in his language. It is not a game that a good athlete can just pick up. Yet all the strategic ramifications and tactical decisions resolve to a hand-to-hand combat for the possession of land.

This fundamental nature of football sets it apart from other sports. A man can play many other games to test his speed and coordination. But if he wants to test his courage, his ability to perform high-level skills in the face of punishment, he goes to football. Such a situation places a nearly moral implication on the outcome of a football game.

Winners are not only considered more skillful, but superior in courage, character and desire. Even in this day of high professionalism, there is still much of Frank Merriwell in the sport.

These moral overtones pervade the entire field of football strategy. The most basic question in the game is whether running or passing is the best way to move the football, and any discussion on this topic usually becomes one of ethics rather than efficiency. Over the years there have been many men who simply felt that throwing the ball was cheap, even cowardly, and that no real football team would rely on the tactic.

Pop Warner, one of football's great coaches in the first half of the century, put this thought clearly. "I think passing should be illegal," he said. "Something should be done to curtail the wild, promiscuous, glorified football that some teams now indulge in. They throw long forward passes and figure on a percentage basis that if one of these connects they will fluke a touchdown and win the game. That's what I'm against. I think a game of football should be strictly on a merit basis."

This attitude creates a contradiction within the game. It is not always clear whether football players are trying to score the most points or to prove who is the most manly, and few players are satisfied with the points if they haven't established their character.

In 1936, Cliff Battles of Boston Redskins cuts between side-body blocks.

Professional football in its early years of the Twenties and Thirties was clearly caught up in this straight-laced moral attitude. They moved the ball by running, and they ran between the tackles. The game in those days was extremely confined. The linemen were shoulder-to-shoulder in a stance that looked like a cross between a deep crouch and an ostrich. As soon as the play started nearly everybody was on the ground and the runner was not so much tackled as dragged under by the collapsing mass of arms and legs.

Offensive thinking was conservative then and a man could lose his social standing for calling a pass at the wrong time, which was nearly any time. The ball was fat and difficult to hold and the passer had to be at least five yards behind the line. Passing was not easy.

Most coaches gave their quarterbacks field diagrams with precise instructions detailing which plays to use in which spots. It all boiled down to one admonition—when in doubt, punt. It was so difficult to make any yards slogging through the ruck at the line of scrimmage that most coaches preferred to wait for their opponents to drop the ball rather than try to push it down the field themselves.

Blocking and tackling in these early decades were executed with the shoulder or with the side of the body. Since the helmets ranged from flimsy to non-existent, very few players went charging head-first into people like they do today. A head-first block or tackle like that was an invitation to concussion and facial rearrangement. Nor did the runner of that era attract the hornet-swarm of punishment that he does today. If one defender were pulling a runner down, the others would watch him do it. With weak equipment and the need for each man to play all 60 minutes, no player was going to waste himself in a collision that wasn't altogether necessary. Nor did all defenders chase every play, again because a long game didn't encourage extra expenditure of energy.

It was a rough sport. Everybody had to play both on offense and defense and it was a personal affront to be pulled out of the game. It was a simple game, a game in which endurance, courage and character were the decisive factors.

The basic offensive formation was the single wing. The philosophy of this formation was simple—get there first with the most men and run the defense down. There were some reverses and even a pass or two, but the big play was a gang-busters attack off tackle.

In the '20s, Melrose defender uses classic shoulder tackle on Canton Bulldog.

Linemen did not pursue runners like they do today, but they weren't needed if linebacker tackled as perfectly as this Redskin did against New York Giants.

In a photo from the '20s (above) the offensive linemen (facing camera) crouch leg-to-leg in single wing formation. The defensive safety is 20 yards behind single linebacker. Until 1933, if runner were downed near sideline, play started from that point (photo below).

Any running offense must begin with this off-tackle play. A defensive line is weakest right at the corner, between tackle and end. The end has no help to his outside so he is always worried that a play will get around him. Therefore, he plays wide and there is a natural gap between him and the tackle.

The single wing was beautifully built to assault this weak spot. The tailback would take the pass from center and follow four men into the hole. To the defensive end, the play would look like the business end of a buffalo stampede. The offensive end and wingback would both block on the tackle, sealing him to the inside. The fullback and quarterback would hit the defensive end, sealing him to the outside. The tailback would follow the guard through the hole created by the two seals. Blocking in the single wing was usually of this double-team variety, that is, two blockers on each key defender.

Once a team could get this off-tackle smash working, other things would open up. If the end pinched

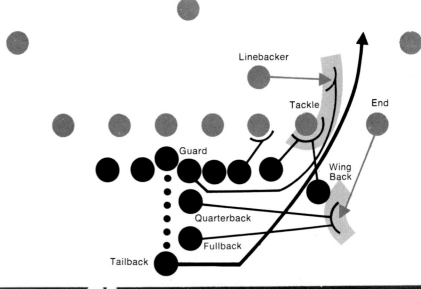

Linebacker

Tackle   End

Guard

Wing
Back

Quarterback

Fullback

Tailback

The Packers run the off-tackle play, with the blockers sealing two Giants (21 and 33) away from the hole.

Hutson's speed and fakes usually put him in the open.

On his first pro play, Hutson ran a deep pattern. Packer tailback Herber faked to power runner Clarke Hinkle, looked at Blood, then threw Hutson an 83-yard touchdown.

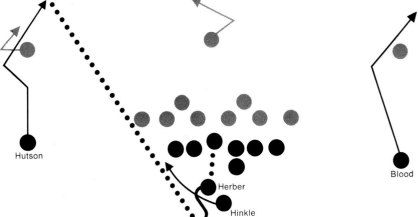

Hutson

Herber

Hinkle

Blood

A diagram of the single wing off-tackle play. Two blockers seal the defensive tackle to the inside (gray tone), two more seal defensive end to outside (gray tone) and tailback cuts into open alley.

Another view of off-tackle play, with a freight train of blockers including Buddy Parker (4) leading Lion tailback Dutch Clark (7) against College All-Stars.

in to shut the play down, then the tailback could go wide around him on an end run. If the defensive linemen in the center lined up wider to stop the off-tackle play, then the fullback could plunge straight through the weakened middle.

This was the game of the Twenties and Thirties, of Jim Thorpe and Red Grange, of Mel Hein and Beattie Feathers. But it is hardly the game of pro football's mid-century. For football, uniquely among sports, has strategically expanded as America has developed. A straightforward test of endurance and desire was a satisfactory game in a simpler time. But as America has metamorphosed into a complex scientific and technological culture, pro football has kept pace, adding layer on layer of sophistication to its brute base.

Two unlikely looking football players initiated the first step in this evolution. Don Hutson came to the Green Bay Packers in 1935 and Sammy Baugh joined the Washington Redskins in 1937. They were both tall and thin and, if they stood side by side, looked about like one football player. But bulk they did not need, since their wh⸺ need, since their wh⸺

was that physical power is not the totality of football.

Hutson was an end, a pass receiver, in the era when passes and short skirts were viewed in about the same light. He was very fast and a sure receiver but his contribution was the discovery of faking. Any defender covering him was sure to get lost in a melange of shifting shoulders, jiggling hips and false steps. Hutson would get to where the ball was supposed to be and he would get there alone. When he first came up his passer was Arnie Herber, the first great long passer, who threw the ball with the arching back and pin-wheeling arm of a javelin thrower. With Hutson to the left and Johnny Blood to the right, the 1935 Packers looked a lot like a modern team, with receivers spread out, although their backs lined up in the Notre Dame "box" formation, not the T. On his first play in NFL football, Hutson got under a Herber pass for an 83-yard touchdown and beat the Chicago Bears, 7-0 (see Diagram). In the next 11 years, the other teams all ⸺ similar tr⸺

Sammy Baugh threw sidearm from a wide stance with amazing accuracy. Here he hits wingback on a crossing pattern.

If Hutson expanded football's theories of pass receiving, Sammy Baugh did the same for passing. Slinging Sammy they called him, and it was an accurate description of his wide, side-arm delivery. Baugh had a quick arm, a good sense of timing and sure accuracy. He did not have to wait for a receiver to get several yards open before risking a floating pass. He threw as his receiver made his turn and the hard pass would arrow into tight spots. This type of passing was revolutionary because it meant that Baugh could rely on passes for short yardage the way other teams relied on the off-tackle slant.

For most of Baugh's career in Washington, the Redskins operated out of a double wing formation. This was a big advantage for the passing game because four receivers, two backs and two ends, could get downfield quickly. In the normal defenses of the day, there were only three backs. Baugh would often look at one of his ends and, when the one safetyman ran to that side, he would throw to the other end (see Diagram). Another aid was the fact that in those days linebackers were tough against the run but not very fast. They could not back up quickly enough to be much of a factor against passes. Baugh matched his skills to this situation so well that he still ranks second in all-time completion percentage.

If Baugh and Hutson as men were challenging the old moral structure of the game, disdaining the crush at the line for the freedom of the air, in Chicago a new strategic concept was brewing which would add to the revolution. This was the T-

formation, the oldest system in football, which got a sharp refurbishing and suddenly blew up the football world in 1940 when the Chicago Bears beat the Washington Redskins 73-0 for the league championship.

The T is so old it actually came from rugby. In rugby, half of the players of each team clump around the ball trying to kick it backwards through their legs. When the ball pops out of the pack, one man, known as the scrum half, picks it up

and laterals it out to one of his backs. When rugby became football, and one team had clear possession of the ball before the play started, the scrum half turned into the quarterback. He stood near the line, was passed the ball by the center, and then gave it to another back.

Chicago Bears coach George Halas had used the T-formation since the day he helped found the league in 1920. The center handed the quarterback the ball between his legs rather

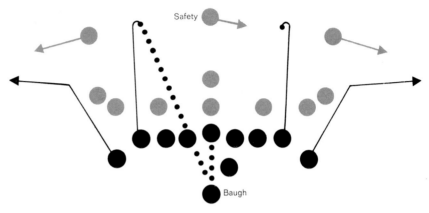

The basic Baugh pass, in photograph and diagram. Operating from a double wing formation, the Redskins sent four receivers downfield. Baugh would hit whomever came open, usually one of the ends.

Safety

Baugh

than throwing it back through the air to the tailback, as he did in the single wing. Unfortunately, the early T-formation was a tight, stodgy affair which had trouble getting around the ends. In 1930 Halas and his partner, Dutch Sternaman, replaced themselves as coaches with Ralph Jones from Illinois. Jones spread the ends and halfbacks a couple of yards, to loosen the formation a bit, but his major contribution was to have one of his halfbacks trot out to the side

of the formation just before the play started. This man-in-motion idea had been used by single wing teams before, but never with the T. The halfback in motion could either go down for a pass, or crack back on the defensive end if the play were a run around end. Still the T was not noticeably more successful than the dominant single wing, or other formations then in use like the Notre Dame box, the double wing or the short punt.

Jones left the Bears in 1933 and Halas resumed coaching the team. He struck up a friendship with Clark Shaughnessy, then coaching at the University of Chicago, and that friendship was to prove of pivotal importance in the evolution of the professional game. Shaughnessy, who played in an early box-T-formation in 1908 and was still active at football's mid-century celebration, was a football genius, a man who delighted in hours of detailed study of football's geometry. He pondered the T-formation, or any football problem, like a chess player will worry over a difficult position—and made piles of notes on all possible eventualities.

Over the Depression decade, Shaughnessy made a number of suggestions to Halas for play design and in the use of precise terminology to control the movements of the players. But it was in 1940, when he collaborated with Halas on the plan which ruined the Redskins (see story on page 166) that the T suddenly burst into prominence. By the end of the Forties, nearly every pro team had changed over to the Chicago system.

In the T-formation, quarterback takes ball directly from center.

The "modern" T-formation has some clear advantages over the single wing and other formations, and all the advantages moved the game further in the direction of speed and agility and away from the ponderous confrontations of the past. The T is a formation oriented to quick-striking. Rather than wait for half the team to get in front of the ball-carrier and mow the opposition down, the T works by shooting the runner through the line before the defense can get moving. On such "quick-openers" there are no longer two blockers trying to shove each key defender out of the way. Instead one blocker pops out at each man and hits him a good blow to keep him busy for an instant. In that instant the ball carrier is past.

The T also solved the basic problem of the single wing, which was that the tailback had to be a genius. A tailback had to be able to run with power and with speed and throw the ball. In the T, the fullback does most of the power running, the halfbacks are available for speed and the quarterback throws. It is much easier to find three people each of whom can do one thing well, than one person who can do it all. Finally, the T is very confusing to the de-

fense because three backs can zip past the quarterback, and even from the stands it's hard to tell which of the four men made off with the ball.

By the time World War II was over and a new football generation had come up through high school and college, the influence of Hutson, Baugh and the T-formation transformed the nature of the game. The pros were flooded with people who had been running fake-filled pass routes, throwing hard passes and practicing quick openers since they were ten. In 1949, the NFL made room for all this diversified talent with the most important rules change in the game's history: free substitution. Under this rule, which was adopted permanently in 1950, players could shuffle on and off the field with the freeway-frequency familiar today instead of being trapped on the field for most of the 60 minutes. Now a man who was a whiz as a pass receiver but not much at tackling fullbacks could perform his specialty and then get off the field.

The Chicago Bears, the oldest T-formation team. Here fullback Bronko Nagurski takes handoff from quarterback Carl Brumbaugh.

The best of the late '40s halfbacks, Steve Van Buren of the Eagles, runs over people.

The Giants demonstrate T faking in early Fifties as FB Eddie Price and HB Kyle Rote (44) cut past QB Charlie Conerly.

A diagram of the T-formation half-back quick-opener; man-in-motion shown by dotted line. In photo below, from modern era, Dick Bass of Rams shows speed necessary on quick-opener.

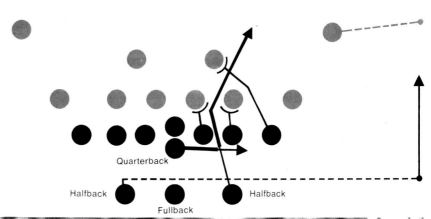

Quarterback

Halfback

Fullback

Halfback

Mac Speedie of Browns catches the sideline pass which he and Otto Graham (far right) invented.

Crazy Legs Hirsch catches bomb.

Berry ran patterns to the inch.

Game breaker McElhenny of 49ers ran with rare grace and elusiveness.

The result was startling—and extremely depressing to people who defined football in terms of the morality of man-to-man power struggles. With the T-formation as a platform for all the young talent, there was an offensive explosion. Clark Shaughnessy, who had moved into Los Angeles as head coach, established the first version of today's "three end" attack by putting halfback Elroy Hirsch wide to one side, end Tom Fears wide the other way and keeping end Bob Shaw in tight. For passers the team had Bob Waterfield and a rookie named Norm Van Brocklin. The Rams won the Western title in 1949. In 1950 and 1951, under head coach Joe Stydahar and offensive coach Hamp Pool, they set scoring and yardage records which still stand.

The impact of the Rams on strategic thinking was total. Rather than rely on running and only pass when necessary, they threw the ball for a living. They were Pop Warner's bad dream come true—three long passes and punt. They were disliked around the league, derided as glamour boys and Hollywood sissies. In the 1949 championship game, heavy rain drowned the Ram racehorses and the crunch-running Philadelphia Eagles humiliated them to the delight of many football purists. But Los Angeles threw its way into the next two championship games anyway and those two matches against the Cleveland Browns (see page 170 for the 1950 game) solidified passing as the new way to move.

For the Browns also were a passing team. Coach Paul Brown had molded quarterback Otto Graham and receivers Mac Speedie, Dub

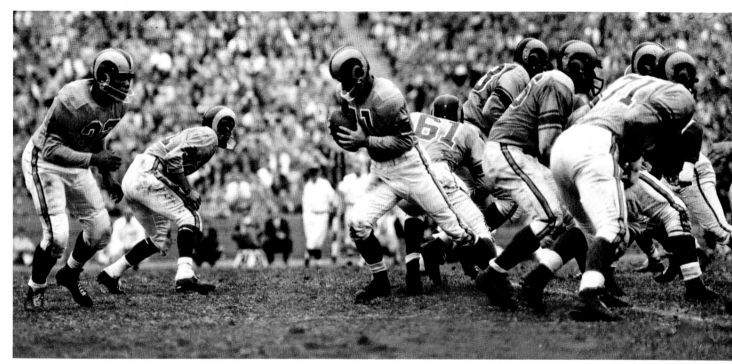

A great '50s quarterback, Norm Van Brocklin, drops back as Rams line forms protective cup.

Jones and Dante Lavelli, into a co-ordinated passing machine. Although they could throw the long pass, they were not as wild as the Rams. They specialized in a controlled attack. Graham was a master at throwing just as his receiver turned around and he and Speedie invented the sideline pass, where the receiver goes down the field ten or 15 yards and then breaks square toward the sideline. This play was a staple in pro ball until well into the Sixties.

Between them, the Rams and Browns broke down the old moral taboos against throwing the ball and other teams followed along

using the three-end system developed in Los Angeles. Great receivers like Harlon Hill, Billy Wilson, Bobby Walston and Bill Howton sprouted all over the league, taking the passes of a new generation of quarterbacks like Y. A. Tittle, Bobby Layne, Adrian Burk, Ed Brown and Tobin Rote.

In the middle of the decade, John Unitas came up from the sandlots to team with Raymond Berry in Baltimore and redefine passing. Unitas' conceptions and throwing skills were a perfect match to the tight precision of Berry's fakes and hands. Together they destroyed the defenses of the day with a timing and consistency borne of dedicated practice.

While the passers and receivers were asserting themselves, runners were trying to keep up. The old straight-ahead type of runner who

could also play linebacker began to disappear. In his place came a swivel-hipped speedster. Game-breaking open-field runners like Hugh McElhenny, Ollie Matson, Jon Arnett, Willie Galimore and Lenny Moore thrilled the crowds and dismayed the defenses all around the League. Even fullbacks like Dan Towler, John Henry Johnson and Joe Perry had quick feet and intense speed.

As the offenses ran amok, there began a search for a new balance in offensive and defensive football. Shaughnessy says, "We had to find some way to kill the ogre we had created." Up until 1950, there had not been much in the way of defensive strategy. Almost all teams used the same alignment and they only spent about 20% of their practice time on defense. But then, for a long time, there was not much for defenses to worry about.

The earliest defense, in the Twenties, was as simple as possible. The seven linemen from offense also played on the defensive line. Their only change was that the ends played a little wider than on offense, in order to box in any end runs. One back, usually the fullback, positioned himself back of the line (as, naturally, a "linebacker") to clean up any runner who got through the scrimmage pile. Two halfbacks played wide watching for escaping end runs or passes and the safety played very deep as a last line of defense and to field the frequent punts and quick kicks.

Defensive development since then has been to increasing mobility. The first change was to pull the center out of the line and team him with the fullback as a second linebacker. Linebackers can move sideways quickly, since they are not bogged down in the scrimmage pile-up, and can therefore get in front of more plays.

When New York Giant center-linebacker Mel Hein came into the pros in 1931 this 6-2-3 (six linemen, two linebackers, three backs) defense was becoming popular. He remembers the next big move. "Steve Owen (the Giants' coach) brought in the 5-3-3 in 1937 and we first used it extensively

Mel Hein of the Giants demonstrates the clean-up function of a linebacker as he plugs a hole against Andy Uram of the Packers in 1940.

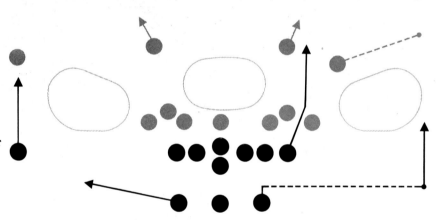

1. The "Eagle defense," a 5-2-4 arrangement, left holes in the middle and flats when stretched out by a man-in-motion and a split end.

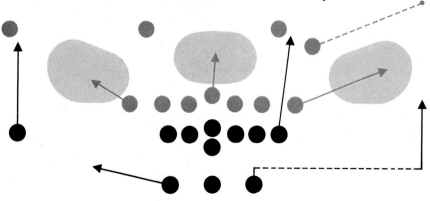

2. Steve Owen's "umbrella defense," a 6-1-4 alignment, had a middle linebacker and dropped the two ends off in the flats, thus stopping short passes.

The Chicago Cardinals line up in the 5-3-3 defense against the tight T-formation of the Philadelphia Eagles in the 1948 championship game.

in 1938," Hein recalls. "Owen figured he had three good linebackers in John Dell Isola, Nello Falaschi and myself. The 5-3-3 was especially effective against Chicago's T-formation. Since we had linebackers left, right and center, none of us had to go running after the first fake. We could wait in our positions to see if the play were coming. Also, we ran stunts from this defense, with the linebackers and linemen criss-crossing as they rushed."

The 5-3-3 was widely used through the Forties. It was effective against T-formation running but it got into trouble with the pass. There were only three defensive backs, so if a quarterback sent out both ends and both halfbacks one of these fast receivers would have to be chased by a slow linebacker. It was an unfair race and as more accurate passers like Sid Luckman and Paul Christman came into the league, something had to be done.

In Philadelphia, Greasy Neale invented the first answer to the problem. He took out a linebacker and substituted a fourth back. This 5-2-4 alignment, or "Eagle defense," with which he won championships in the late Forties, was soon widely copied. The four backs could handle all the fast receivers and the two linebackers helped out also by holding up the ends if they tried to get downfield. But, as Neale says, "This defense was most effective against the tight T-formation. A man-in-motion or a flanker spread it out."

The Cleveland Browns proved this the first time they played the Eagles, in the first game of 1950 (see page 168).

The Browns spread Mac Speedie one way and sent Dub Jones the other. Suddenly the Eagle defense was full of holes. The two linebackers could not cover the middle nor could they get out to the flats (see Diagram 1). The two defensive halfbacks had no help trying to cover Speedie and Jones, making their job nearly impossible. Hutson had proven that good fakes could lose any one defender. Soon the Browns and Rams and other passing teams were bombing the 5-2-4 defense. Something had to happen or one of those Fifties offenses would have scored 100 points.

The first step actually came in 1950 but it took years to consolidate. The leader again was the Giants' defensive genius, Steve Owen. Tom Landry, now coach of the Cowboys but then a defensive back for Owen, remembers, "The first time we went up against Cleveland, Owen went

back to a six-man line, kept the four defensive backs and had only one linebacker, in the center. But the secret was that the two ends on the line often dropped back into the flats like modern linebackers. The two ends and the four backs fanned out and reminded sports writers of an open umbrella. So it was named the umbrella defense." Those two ends dropping off got in the way of Otto Graham's sideline passes to Speedie and Jones and disrupted the Cleveland passing attack. Meanwhile, the one linebacker patrolled the center (see Diagram 2). It was effective. The Giants held the Browns to 21 points in three 1950 games, winning the first two but losing a conference playoff, 8-3.

Billy Ray Smith, defensive tackle for Colts, shows the speed and agility of modern linemen while chasing Gary Lewis of 49ers.

More importantly, this umbrella defense was the forerunner of the modern 4-3-4. The two ends on the six-man line became linebackers, leaving only four defensive linemen. This was the most feasible alignment against all the threats the spread T-formation presented, but before it became fully effective, a new breed of athlete had to appear. Since there were only four defensive linemen, those four had to be tremendously big but still mobile. Otherwise they would be either run over by a ground attack or left standing on the line by a passing attack. Also, the three linebackers had to be nearly as big as linemen, to stop the runs, and nearly as fast as backs, to cover passes. Few of these specimens grew naturally in the Fifties. Finally, fast and intelligent people had to be put into the defensive backfield. With receivers like Hirsch, Howton and Hill coming down the field, coaches could no longer allow offensive rejects to man the defensive secondary. They would be slaughtered.

But better players in a better alignment was not enough to stop the

race-horse offenses. New theories had to be evolved to combat the advanced offensive thinking. In the early decades, defenders had diagnosed plays simply by watching the ball. This was not too difficult with the single wing, where the ball was passed openly through the air to the runner and handoffs were few. But in the T-formation, the quarterback took the ball, turned his back and dealt out fakes like a 4:00 a.m. poker player. Defenders who tried to watch the ball got eye strain and few tackles.

The first defensive answer to this was fairly simple. Ernie Stautner, all-pro defensive tackle of the Fifties, remembers, "When I first came up the idea was that you acted against pressure. If a blocker tried to push you one way, you fought back in the opposite direction, where the play was supposed to go." But this type of tactic was only rudimentary as a method of play diagnosis and soon another idea was in use.

This was the theory of "reading." Defensive coaches figured, as Merlin Olsen, a Sixties all-pro tackle, says, "The offensive play is a total design. Each player has a part. So if we on

defense watch the parts and react accordingly, we should all act together to stop the play. We all listen to different music, but we come out together." Thus, defenders began to "read" plays, watching the blockers instead of the ball, on the theory that the ball would eventually follow the blockers. Each defender was given one or two offensive people, or "keys," to inspect. Each move that these "key" people made was supposed to tip off the play that was coming.

This was the basis of the reading and reacting defenses which developed in the Fifties and were still widely used after fifty pro years. The key to the successful reading defense was the speed with which the defenders converged on the attack spot. This was known as "pursuit," and that word became the chief verbal lash of defensive coaches. A big lineman was useless if he couldn't pursue plays swiftly and lumbering giants got thrown out of training camps in

Steelers (white) play 4-3 defense against Redskins. Outside linebackers (34 and 69) used to be ends.

The three defensive units, linemen, linebackers and backs, represented by Ed O'Bradovich (87), Dick Butkus (51) and Richie Petitbon (17) of Bears.

the first week. Soon Sunday crowds began to buzz at the sight of huge men like the 295-pound "Big Daddy" Lipscomb sprinting 70 yards down-field to catch a speedy flanker like Del Shofner at the goal line. A game which had once resembled a gang-fight in a closet now had 22 fast men colliding in all corners of the field. Ball carriers used to have one man at a time to worry about. Now they drew crowds of tacklers the way fresh meat draws piranhas. Defense was striking back.

Not all the defensive changes were up front. The pass defenders clearly needed help in chasing the tricky speedsters who raced out to catch footballs. The faking by the receivers was the big problem and to nullify this, many teams began to use zone defenses. In a zone, a pass defender does not stay with any one receiver, but rather he stays in one area, or zone, of the field. A receiver can come down and fake his helmet off, but the defender calmly runs to his assigned spot and awaits develop-ments.

The most common type of zone is the "four-short, three-deep" variety One of the defensive halfbacks runs up to cover a short zone and the three linebackers each take another short zone. The other three defensive backs split the field far from the line of scrimmage into three zones. This arrangement has one tremendous advantage. Since the three deep defenders ignore faking, it is almost impossible for a receiver to get behind them for a long pass. On the other hand, with each defender covering a zone, there are spaces between them. If a receiver can find one, he is an easy target for a medium-distance pass. A zone defense there-fore requires a strong pass rush to keep a passer from finding his re-ceivers in these cracks between the zones.

Across the Fifties, better personnel and improved theories raised the level of defensive play greatly. The Detroit Lions took their best athlete, Jack Christiansen, and put him at safety. He was joined by Jim David, Yale Lary and Carl Karilivacz in the first great defensive secondary which,

through heavy use of zone defenses, helped the Lions to championships in the early and middle Fifties.

The Giants first fought to full acceptance in New York on the strength of a great defense. The front four linemen featured Andy Robus-telli and Roosevelt Grier. The line-backers were strong in the center with Sam Huff and quick on the sides with Harland Svare and either Bill Svoboda or Cliff Livingston. The backfield, starring safeties Emlen Tunnell and Jim Patton, was first-rate. Coached by Tom Landry, this group was so effective that, by the second half of the decade, it was getting the cheers which had here-tofore been lavished only on offenses.

As professional football went into the Sixties, the defenses had gone a long way towards stopping the high-point offenses unleashed around 1950. This helped reassert the old moral balance of the game. Too many points are not good because each point is cheapened; nothing which comes easy is worth much. In the early Fifties, the offense had been avoiding the old man-to-man power struggle in favor of the cheap bomb and the tricky run.

But by 1960 most defenses had bottled up the end run and shut off the long pass. Bigger, faster defensive specialists, following subtle new designs, countered each of the offensive threats from sideline to sideline. Tom Fears, all-time end and ex-coach of the New Orleans Saints, says, "We've run out of room. The quick defensive backs and linebackers have filled up the field. There's not much space out there any more."

As the field seemed to shrink, the pros were forced back into elemental confrontation, but at a much higher level of strategic complexity. The offense could no longer sail around or over a tight and slow-moving defense. Instead, it had to strike directly into the enemy, creating cracks with an ever-varying mixture of muscle and guile. The game was coming back to moral balance, but with so many added elements of skill and concept on each side that it bore only slight relation to the constricted game of the sport's earliest era.

Over the Sixties, both the offense and defense have continued to evolve. Colt quarterback John Unitas can

The aggressive Ram defenders go after backs like Donny Anderson of Packers believing they have an equal right to the ball.

speak for the new offensive problems. "The offense no longer has the initiative," he says. "When I first came up, defenses would get into one picture and sit in it. The quarterback knew what he had to deal with. Now, the defenses change every play, even after the play starts. Everybody on the offense has to adjust after the play has begun."

Defense has thus lost much of its passive character. Even a team like the Green Bay Packers, which used a simple reacting defense throughout the decade, played with an aggressive attitude. They read plays so well and reacted so fast that they snapped shut on offensive plays like a bear trap.

In other NFL cities, the whole idea that the defense should wait for the offense and then react was given up as moral surrender. Why let the offense lead as if a football game were a fox trot? Clark Shaughnessy, Chuck Drulis, George Allen and other

coaches decided that defenses should go on offense, smashing recklessly through a pre-determined pattern, ruining whatever play the offense happened to be using. As defensive coach of the Chicago Bears in the late Fifties, Shaughnessy was one of the originators of the trend. "After all those years on the other side," he explains, "I knew that the biggest problem for an offense is not knowing where the defenders will be and what they will do. So in our defense we used a lot of shifts and stunts. The defensive linemen 'muddled'—that is, they criss-crossed, muddling up the offensive blocking assignments. The linebackers lined up anywhere along the line and we had many combinations of blitzes

Mel Farr of the Lions steps into the palpable hostility of a '60s scrimmage battle.

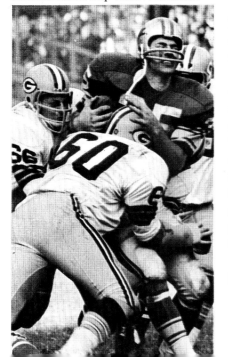

Packer backers Nitschke, Caffey
and Robinson trap Lion Nowatzke.

(where linebackers rush the passer). In the secondary, we used various combinations of man-to-man and zone."

Chuck Drulis, who handled the St. Louis Cardinal defense throughout the Sixties, found a wildman safety in Larry Wilson. Soon he had Wilson crashing in at the passer like a linebacker as the eighth man in a terrifying all-out blitz. Although few men were left to cover pass receivers, the quarterback rarely remained vertical long enough to throw.

Into Los Angeles, George Allen brought some of Shaughnessy's ideas, added his own refinements and emotional fervor, and put on the field a football-grabbing defense which had ball carriers worried as much about holding onto the football as about gaining yards. The field leader was linebacker Maxie Baughan, who says, "We want the ball, and we have more than 300 defenses we can use to try to get it." Reversing the usual cat-and-mouse roles of offense and defense, Baughan points out, "We will deliberately show them a defense with a weakness. Then, when the quarterback goes after the weakness, we change up to cover it and try to knock the ball away or intercept."

149

Only one successful defense of the Sixties was not imbued with this kind of attacking personality. This was Tom Landry's "Doomsday Defense" in Dallas. Landry, an intricate football mind and true successor to Shaughnessy as a strategic philosopher, developed a complex defense around a simple premise. "There are eight gaps along the line of scrimmage, six between offensive linemen and one in each flat. In each of our defenses, one man is assigned to each gap. If the play comes in a defender's direction, he covers his gap, rather than going directly for the ball." In this defense, a defender never over-reacts. He doesn't chase the play too soon and leave an open space behind him. It was these haphazard open spaces which the good Sixties runner could find (see Diagrams 1 and 2). "We believe," says Cowboy defensive coach Ernie Stautner, "that we have the only defense that can cover every running play."

A problem with this gapping, or "partnership," defense was that it placed an unnatural strain on a football player's instincts. Any good man wants to get into the action as fast as he can, but in this defense there was often some delay. "It's easy to play the run this way," reports Cowboy all-pro tackle Bob Lilly, "but at first we had trouble getting a quick pass rush or good pursuit. We were waiting too much. But now we know the defense so well that I believe we are as quick as anybody. It's a great system."

A quick and powerful pass rush was certainly a necessity for this defense or any other because it was the pass rush which finally forced the passing game back into moral unity

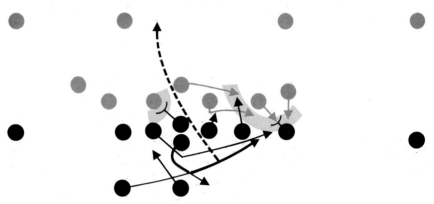

1. A good reacting defense may move so fast to the offense's planned hole (here, right tackle) that the runner finds an open spot (dotted line).

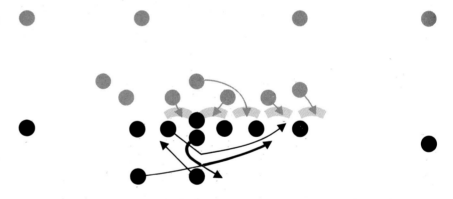

2. In a gapping defense, each defender covers one assigned spot and no accidental hole opens up.

with the rest of football. In fact, in the Sixties the front line battle for the quarterback's life had become the pivotal struggle in pro football. A mobile and massive front four in Detroit, led by tackles Alex Karras and Roger Brown, first popularized the fact that a crushing pass rush could control a modern professional game.

There is a metaphysical position in some philosophies which states that opposites, like the beautiful and the ugly, are actually two parts of the same thing. In the last ten years this metaphysic was embodied in the professional passing game. The classic beauty of a soaring pass and graceful catch was totally dependent upon the brutal, rending warfare in front

of the passer. No pass was cheap anymore. Any throw completed despite the rush of high-speed destroyers like David Jones or Carl Eller was yardage well and manfully earned. Passes no longer circumvented the basic physical character testing of football. It was still true that a quick score would occur more frequently passing than running. But a successful precision passing attack now meant not just that defensive backs were being fooled but also that the war of the lines was being won. The moral victory for passers was as total as if the runners jammed down the field between the tackles.

Even with this emphasis on the pass rush, modern defensive theorists expended great amounts of energy

David Jones (75) of the Rams shows why the modern passing game is no easy matter.

developing new theories of pass coverage. The art of chasing pass receivers changed perhaps more than any other facet of the game. Modern thinkers finally concluded that it is simply impossible for any one defender to successfully follow one receiver. The receiver's preknowledge of the play is an advantage which cannot be overcome. Unfortunately, plain zone coverage, although it relieves the pressure on any one individual, is also unsatisfactory because there are gaps between the zones into which any modern passer can slice his throws. Since neither of these straight-forward plans was feasible, modern defenses turned to confusion as a basic tactic. Sometimes they used a zone, sometimes man-to-man, sometimes various combinations of the two. The swift linebackers were vital to these defenses, sprinting back into the pass coverages to get between the thrower and his receiver. Receivers still got

The Falcons' Tommy Nobis—even the toughest linebackers are mobile.

open, but a quarterback had only three or four seconds to figure out just what defense he was up against and then remember which receiver was likely to get open against that particular defense. It was not easy, with the hungry monsters clawing at him as he tried to decide. Many a time the passer mis-read the defense and saw an open man, only to have his throw intercepted by a defender whose assignment for that particular defense happened to send him right into the ball.

These confusing defenses were being made even more effective by intelligent use of reserve ball players. Taking advantage of the large 40-man squads, many coaches have followed the lead of Jim Dooley in Chicago and sent in more defensive backs in obvious passing situations. As many as seven at one time have been seen scurrying around, looking for errant footballs.

Faced with these shifting, aggressive defenses, modern offenses were forced into many modifications. Every nuance of power, precision and subterfuge had to be employed in order to rip yardage from the control of the defense. Every incursion into the enemy's hostile environment had to be perfectly planned and vehemently executed or swarming destruction was the sure result.

The strategic creativity was so complex that computers were pressed into use. These computers are used to analyze and read out the strategic ideas and tendencies of the home team and its opponents. Final results give accurate odds, for instance, on which play Sonny Jurgensen is most likely to call on third and seven on his own 26-yard line with the ball closest to the left sideline and his team behind in the second quarter.

Based on these "tendency charts" of an opponent's offense and defense, a coach does his planning. He has at his disposal scores of basic runs with many blocking variations, and scores of basic passes with many more pattern variations. These hundreds of potential combinations are learned by the team in the summer training grind. Yet, during the season an entire new set of plays often has to be developed specifically for a new quirk found by studying the films of opponents' games. The decision on which plays to pull from the repertoire and which new ones to install is crucial, difficult and time-consuming. Few coaches have much free time during the season.

Systems this complex must have simple and solid premises or they·

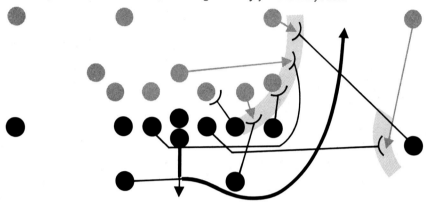

The power sweep—the defensive halfback is sealed to the outside and other defenders to the inside, creating an alley for the halfback.

Three Dallas linemen pull out in perfect synchronization on a power sweep left, leading halfback Dan Reeves.

will fly apart into thousands of uncoordinated pieces. This was the genius of Vince Lombardi. Given the Green Bay job in 1959, he saw that defenses had essentially shut down free-and-easy offenses. He went back to the basics, back to the root of the game, back to the physical-emotional confrontation of strong men on a field of battle. Lombardi kept enough of the modern offensive capabilities to take advantage of any glaring defensive weaknesses. But his main thought was to take simple plays

and crunch straight through his opponents on the strength of superior execution and desire. The continual pounding of his archetypal tough backs, Jim Taylor and Paul Hornung, behind a smoothly meshing line eroded an opponent's confidence and self-image. Eventually defenders either gave in, or ill-advisedly over-balanced their defense. At this latter opportunity Lombardi's quarter-

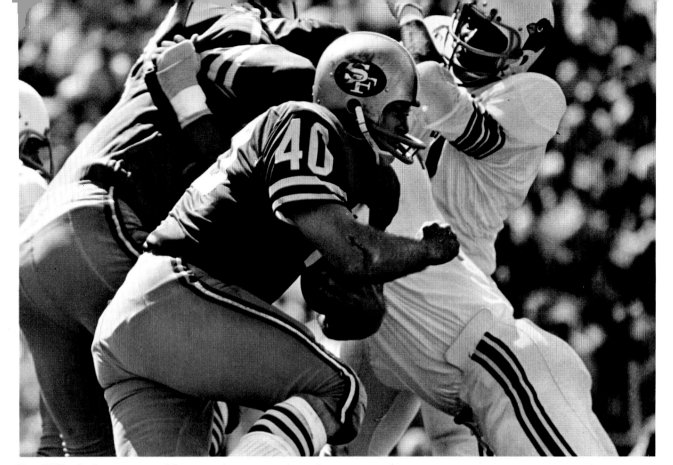

Ken Willard of 49ers, one of latest and meanest of tough scrimmage runners.

Power backs—Hornung and Taylor.

back, Bart Starr, would appreciatively dispatch a touchdown pass into the vacated spot.

The most important Lombardi play was the famous power sweep. This powerful end run, featuring either Paul Hornung or Jim Taylor, was actually a modern version of the old single-wing off-tackle play. In a Sixties defense, the job of containing an end run was no longer handled by the end or even the linebacker. The game was so spread out that it was the defensive halfback who was supposed to race up and force the run back to the inside. The power sweep therefore turned up inside that halfback just like the old off-tackle play used to turn inside the defensive end.

On one version of the sweep (see Diagram) the right guard pulled out to seal the halfback to the outside. The fullback, tight end, left guard and flanker sealed the defensive end, linebackers and safety to the inside. The halfback turned up the field in the gap. Such a sweep made no attempt to get completely around the defense, because it was almost impossible.

Lombardi and the Packers made famous another idea of how to gain yardage on the ground. The rising defenses of the Fifties had developed their abilities to "read" and react so well that most running holes were clogged with defenders before the ball carrier got there. Some runners got badly mauled in this situation but others reacted by giving up on the assigned attack point and branching out on their own, looking for some space anywhere they could find it. On a play which was supposed to go over right tackle, for instance, the defenses would react so quickly that the only available clear spot might be over center. Runners who could only plow down pre-designated paths were soon replaced by men who could find some "daylight" and get into it in a hurry. Dick Bass remembers, "When I first came up, I used to run where the play was designed. Got a lot of headaches, too. Then I learned to scuffle around and find an opening." By the late Sixties, even the huge power backs like Jim Grabowski and Ken Willard were cutting and veering like the best old-time scat backs. Lombardi called this tactic "running to daylight," and it was in reaction to this offensive trend that Tom Landry developed his previously mentioned gapping defense.

Not only the runners had to change their styles. Another vast change came in the way coaches taught their offensive linemen to move defenders. The strength and guile of defensive linemen was such that any spot the offense tried to clear out would soon be full of them. The very attempt to clear out any one spot would draw a crowd to that place. There were two reactions to this.

One was the development of option blocking. Blockers were told to let their defenders choose a direction and then just shove them the same way. The runners were strictly on their own, and the ones who lasted were the ones who found some space. The second reaction was the development of a series of plays in which only some of the blockers or, in extreme instances, none of them, actually blocked out the hole for the runner. Instead, these blockers ran off in strange directions to confuse the defensive readers and induce them to move out of the way all by themselves. If a defensive tackle watches the guard opposite him go racing off around end like he does on a sweep, the tackle is very likely to be fooled by a trap block or even by a runner who slices into his territory with no blocking escort at all (see Diagram).

These "cheater" plays have a dual purpose. Often they hit for big yardage since the defense is pulled out of position by the false blocking pattern. But even if they do not, they confuse defenders enough that they will slow down their reactions to normal running plays. A successful running attack is usually subtly balanced between the two types of plays.

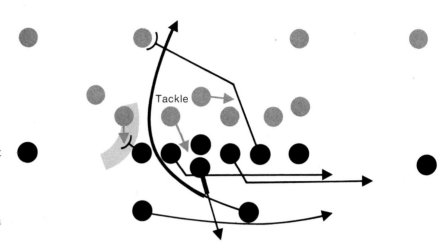

The St. Louis Cardinals run a "give" play or "cheater" play (diagram and photos). Both guards (54 and 66) pull to right as on an end sweep. Defensive tackle (84), who is not blocked, starts to follow guards as instructed and misses the fullback (39) slicing through his hole.

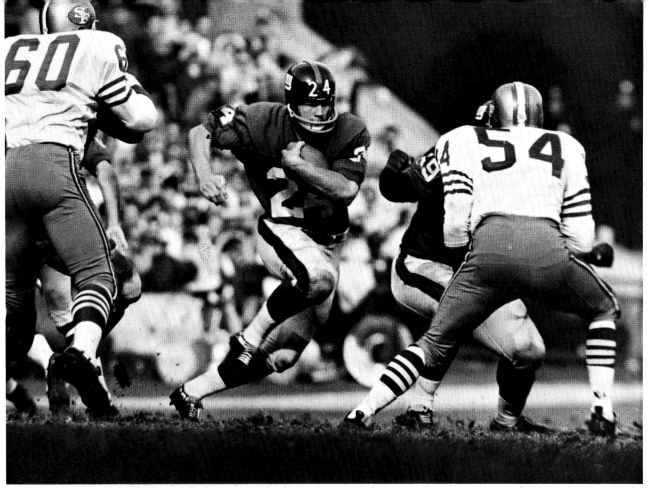

A young power back, Tucker Frederickson of Giants, runs for daylight.

The great Jim Brown looks for a hole behind option blocking.

Thus, in complicated ways, the offense reasserted its power image. With the re-establishment of strong running, despite the ferocious new defenses, the sport completed its return to a basic confrontation test. Both passing and running had lost their track-meet connotations and rooted themselves firmly in the basic scrimmage struggle.

This was shown by the fact that the key to a successful offense in the Sixties was an intelligent integration of the passing attack with the running attack. Passes were used in any situation, which meant that defenses could never be sure whether a run or pass was coming. Teams which could generate a powerful running attack forced defenders to crowd in, and this made passing easier. Many pass plays were disguised as runs, with fake handoffs and false blocking.

Passing was no longer either a moral evil or an easy way out. Passing and running became two sides of one coin. Is running or passing the best way to move the ball? The modern answer was, Yes.

John Unitas gives some idea of the problems of operating a passing attack. "A good arm doesn't get you anywhere by itself," he says. "You have to know your men and theirs, to know how to control their defense with your patterns, to be able to read their defense and adjust on the move." And a quarterback had to do all this with the cool courage of a Unitas, throwing with synchronized accuracy in the sure knowledge of impending punishment.

The basis of passing strategy changed as defenses changed. When defenders gave up on man-to-man coverage they changed the problem for the offense. The passer could no longer wait for his receiver to throw good fakes on the defensive halfback and then break wide open. It didn't do any good just to beat one defender because, one way or the other, that defender usually had help. So a modern passer had to try to beat the design of the entire defense.

One way of expressing this total design concept is the phrase, "linebacker control." Bart Starr says, "We don't try to beat the deep backs. We can always get a step there. We concentrate on the linebackers. We use fake runs or send backs out of the backfield to force the linebackers to do a job. When the linebackers are forced to move, you can see just what defense the other team is using and throw accordingly." The new linebackers were so fast that if they were not controlled in this way, they were always popping up in just the wrong place. A flanker might run a great pattern 15 yards down the field, fake his halfback into the stands, and wind up with a linebacker right in front of him (see Diagrams 1 and 2).

A second problem presented by modern pass defenses was the fact that they changed from play to play and often after any one play had started. As the quarterback lined up he might see the defense arranged to run a certain type of zone and by the time he had taken the ball back seven yards into the pocket, the defenders might have run off into some other type of combination altogether. By watching carefully

As Cardinals' safety Larry Wilson (8) blitzes, Cleveland Browns work on linebacker (34). Linebacker is supposed to help his defensive back (26) on Brown tight end (89). But when he does, fullback Charley Harraway (31) swings open up the middle to catch pass from Bill Nelsen.

the movements of as many of them as he could (Unitas tried to follow the strong side linebacker, halfback and safety) the quarterback had to "read" what defense was being used. So did the receivers. Often a flanker had to change his pattern if he saw that the defense was going to negate the pattern he was going to run. Thus, in the two or three seconds after the snap, both the passer and the receivers had to figure out what the defense was doing and make the correct decisions. If the receiver went one way and the passer threw another, it looked awfully bad on instant replay. "Football," says

Unitas, "is a game of adjustments."

In the face of this defensive complexity, many pro offenses went the way of Lombardi, streamlining and simplifying to avoid mistakes. But there was a more adventuresome answer, which was to make the offense so complicated that it could handle anything the defense did and even force the defense into certain vulnerable situations. This type of thinking prevailed in Dallas and Baltimore, where Tom Landry and Don Shula lined their teams up in many strange variations of the T-formation and salted their basic attacks with a number of odd-looking plays.

The goal of this offensive complexity was to give the defense so

In the war between linebackers and quarterbacks, Lee Roy Jordan of Cowboys (55) gets between Washington's Sonny Jurgensen and his receiver (blurred helmet just to Jurgensen's left) who is slanting into the middle.

many problems that it would have to cover each offensive pattern only one way. Then the offense would know what it had to deal with. Dallas, for instance, overloaded one way in order to leave the sprinting end, Bob Hayes, with only one defender covering him. If the defense insisted on putting two men on Hayes anyway, then the Cowboys worked on the weakness this created on the other side of the field. Either way, they forced the opposition into a compromised position. Instead of going into a simple shell and letting the defense take the initiative, this type of offense prodded and challenged the defense, trying to force errors. It was difficult to do, but in Baltimore and Dallas, at least, it worked well.

As pro football entered its second half century, there was no end in sight to this strategic escalation. Football is an open-ended proposition and only the limits of man's creativity and technology bound the theoretical possibilities on the field. Yet as the game grew more scientific and refined, it also became more intensely violent. Bigger, stronger, faster men in lighter, more effective equipment crashed together with a muscular vitality that steadily increased.

The game allows men to exercise their mental quickness and bodily grace in the face of an elemental physical brutality. It is a magnificent spectacle and in pro football's second half-century fans wait expectantly for the latest modifications in a sport which continually changes for the right reason — there is always a better way to play the game.

1. Modern linebackers back up quickly, casting a "shadow" between passer and his receivers.

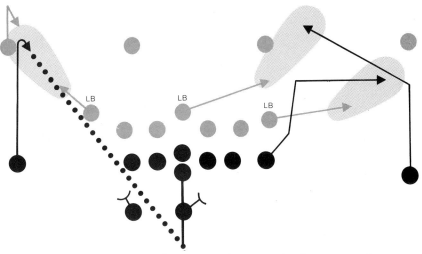

2. By sending backs out into the pattern, the quarterback can control movements of linebacker, opening up a wide receiver for hook pass.

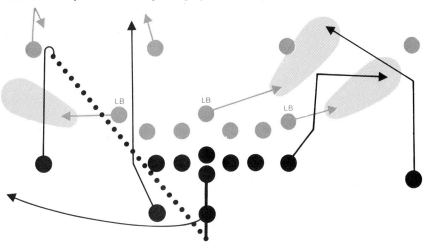

Ten That Mattered

In the fifty NFL seasons there have been thousands of games. Their quality is implied in the continual growth of the sport's popularity from a sandlot pastime in small towns to a leisure-time focal point for an electronically united nation. Yet in this long series of games, a relative few can be singled out as of pivotal importance, games which were more than exciting in themselves or significant in a championship race.

This section of the book is devoted to ten of those games. They are contests which have had a lasting impact on the development of the sport. They either initiated change in themselves or else summed up dramatically trends which were occuring at the time. The games were not chosen merely because they became well-known or were unusual. Most of them were championship meetings, for two reasons. In the first place, the championship brings together the best teams and coaches in a situation demanding top performance. Secondly, what happens in a championship game gets wide publicity and is long remembered, so that the effect is greater both on fans and on the football world.

Ten games have been chosen mostly because our mathematics works to a base of ten rather than, say, seven or 16. It is an artificial stopping point, used for convenience. Nor is this the only list of ten that could be compiled. But each of these games has a solid claim for inclusion.

The Bears-Giants game of 1933 was the first official championship play-off and showcased important rules changes; the Redskins-Bears game of 1937 celebrated an inaugural season in Washington, D.C., and brought to prominence Sammy Baugh and George Preston Marshall; the Bears-Redskins game of 1940 changed the sport over to the T-formation; the Browns-Eagles game of 1950 answered the contentious question of Cleveland's ability to play in the NFL after four years as AAFC champion and, along with the Browns-Rams game of the same year, made passing the dominant method of moving the ball; the Colts-Giants game of 1958 signaled the importance of the marriage between pro football and television and introduced the game's all-time quarterback; the Bears-49ers game of 1961 sealed the doom of the only challenge to the T-formation in thirty years; the Packers-Browns game of 1966 highlighted dramatically the return to the running attack instigated by Vince Lombardi; the Packers-Cowboys game of 1967 presented pro football at a level as near perfection as the modern game can be played; and the Jets-Colts game of 1969 established the equality of the two competing leagues, unifying pro football as it enters its second half century.

Bert Bell, league commissioner from 1946 to 1959, once expressed a thought which, because it is accurate, has become one of the classic cliches of sports: "On any given Sunday, any one team in the NFL is capable of beating any other." Once each autumn week, professional football presents a full card of dramatic adventures.

The following ten-game exploration is a symbolic salute to all the men who make these Sundays possible.

The Games

December 17, 1933	Chicago Bears vs. New York Giants
December 12, 1937	Chicago Bears vs. Washington Redskins
December 8, 1940	Washington Redskins vs. Chicago Bears
September 16, 1950	Philadelphia Eagles vs. Cleveland Browns
December 24, 1950	Cleveland Browns vs. Los Angeles Rams
December 28, 1958	New York Giants vs. Baltimore Colts
October 22, 1961	Chicago Bears vs. San Francisco 49ers
January 2, 1966	Green Bay Packers vs. Cleveland Browns
January 1, 1967	Dallas Cowboys vs. Green Bay Packers
January 12, 1969	New York Jets vs. Baltimore Colts

Chicago Bears	3	3	10	7	23
New York Giants	0	7	7	7	21

Wrigley Field, Chicago
December 17, 1933

In a historic photograph, Bear end Hew

The National Football League's first championship game was as good as it should have been. There are great occasions and great games, but they rarely get together. In 1933 they did, as the Chicago Bears beat the New York Giants, 23-21.

The previous spring, following an idea of Washington Redskin owner George Marshall, the league had split into two divisions. This increased interest by providing two championship races and also set up a natural championship game. Pro football had also adopted three playing rules in 1933 which opened the game up. One rule brought the ball in at least ten yards from the sideline on every play, so the players would not get cramped on one side of the field. Also, passing was made legal from any point back of the scrimmage line. Previously, a passer had to be standing at least five yards behind scrimmage before he could throw. Finally, the goal posts were moved up to the goal line, making field goals ten yards easier.

These changes had been made to increase the movement and excitement of football. In the first NFL championship game, the new rules proved out.

The New York Giants had won the Eastern division title with a diversified offense and a defense anchored by Hall of Fame center and linebacker Mel Hein. On attack, the Giants used the single wing. Tailback Harry Newman was the quick and tricky type with one of the league's best throwing arms. There was another Hall of Fame choice, Ken Strong, providing inside power, and ends Morris Badgro and Red Flaherty along with wingback Dale Burnett were fine receivers. With so many threats, New York was tough to defense.

In Chicago, George Halas was building his Nagurski machine. Bronko ran from fullback in an early version of the man-in-motion T-formation. The offense was designed to take advantage of the damage Nagurski did with his 235 pounds when he was sent piling into the line. If the opponents could ever find enough bodies to throw in front of Nagurski, then the Bears would fake to him and pitch out or pass into areas where defenders should have been. The team had a lot of other talent, Red Grange at halfback, Bill Hewitt at end, Link Lyman in the line. But the 1933 Bears were a Nagurski team.

They were two good teams playing on a meteorological accident, a good field in Chicago in December. About 25,000 came out, the largest crowd since Red Grange first came up, and the game they saw was worth the price.

It was a wide open game which the Giants led, 7-6, at halftime. Newman, who had a big day (13 for 19, 201 yards, 2 TDs) threw a touchdown to Badgro in the second period to offset two Bear field goals by "Automatic" Jack Manders. Nagurski set up the first kick with an interception and Manders booted the second 40 yards.

...terals to Karr for the winning touchdown.

Chicago Bears 23
New York Giants 21

One of the game's strangest incidents was a center-eligible almost-pass in the first quarter. As Giant center Hein remembers it, "This was a play we had to alert the officials about ahead of time. We put all the linemen on my right except the left end. Then he shifted back a yard, making me end man on the line, while the wingback moved up on the line on the right. Harry Newman came right up under me, like a T-formation quarterback. I handed the ball to him between my legs and he immediately put it right back in my hands—the shortest forward pass on record. I was supposed to fake a block and then just stroll down the field waiting for blockers, but after a few yards I got excited and started to run and the Bear safety, Keith Molesworth, saw me and knocked me down. I was about 15 yards from the goal, but we never did score on that drive."

In the third period, Jack Manders hit his third field goal through those invitingly close goal posts, a large total considering that the season's record until the Fifties was only ten. The Bears now led 9-7, but action was barely beginning.

Newman got hot, throwing the Giants 73 yards down the field to a one-yard touchdown buck by Max Krause. The Giants were ahead 14-9, after four lead changes. On the next series, the Bears had long yardage on third down and went into punt

Bear QB Brumbaugh escapes Strong on a first quarter end run.

formation. But it was a fake and George Corbett threw to quarterback Carl Brumbaugh for 67 yards to the Giant eight. On third and six, the Bears went to their strongest play. The ball was given to Nagurski who faked straight into the line. Then, taking advantage of the new passing rule, he stopped just short of the line and popped a quick jump pass to right end Bill Karr. Massed in front of Nagurski, the Giants watched helplessly.

Behind 16-14, Newman again went to the air, completing four straight passes to the Bear eight and setting up one of history's strangest plays (see Diagram 1). As Ken Strong tells it, "Newman handed off to me on a reverse to the left, but the line was jammed up. I turned and saw Newman standing there, so I threw him the ball. He was quite surprised. He took off to his right, but then *he* got bottled up. By now I had crossed into the end zone and the Bears had forgotten me. Newman saw me wildly

waving my hands and threw me the ball. I caught it and fell into the first-base dugout." The Giants later put this play in their offense, but it never worked again. This time, it put them in front, 21-16.

The game was almost over when a New York punt sliced away and the Bears took over on the Giant 47. A short pass and Nagurski got a first down on the 33 and then the Bears went back to their big play. Nagurski faked and jumped one to left end Bill Hewitt. When halfback Dale Burnett raced over to make the tackle, Hewitt lateraled to Karr who cut behind Gene Ronzani's block on Strong to score. The score was now

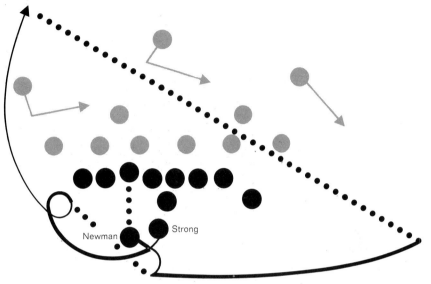

1. *Newman to Strong to Newman to Strong—impromptu Giant razzle-dazzle.*

Newman

Strong

final, Bears 23, Giants 21, but there was one bit of action left.

On the last play of the game, Newman threw to Dale Burnett. Says Red Grange, who by then was one of football's best defensive backs, "I was alone in the defense and Burnett was coming at me with somebody on the side of him. I could see he wanted to lateral, so I didn't go low. I hit him around the ball and pinned his arms. I never did throw him."

Play ended in this static two-man vignette. But the game had already shown the fast-moving, high-scoring excitement of pro football's future.

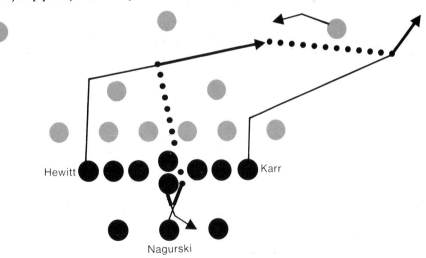

2. *A jump pass followed by a lateral won the game for Chicago.*

Hewitt

Karr

Nagurski

2

Washington Redskins	7	0	7	14	28
Chicago Bears	7	7	7	0	21

Wrigley Field, Chicago
December 12, 1937

A national sport has to play the nation's capital. It was in 1937, as the NFL settled towards solid organization, that pro football moved into Washington, D.C. The elements for the inaugural season were fitting— a dynamic owner, a spectacular rookie and a world championship.

The owner was George Preston Marshall, and the ring of his name tells much about him. He was dynamic and dramatic, a some-time actor and friend of politicians who had both the desire and the talent for generating public acceptance. Marshall bought the Redskins in 1932. The team was in Boston then, but the people there found other things to do with their Sundays, even when the team won an Eastern title in 1936, so Marshall moved south.

In the more appreciative atmosphere of Washington, Marshall's genius for promotion developed rapidly. "He had the proper concept of pro football," remembers Wellington Mara, New York Giants owner. "He was way ahead of everybody. He saw that pro football should be a family game. The wife should demand to go out to the stadium on Sunday. So he developed the first marching band in pro ball and gave each man an Indian headdress. He had a team song. He staged parades. He had an Indian medicine man get out on the field and sprinkle powder in front of the guy that was kicking off. Anything to make a show. Even for his laundry business he had a motto, 'Long Live Linen.' "

Slinging on the move, Redskin Baugh fires one of his 33 passes.

Baugh to Millner for 77-yard touchdown.

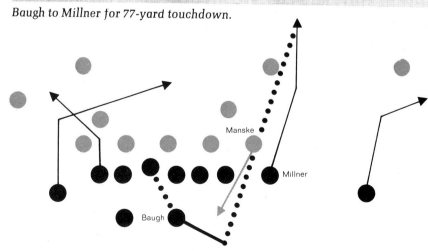

Battles fights Bears on a reverse left.

Marshall's impact was not limited to the trappings of the game. He knew the sport itself had to be highly saleable. When he first joined the league he teamed with George Halas on the important rules changes of 1933 which made for faster, more exciting football. Then, as he moved to Washington, he brought in a rookie ballplayer whose style opened the game even further.

Sammy Baugh left Texas after establishing a reputation at TCU as the best passer in football history. Whipping the ball sidearm out of a wide stance, Baugh could throw accurately from any position. "I practiced it that way" he says, "running sideways or backing up. You do it the hard way during practice and it comes easier during the game." His timing was so good that he could drive a team on a series of short passes — heresy in a day when passing was conventionally considered a desperation weapon.

Passing like that was all the Redskins needed. They had already won the 1936 Eastern crown with a crunching ground attack led by Hall of Fame halfback Cliff Battles and featuring strong blockers and runners like Ernie Pinckert and Riley Smith. The new combination was smooth. Battles led the league in rushing in 1937 with 874 yards and Baugh led in passing with a record 81 completions.

The Redskins went into the championship game against a resurgent Bear team. Bronko Nagurski was in his last year but George Halas was building back to the top with tough runners like Jack Manders and Ray Nolting, and Hall of Fame linemen like Joe Stydahar and Danny Fortmann. In 1937 the Bears went 9-1-1 in the division with the Hutson Packers and were probably good enough to take anybody but Sammy Baugh on a good day.

Sammy had just that, hitting 18 out of 33 for 335 yards and three touchdowns despite, in his words, "the worst field I ever saw. The field had been torn up the previous week, and it froze solid with jagged clods sticking up. I've never seen so many

people get cut up in a football game."

As the game opened, Baugh passed the Redskins down to the Bear seven. Then, when Chicago put on a desperate pass rush, he slipped the ball to Battles on a reverse for the touchdown. But the Bears were tough. They left at halftime leading 14-7 as halfback Manders scored all the points on a touchdown run, a touchdown pass reception and two extra point placements.

In the second half, Baugh took over. Mixing short and long passes, and ignoring the icy field with off-balance accuracy, he chewed up the Bears' special defense. Chicago used five defensive linemen, one less than normal for that period, and covered with six people, but it was no use. Hall of Fame end Wayne Millner escaped with two long touchdown receptions, good for 55 and 77 yards. The Redskin double wing formation let four receivers downfield quickly and the rudimentary pass defenses of that time could not cover them all. On Millner's second touchdown (see Diagram) he beat his man deep and although Bear end Ed Manske charged straight in at Baugh, Sammy laid the bomb out accurately while backing away.

With the score tied 21-21 in the fourth quarter, Baugh looked one way, then wheeled and threw the other to hit wingback Ed Justice in the corner 35 yards away with the winning touchdown.

In his rookie year, Sammy Baugh had beaten pro football's best with a style of play 15 years before its time. And in his first year in prestigious Washington, George Preston Marshall ran up a championship flag. Pro football was getting its base.

Chicago Bears	21	7	26	19	73
Washington Redskins	0	0	0	0	0

Griffith Stadium, Washington, D.C.
December 8, 1940

On a Sunday in the 1940 December, the Chicago Bears played perfect football for a greater percentage of the official hour than any team before or since. In the championship game, as an underdog to a team which had just beaten them, the Bears made an eleven-touchdown pile and used it as a pedestal to raise the NFL to view in all corners of the country.

Seventy-three to nothing. 73-0. And it really does not reflect at all on the Washington Redskins, who just happened to be the closest witnesses to the sudden flowering of the T-formation. George Halas had been using lesser versions of the T for twenty years. But in this game, the formation reached a new peak. Within five years, most teams in the country, high school, college and pro, were using the T.

Halas had undoubtedly put together a great team in 1940. Around Bulldog Turner in the center of the line were such other Hall of Famers as guard Danny Fortmann and tackle Joe Stydahar. In the backfield was the first modern T quarterback in professional football Sid Luckman. The league's most dangerous open field runner, George McAfee, was at right halfback, with Ray Nolting at left halfback and Bill Osmanski at full. And the Bears were so deep that most opponents would agree with Jim Lawrence, a Philadelphia lineman and later Pittsburgh coach, "It was worse when the Bear second string came in because they were breathing fire trying to prove they should be first string."

But the Washington Redskins were a good team, too, improved over the 1937 championship squad by Sammy Baugh's increased experience. The Redskins double wing formation got four receivers quickly down field against the three defensive backs standard in that era, and Sammy found the open one regularly. And Baugh had a lot of help from teammates such as backs Jimmy Johnston, Max Krause and Ed (Chug) Justice and end Charley Malone.

How one of these teams came to treat the other like a collection of tackling dummies is no easy thing to answer. It starts with one of the last League games in 1940, which featured the same two teams. The Redskins won by the oddly anagramic score of 7-3, but the Bears screamed loudly on the field and for several days thereafter that they had been done out of the winning touchdown by a referee's mistake. Redskins owner George Preston Marshall, who wasn't the quietest either, announced publicly that the Bears were "crybabies," and "first-half ballplayers." Marshall's quotes made interesting wall paper in the Bears' dressing room.

Justice stops Bear back Nolting.

But the championship game was not just an emotional outburst by Halas' men. It was also a carefully planned and executed strategic concept. Halas flew in his long-time advisor, Clark Shaughnessy, who was resting up before taking his Stanford team to the Rose Bowl. Shaughnessy, cleaned out some dead wood in the Bear attack and introduced a new communications system. Also, after long study of the films of the Redskins defeat, he put in a whole new series of plays. Since the Redskins shifted their linebackers which ever way the Bears' man-in-motion went, Shaughnessy figured that counter plays to the other side were obviously in order. By the time they were done, Halas says, "We had a two-ply game plan. One was perfectly fitted to the Redskin defense we had just seen. We were quite sure they wouldn't change something which had worked so well for them. If they did, though, we had a more general plan to put in."

Game day came up warm and sunny. The Bears came out ready both emotionally and mentally. "There was a feeling of tension in the air," says Sid Luckman, "as though something tremendous was about to happen." Before the first quarter was over, it had.

On the second scrimmage play, while the Bears were still checking the Redskin defense to see if it was the same, fullback Osmanski suddenly streaked an off-tackle play into a 62-yard touchdown. Although this play has usually been remembered and written as one of Shaughnessy's counter plays against the man-in-motion, films at the Hall of Fame show otherwise. Right half McAfee

Fullback Osmanski passes Justice (13) and Johnston (31) sprinting to 1st TD.

The Osmanski touchdown as recorded on film at Hall of Fame.

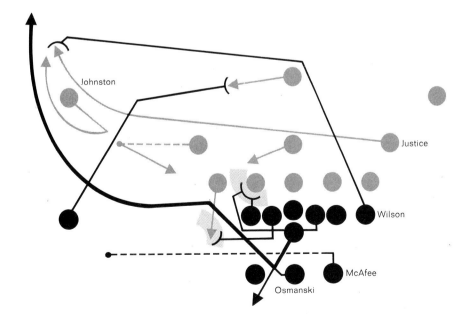

went in motion to the left and drew the Redskin right linebacker out with him. Osmanski took the ball on a straight smash at left tackle and the hole opened wide. He zipped through, made a great cut to the outside and swung down the sideline. Two men were chasing Osmanski and Chug Justice had a diving chance at the runner's heels, but Bear end George Wilson decked both Redskins with a crushing high shoulder block.

The Redskins came right back on a big kickoff return and a series of inside reverses until, on third down, Baugh threw his first pass. The ball came down to Charley Malone, open on the four, right out of the sun. It got away. The Bears immediately countermarched 80 yards on 17 crunching plays. Luckman threw only once, to McAfee, who carried the quick pass 15 yards to the two. Luckman sneaked over for 14-0. On the next series, the Redskins again dropped a Baugh pass on third down. Luckman took over on the Redskin 42, pitched out to second-string fullback Joe Maniaci, and Maniaci took it in. 21-0 in the first quarter.

The Redskins sensed it. Baugh was taken out and played little the rest of the game. By the second half, the Bears were scoring on interceptions, bucks, long passes—seven touchdowns in one half. In the final totals, the Bears had 347 rushing yards, the Redskins three. The Bears completed six of eight passes and intercepted eight by the Redskins. And the final score was 73-0.

Pro football, the T-formation and the Chicago Bears were the sudden sports news of the year.

4

Cleveland Browns	7	7	7	14	35
Philadelphia Eagles	3	0	0	7	10

Municipal Stadium, Philadelphia
September 16, 1950

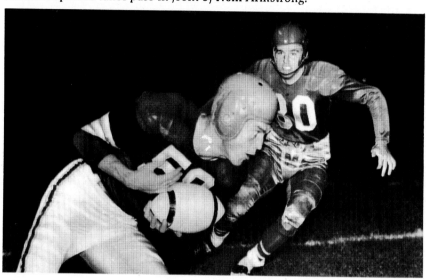

Brown's Speedie takes pass in front of Neill Armstrong.

The game was a natural anyway — the 1949 champions of the NFL, the Philadelphia Eagles, against the 1949 champions of the All-America Football Conference, the Cleveland Browns. But when the two leagues merged, NFL commissioner Bert Bell heightened the drama by scheduling their meeting as the first game of the 1950 season, all alone on the Saturday night before the first league Sunday.

The idea was to stir up interest, and it worked like a nationwide osterizer. By game time the papers were full of "The most talked about game in NFL history."

The Philadelphia Eagles had won three straight Eastern Conference crowns and the last two world titles with an authentic powerhouse. Head Coach Greasy Neale had developed the latest defense, a 5-4 alignment widely copied around the league as the "Eagle Defense," and manned it with tough people like Bucko Kilroy, Hall of Fame linebacker Chuck Bednarik and All-Pro halfback Russ Craft. The offense also stressed solidity, with an efficient quarterback in Tommy Thompson, a clutch-catching end in Pete Pihos, and a crushing runner in Hall of Fame halfback Steve Van Buren.

The Cleveland Browns — well, the Browns had torn up the AAFC, but could they stay with NFL competition? Few teams threw the ball around in the NFL the way the Browns had. Their pass protection was supposed to break down against a real rush. Their defense couldn't stand against a professionally punishing attack. But it turned out otherwise. "That game wasn't really a sporting proposition for the Eagles," Cleveland's coach Paul Brown thinks back. "The

press and the public were saying how we were going to get whipped 50 to nothing, and this would take a little doing when we had guys like quarterback Otto Graham, fullback Marion Motley and receivers Dante Lavelli, Mac Speedie and Dub Jones. Besides, this was the highest emotional game I ever coached. We had four years of constant ridicule to get us ready."

By kickoff time, the entire football nation was waiting for the outcome. In the middle of Philadelphia's most memorable baseball pennant race, the Eagles sold 60,000 tickets in advance and welcomed 71,000 people into Philadelphia Municipal Stadium. None of them quite expected what they saw.

The Eagle defense was indeed tough against the run — in the first half. The Browns lost yardage on two of three first quarter carries and fumbled on two of five second quarter carries. But at the half, it was 14-3, Browns. Otto Graham hit two big plays, a 41-yard touchdown to flanker Dub Jones, and a 26-yard touchdown to right end Dante Lavelli. The Eagles,

playing without their star halfback Van Buren who was out with a foot injury, were moving the ball but not scoring. When Graham came out in the third quarter and drove to a 13-yard touchdown caught by the third of his three great receivers, left end Mac Speedie, the game was really over. The Browns turned to Motley and the running attack and churned out the clock, piling on two more touchdowns as incidental benefit. At the end it was 35-10.

In this era, teams did not exchange films and the Eagles were surprised by the nature of the Cleveland passing attack. Eagle defensive halfback Russ Craft, many times all-pro, says of the problems the Browns created, "We never met such a spot passing program as they had. We would be on top of the receivers, but they caught the ball anyway because the pass was so well-timed. This was something new in football." On a sample play, the Browns would have Speedie hook straightaway, Lavelli to the inside, and Jones go in motion and then square out. With "three Don Hutsons," it was impossible to

1. A typical Cleveland pass pattern.

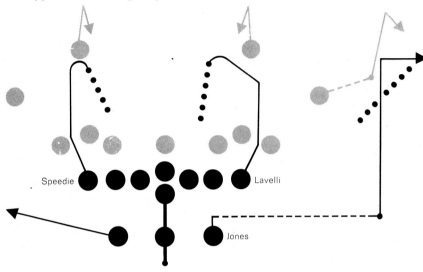

Speedie   Lavelli

Jones

2. The Motley trap through a widened Eagle defense.

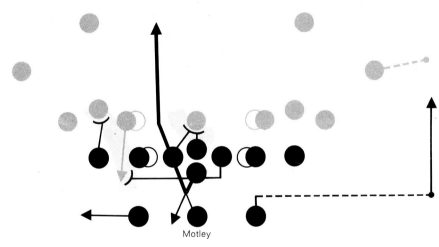

Motley

double cover all of them. Cleveland end Dante Lavelli says, "We always felt it would take more than one person to cover us. I still think no one man can cover even a mediocre receiver." Not when the timing is perfect (see Diagram 1).

Cleveland got its running attack smashing in the second half with the help of a stratagem by Coach Brown. "In the four years we waited for this game, we gave a lot of searching thought to the Eagle 5-4 defense. Its problem, against both run and pass, is that there is no middle linebacker, so the center is weak. On runs, what we did was to keep spacing our tackles a few inches wider on each play. The defensive tackles would keep moving out, too, and this created natural spacing in the line. Every now and then, we could zing Motley through on a trap" (see Diagram 2).

For the game, the Eagles actually earned more first downs than Cleveland, 24-23. But Cleveland was hitting the killing play, behind Graham's final total of 346 aerial yards. Later in the year, the Eagles adjusted and prevented Graham from completing a single pass, but lost 13-7 on an interception. The New York Giants also gave the Browns fits, allowing only 13 points in two regular season games, winning them both.

But in the match-up of titans, the first game of 1950, the Browns shocked the football world. In December, in a playoff with New York and then in the championship, the Browns would show that if they weren't the unstoppable machine they seemed in September, they were at least the champions.

And that's enough.

5

Cleveland Browns   7   6   7   10   30
Los Angeles Rams   14   0   14   0   28

Cleveland Stadium, Cleveland
December 24, 1950

QB Graham, about to collide with Woodley Lewis, ran often in the clutch.

When the Cleveland Browns scuffled their way into the 1950 championship with a squeaky playoff victory over the New York Giants, they brought the old question of their NFL-worthiness to its final test. The Los Angeles Rams, a team which itself had been based in Cleveland only five years earlier, would make this last case for the old-line NFL teams.

But when Cleveland coach Paul Brown remembers it as "the greatest game I had ever seen," he is not thinking as much of the inter-league context as he is of the aerial exhibition put on by both clubs. The Browns and the Rams were the two leaders in the modern passing revolution and in their first head-on collision they threw the ball for sixty minutes solid.

Never before this game and rarely since has such a collection of receivers peopled one field. The Browns, first specialists in the precision passing game, had Mac Speedie, Dante Lavelli and Dub Jones. The Rams, who were making the long pass as routine as the off-tackle slant, countered with Tom Fears (whose 1950 total of 84 catches was a record until 1964), Hall of Fame flanker Elroy Hirsch and Glenn (Mr. Outside)

Davis. Los Angeles had won its way into the second of three consecutive title games with a backwards offense. "We reversed the usual procedure," says their offensive coach of that era, Hamp Pool. "Instead of our running setting up the passing, our passing set up the runs, such as draws and the statue of liberty. In the championship game we ran the statue several times (see Diagram 1). Our quarterback would fake a pass and hand off to one of our quick little halfbacks on a reverse." In the memory of Hirsch, "Our 1950 Ram team was man for man as fine a football team as I've ever seen." Yet this day, the Browns won. It was not bad football.

The game started fast, ended wild and looked like a pack of rabbits on amphetamine in between. Both teams scattered receivers all over the scrimmage line in an assortment of forma-

tions rivaled by few half-time bands. On the first play, the Rams established their credentials with an 82-yard touchdown pass from Bob Waterfield to Davis (see Diagram 2). Offensive coach Pool remembers, "That first play took advantage of their 5-3-3 defense. We sent a man-in-motion to the right and had our left end, Tom Fears, break inside. Our left halfback, Glenn Davis, gave a first picture that he was going to block. The Brown linebacker was supposed to cover Davis, but when he took his eyes off him to follow Fears, Davis sneaked out and took Waterfield's pass for the TD." Shaken

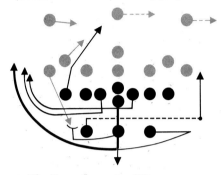

1. A Ram Statue-of-Liberty play.

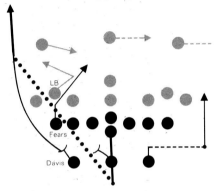

2. The Rams' opening TD.

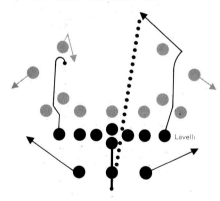

3. The Third Cleveland TD.

not the slightest, Otto Graham brought the Browns right back, firing 31 yards to Dub Jones to tie the game 7-7 after only three minutes.

And this was just for openers. Waterfield finished the day 18 for 22 for 312 yards and a touchdown. And this against the first technically refined pass defense, coached by Brown's assistant, Blanton Collier. Graham made 22 of 33 and accounted for all four of the Cleveland touchdowns. His right end, Dante Lavelli, caught eleven short and long and scored twice.

Pool explains that, "The Browns hurt us a lot by isolating their inside ends, Lavelli and Speedie, on our two safeties. Lavelli got a touchdown when Graham had both his halfbacks flare wide out of the backfield (see Diagram 3). This occupied our halfbacks. Then Speedie hooked, to hold one of our safeties, and Lavelli ran a deep post on the other safety. No one man could cover this, if the ball were thrown straight. And Graham was very good at hanging the ball up and letting his receiver run under it."

Until the end, the Browns were ahead only once, 20-14 in the third quarter, but the Rams soon ended that, piling up 14 points in 21 seconds. First, fullback Dick Hoerner ended a 71-yard drive, carrying seven consecutive times from the 17 to a one-yard touchdown. On the next scrimmage play, Ram defensive end Larry Brink picked up a fumble

by fullback Marion Motley and carried it to the 28-20 touchdown.

The Browns were down eight points in the fourth quarter, but they had two effective weapons for the situation. One was their disciplined short passing attack. "The defenders couldn't afford to come up fast," says coach Brown, "or Graham would have faked a quick one and thrown deep." Also, and decisively, quarterback Graham was given the express go-ahead to run any time necessary. Remembers Brown, "Only in the deepest pressure would you gamble your quarterback's body." The gamble paid off in key runs on both of the last drives as Graham pushed the Browns to a touchdown and then, starting on his own 32 with 1:50 on the clock, moved the team into position for Lou Groza's 16-yard field goal with 28 seconds left.

After the field goal, the fans had to be cleared off the field to finish the game, but the action was finally over. The Browns had shown the NFL that they did, indeed, belong. But more importantly, both teams had shown all of football that there was a new way to play the game.

6

Baltimore Colts 0 14 0 3 6 **23**
New York Giants 3 0 7 7 0 **17**
Yankee Stadium, New York
December 28, 1958

Baltimore's Berry leaps for one of his 12 receptions.

This is the game that did it for NFL football. It has been called the greatest game ever played, and maybe it wasn't, but there never was a more important one. As John Unitas crafted the sudden-death drive to its bravura touchdown, pro football was exploded into the mind of America. The sports public had read and heard of the great games in the past. But it *watched* this one, and seeing is exciting.

Marshall McLuhan says that television has turned the world into a village—everybody can share one experience despite great distances. Some outlying parts of the world may have missed it, but in every corner of America, millions of people turned out to watch the New York Giants play the Baltimore Colts, and the game sold them the sport.

Pro football had risen from the sandlot days through a stage as Sunday pastime. Now it was launched as a significant portion of the mass culture of America. If television programming priorities reflect the country's collective mind, then pro football is this people's major diversion. And it started with sudden-death.

The New York Giants' season had been wild enough already, without the cardiac championship game. In training camp the team looked so bad that assistant coach Vince Lombardi felt he had never been around a worse group. When the season started, the offense died and the defense had to keep the team in contention. Fortunately, this was the great Giant defense. The defensive line was the first to command national attention—ends Andy Robustelli and Jim Katcavage, and tackles

With 20 seconds of regulation left, Myhra ties it 17-17.

Conerly fires past Marchetti.

Roosevelt Grier and Dick Modzelewski. Sam Huff played middle linebacker between two mobile wings, Harland Svare and Bill Svoboda. The backfield was good and experienced, with Lindon Crow and Carl Karilivacz at corners, Jim Patton and Emlen Tunnell at safety.

To get to a divisional tie the Giants had to win the final four games in a row, the last against the rival Browns. They just squeezed them out, beating the Browns in the closing seconds with the NFL's most memorable field goal. Pat Summerall slammed it through a snow storm so blinding nobody knows if it was really only 49 yards. Then the Giants shut out Cleveland in the playoff, 10-0, to stagger into the confrontation with the Colts.

Baltimore had gotten to its first championship with less travail. The Colts had been climbing in the Fifties. A decent team went to the top when in 1956, it picked up halfback Lenny Moore, defensive tackle Big Daddy Lipscomb and quarterback John Unitas and then, in 1957, anchored the offensive line with tackle Jim Parker. The worst for the 1958 Colts came in the sixth week when Unitas broke two ribs and punctured a lung. He sat out one whole week and then came back to bomb Moore a 58-yard touchdown on the first play against the Rams. That set it. By the tenth game, they had the title won and were waiting for a championship opponent.

Baltimore Colts 23
New York Giants 17

The charge of the game was generated by two factors, (1) the scalpel-clean attack of the Colts against the crackless Giant defense and (2) a stirring comeback by each team.

The 25-year-old Unitas brought his whole game to New York that day. Calling beautifully, dropping, wheeling and sticking the ball to his receivers, he played quarterback as though he were inventing the position anew. Early in the game he dropped a 60-yard pass on Lenny Moore despite perfect coverage by Giant corner Lindon Crow. Throughout, he maneuvered 12 passes to Raymond Berry, all of them big, despite aggressive and intelligent play by Carl Karilivacz.

It was a thrilling display and it almost dismembered the Giants. At the half it was 14-3 and Unitas came out in the third quarter throwing to the Giant three-yard line. But the Giants rose up and tore the game from the young master's hands. In four runs, the Colts lost a yard.

A few plays later, Giant quarterback Charlie Conerly found Kyle Rote with a deep slant. Going down on the Colt 25, Rote dropped the ball but halfback Alex Webster grabbed it and took it to the one. Fullback Mel Triplett scored.

The Giants got the ball back and Conerly, functioning out of their archaic tight-T, hit Bob Schnelker for 46 yards and then halfback Frank Gifford on a 16-yard swing pass TD.

The Colts cut off Gifford on an overtime third down, getting the ball for Unitas.

A possible Colt rout was suddenly a 17-14 Giant lead, and the great New York defense went out to win it.

But Unitas put it back together. With two minutes to go, he slashed the ball down the field, going to Berry three times for 62 yards. As the clock ran down, Steve Myhra hit a 20-yard field goal, and the first 60 minutes ended, 17-17. The game went into football's first sudden-death overtime and it was all Baltimore. Unitas was into a white-hot creative state and the team swept to the win with the inexorable esthetic of a Beethoven finale. At the end, well into field goal range, Unitas was still throwing, not because of strategy, but because that's the way it felt — he couldn't have moused it out any more than Van Gogh could have done post card landscapes.

His inspired leadership turned a simple fullback trap by Alan Ameche into the biggest play of the drive (see Diagram). Unitas had been dumped by Giant tackle Modzelewski on second down at midfield. On the next play he rose to throw a vital first down pass and then his thoughts returned to the Giant tackle. He remembers, "Modzelewski had been blowing in there pretty good. When I came up to the line, I saw that Huff was going to back up to try to take away the passes to Berry. I checked off to the Ameche trap." Tom Landry, then coach of the Giants' defense, remembers, "We were look-

Behind Moore's block, Ameche bulls in with the winning touchdown.

ing for a pass and went into a special defense. Both linebackers, Svare and Livingston, were over on the strong side to double up on Moore. Patton and Karilivacz doubled Berry. Huff was playing pass and they caught us." Ameche got 23 yards and put the ball in field goal range. But John Unitas was not thinking field goal.

He threw right to the goal, Jim Mutscheller taking the last pass out of bounds at the one. At eight minutes and fifteen seconds of overtime, fullback Ameche went through a huge hole and the country came to its feet.

Said Raymond Berry, "It's the greatest thing that's ever happened."

The Ameche trap called by Unitas in the overtime drive.

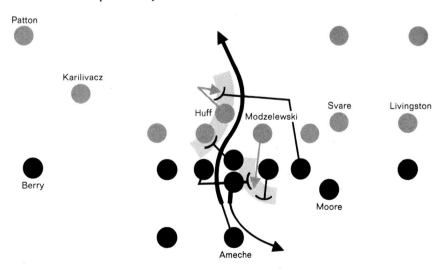

Wrigley Field, Chicago
October 22, 1961

Shotgun tailback Kilmer takes direct pa

In the three decades since the Chicago Bears fell on the Washington Redskins 73-0, the T-formation has dominated pro football. Ends have split wider, halfbacks have moved to the flank, but the quarterback has spent the last thirty years taking the ball from center and turning his back to start the play.

The T is effective. It can't be argued. And yet there's a feeling, a suspicion, that by now everybody uses the T because everybody *else* uses the T. Man's natural tendency to tradition and conformity has been increased by the use of film, which records for easy copying all the ideas of currently successful coaches. Breaking out of this confinement takes imagination and courage.

It's happened once in recent history and the man to do it was Red Hickey. A top pass receiver in his time, Hickey as coach of the San Francisco 49ers watched the great defensive teams in Green Bay, Baltimore, Detroit and New York stunt the scoring of the standard T, and wondered about the possibility of some revolutionary change. Circumstances led him to a sudden decision.

The 49ers were going up against the Colts in Baltimore in 1960. The Colts were two-time champions and Hickey figured there was no way he was going to beat them with the same old stuff. In mid-week he installed the Shotgun. On Sunday he gunned

Baltimore down, 30-22. The Colts never recovered, losing for the rest of the season, and Hickey was the sudden rage of the league with four wins in the last five games. That winter, he drafted for a Shotgun tailback, getting Bill Kilmer from UCLA's single wing, and traded his old passer who was too slow to maneuver in the new formation, Y. A. Tittle.

By 1961, the Shotgun was loaded and when Hickey pulled the trigger, he almost blew the league down. After the first five games of the season, the Shotgun led the league in points, yards passing *and* yards running. Hickey began to rotate his tailbacks, John Brodie, Bill Kilmer and Bobby Waters, on every play and the results were horrendous destructions of the Lions and Rams, 49-0 and 35-0.

The theory of the formation (see Diagram 1) is in, perhaps, three parts. First, receivers are draped all along the line where they can get downfield quickly. Second, the passer is back where he can survey the field from the start of the play. Third, the key maneuver rolls the passer to the side with a free choice to run or pass. This is the option play, football's most effective basic ploy. The defenders don't know whether to come up to stop the run or drop back to cover the pass. Most offensive plays tip themselves off in the first fraction of a second. The option play is disguised until the actual moment of attack.

In the Shotgun, the linemen take wider spaces than normal. One end and the flanker are set wide, and the two "running" backs are nearly on the line as wingbacks. The tailback is five yards deep, very alone. A play starts with a spiral snap to the tail-

back, who can step up to run or hand off on a wingback reverse (see Diagram 2) or he can stand and throw. or roll out on the option.

The 49ers had fullback-types as wingbacks, J. D. Smith and C. R. Roberts, and the Shotgun running attack, a combination of tailback plunges and wingback reverses, went very well. With faster wings, the passing would have been even more effective. The problem with this formation, of course, is to keep the tailback alive. Hickey's final solution

to this was to rotate three of them, keeping them rested. John Brodie usually passed, Bill Kilmer usually ran and Bobby Waters did some of each.

For the first five games in 1961, the combination was too much for the league. Then, with no warning, the Shotgun was suddenly twisted into a useless heap. The Chicago Bears did it, and the man who masterminded the operation was Clark Shaughnessy, owner of the most intricate mind in football's history. "Clark had been scouting the Shotgun for two weeks and making a million diagrams," said Bear head coach George Halas of his defensive coach. "He threw out all our old stuff and outguessed the 49ers."

1. The Shotgun formation.

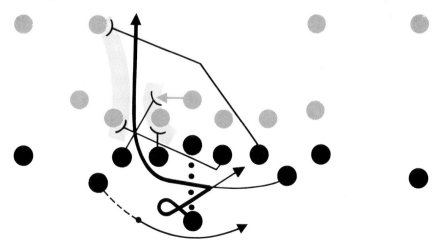

2. A wingback reverse.

Chicago Bears 31
San Francisco 49ers 0

Although Shaughnessy perfected the T-formation, his expertise precedes it and he remembers a fatal weakness of a tailback type of attack. "To pass the ball back to the tailback, the center has to put his head between his legs and nobody in that position can block a man that's on top of him. We put our middle linebacker, Bill George, right over the center. He was a great player with a quick sense of the game. More times than not he just shot right through into the backfield. He had that poor tailback by the throat even before he could hand the ball off."

There was more to Shaughnessy's plan than just Bill George up the middle. Defensive linemen continually jumped around and charged in different directions. This was called "muddling" because it muddles up the offensive blockers. If a wingback went into motion, the defensive ends shifted too (see Diagram 3). In addition, the defense was carefully keyed to the varying skills of the three Shotgun tailbacks. With Brodie, extra deep backs were employed. Against Kilmer, the running defense was beefed up. Waters was given balanced coverage.

The game turned into a classic rout. The first quarter was scoreless, but a short punt and a pass interception set up two fast touchdown passes by Bear quarterback Bill Wade in the second quarter. "By the second half, they were discouraged," says Shaughnessy. "Our new defense surprised them. As I always say, it doesn't make a heck of a lot of differ-

Doug Atkins dumps Kilmer in Bear win.

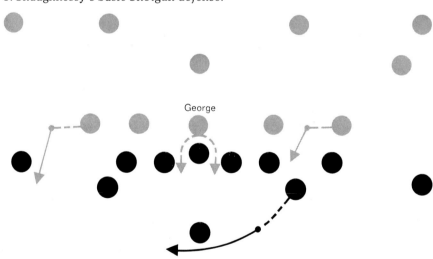

3. Shaughnessy's basic Shotgun defense.

ence what you do, just make it new. Give them something they never faced before. They couldn't cope with it and they just took it for granted that everything they did was wrong."

In the second half futility, the 49ers netted one yard, total. They got one first down, on a penalty. The ball got

away from them on fumbles and interceptions, setting up two more Wade touchdowns and a field goal. At the end it was 31-0 and it was more painful than that to watch.

The Shotgun was plugged, but post mortems still appear. Hickey, for one, isn't convinced. "It wasn't the 'defenses' that stopped our Shotgun," he says. "We stopped ourselves. In that Bear game, we dropped the ball

Hickey confers with three tailbacks, Waters, Brodie and Kilmer.

and threw it away. I abandoned the Shotgun for three reasons. Bob Waters got injured, we were fumbling, and our confidence declined. Basically, the Shotgun had worked because of confidence and aggressiveness. After a while, the kids read so much about the defenses catching up with the Shotgun and solving it, that they began to believe it. If the kids lost confidence in the Shotgun, it was no good to us. But I'll never keep losing with the same attack. Like I said after the Bear game, 'Next week we'll try something new. Blocking.' "

One of Hickey's tailbacks, Bill Kilmer, doesn't downgrade the Shotgun either. "I think it was a good formation. It had a lot of threats. The problem was they could key the quarterbacks. They knew Brodie would throw and I would run. I wish I could have run the option pass more."

Most significantly, perhaps, Shotgun-killer Shaughnessy still likes it. "Hickey never should have dropped the Shotgun, just because we came along and surprised them," says Shaughnessy. "It's a sound formation with good values. He could have changed it enough to take advantage of the new defense. It's too bad."

But regrets are all that are left. Whether it was beaten or just abandoned is not clear. But it's gone. After a half-century of pro football, all the quarterbacks line up right behind the center. The T is the thing.

8

Green Bay Packers 7 6 7 3 23
Cleveland Browns 9 3 0 0 12
Lambeau Field, Green Bay
January 2, 1966

The field and the tough Packer defense kept Jim Brown in check. The Browns slowed Hornung and the Packers until the half.

Football is a world of possibilities. Strategy is computer-complex, skills are highly refined, strength is at a premium and emotional impact is total. Each man can choose whatever fits his personality.

Vince Lombardi brought to Green Bay a highly emotional nature and translated it into a football team. He was a man of strong feelings and sharp mood changes. He was challenged and charged by the need for emotional leadership in the intricate group effort of modern football. He was a good strategist, he was a sound judge of strength and skill. But he was attracted to football by the demands on the character strength of the people involved. In his view, intricate strategy only interfered with the direct challenge football poses for a man's commitment to his team and to victory. Some people like to watch the arc of a long pass. Lombardi liked to feel an off-tackle slant — the blockers knock people back three yards, the runner hacks out three more and the team stalks back to the huddle hitching pants and shifting shoulder pads. These are the hard yards, the proud yards and they are the yards Lombardi loved to get.

He was intelligent enough to win any way he had to. But he would rather win sure in the knowledge that he and his team had demonstrated their superiority in courage, character and commitment.

The Packers took this tough way to the top in the early Sixties. But by 1965, Green Bay had been missing from the championship game two

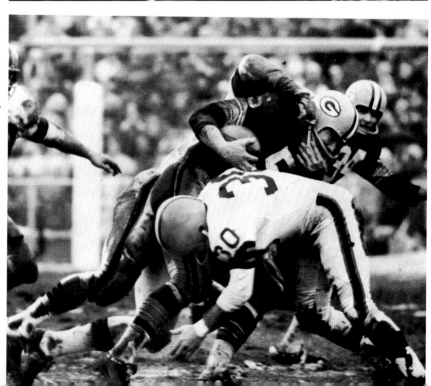

Packer fullback Taylor, veering to daylight, earned 96 yards on 28 carries and the MVP award.

straight seasons, victims of hot years by the Bears and Colts. Even this year had been no waltz. The running game had suffered with injuries to fullback Jim Taylor and halfback Paul Hornung. The Packers just did squeeze an overtime playoff victory past a Colt team that didn't even have a quarterback. The faltering Packer power was underscored at the end of the league season when Lombardi signed two highly-rated college runners, Jim Grabowski and Donny Anderson. The great days of the Taylor-Hornung machine seemed dead.

In the championship game, the Cleveland Browns were a likely team to erect a Green Bay tombstone. The previous year, the Browns had won the title in shocking 27-0 fashion over the Colts. They had the league's best running offense, Jim Brown, and great receivers, Jim Brown, Gary Collins and Paul Warfield. Dr. Frank Ryan at quarterback was a fine strategist and a killing post-or-corner passer. If the Browns could stay close and go with their best stuff, Dr. Frank might easily bomb the Packers out of the game. As the game was

played, it looked just that way right up to halftime.

Then, as the second half started, Green Bay reached back and put it all together again.

Game day was typically Green Bay. They had to get snow plows out to find the field. Warmth was nowhere evident and the footing required a sort of off-speed skate.

Just to be perverse, the Packers came out throwing. Bart Starr threw short to his backs and then, following a prearranged design, he went for the big one to flanker Carroll Dale. The field put two Browns on their backs, Dale carefully moved under the ball and Green Bay had seven quick points.

**Green Bay Packers 23
Cleveland Browns 12**

Hornung cuts inside Taylor's block and follows Thurston on the power play off tackle.

Ryan passed the Browns right back into the game, marching smoothly to a 17-yard Gary Collins touchdown catch in the corner. The Browns muffed the extra point. By the end of the second period, four field goals had been added to the score, two on each side, and the 13-12 game looked like the type to go right down to the final gun. But in the halftime locker room, the Packers made some old-time decisions.

"We realized the field was slowing down the speed of our plays to the hole," says Jerry Kramer. "We decided to go to the straight stuff that got us to the hole quicker." Jim Taylor recalls, "We knew that on that type of field, ball control could win the game. We didn't want to give Ryan too many chances." When the Packers came out for the second half they were ready, in the most fitting way, to grind their way back to the top.

When he could get the ball, Ryan kept bombing away, since Jim Brown was hampered by the field. He had three near misses, the last when Packer middle linebacker Ray Nitschke chased Brown half the field to nick away a touchdown pass. The near-misses were all Cleveland got as the Packers took out a land-claim on the football.

For the second half the Packers outgained the Browns by 148 yards. Final statistics showed that they had run off 69 plays to the Browns' 39 and made 21 first downs to the Browns' 8. The biggest move was a 90-yard drive on eleven third-quarter plays—two passes, seven minutes consumed. Hornung got the touchdown 13 yards around left end. Key plays in the

1. The Packer power play at right tackle.

2. The modified Packer sweep which scored 20-12 TD.

Kramer leads Hornung to 13-yard TD.

Taylor and Hornung on top again.

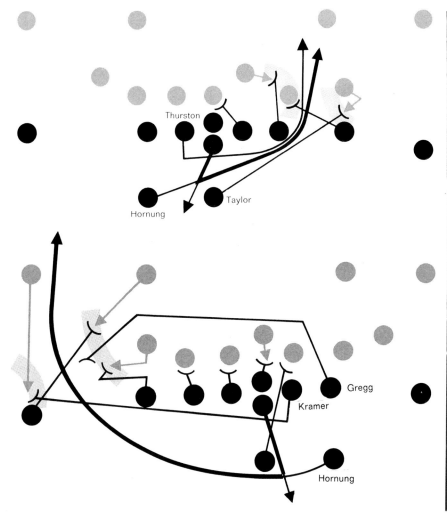

drive were all bedrock football. Paul Hornung got a good portion of the yardage running the straightest type of off-tackle slant (see Diagram 1). Tight end Bill Anderson blocked to the inside, Taylor took the linebacker to the outside and Hornung followed guard Fuzzy Thurston at a hard sprint.

For the 20-12 touchdown the Packers went to a variation of their famous power sweep (see Diagram 2). The usual play sent Hornung wide behind both guards, Thurston and Jerry Kramer. But in this game, only the guard furthest away, Kramer, pulled

out to lead. This seemed to confuse the Browns, especially the middle linebacker, who moved up instead of chasing the end run. Tackle Forrest Gregg circled all the way around to clean up people the other guard usually hit. On the TD run Hornung was not touched.

In this drive and throughout the second half, Taylor grunted and bucked and growled his way to one

messy yard after another. He was working on a bad knee, a bad ankle and a groin muscle pull. He finished with 96 yards.

It was beautiful football if your taste is brutal man-to-man. It was Packer football. "This is a team with character," said Vince Lombardi, and his ride off the field came on the shoulders of Paul Hornung and Jim Taylor.

In the locker room Ken Bowman, the team's new center, recalled the spirit in the huddles. "They kept hollering, 'Just like 1962.' I guess this is how they used to do it."

Cowboys' Perkins fakes left before taking Meredith handoff through the right

The modern game of professional football is a sport of complex calculation and precision dancing set in an environment of organized violence. At its peak it is a spectacle of courageous beauty. At the conclusion of the 1966 season, in the Texas sun, the Green Bay Packers and the Dallas Cowboys took the game to its peak. Playing for the championship, both teams executed at such a high level that 61 points were scored against two of the league's best defenses. It was a game of comebacks, tension, and a last second goal line stand.

The good modern defense leaves only the smallest of cracks, with pain on all sides. This was a day when both offenses were slicing into the cracks. Football can hardly be played any better.

The Packers came into the game after one of the most impressive seasons in an impressive era. They lost only two games in 1966, by a total of four points. Throughout the year, the defense was decisive. The team led the league for the season in points allowed, 163, which is not quite twelve a game. The defense was simply conceived but perfectly coordinated, built around the best group of linebackers in football, Ray Nitschke, Dave Robinson and Lee Roy Caffey. To go with this flexible linebacking nucleus, the Packers had a quick front four, led by end Willie Davis, and an efficient secondary starring cornerman Herb Adderley and safety Willie Wood. As a group, they didn't give an offense much to work on.

The 1966 Packer offense was a more modest affair. Quarterback Bart Starr's startling 62% completion average was a product of a conservative pass offense that threw more to fullback Jim Taylor than anybody else. And the running offense had been less than overpowering. Paul Hornung had missed most of the year with a nerve injury.

On the other hand, the Cowboys came on as a flamboyant offensive outfit, emphasizing speed and confusion. Sprinting end Bob Hayes required either two men or iron shoes to keep him down. Backs Don Perkins and Dan Reeves provided the intelligence and versatility necessary in Coach Tom Landry's multiple offense and quarterback Don Meredith was acquiring the eminence long predicted for him.

Despite the offensive show, the Cowboys were also constructing one of the league's top defensive units. They were perhaps a year away from

Fullback Taylor had good day running and receiving.
Cowboys clean out Packers for Reeves' TD.

perfect adjustment to Landry's partnership conception of defense, but led by Bob Lilly in the line, Lee Roy Jordan and Chuck Howley at linebacker and Mel Renfro and Cornell Green in the secondary, the Cowboys had finished fifth in defense in 1966.

In this setting, Landry for the Cowboys and Vince Lombardi for the Packers put together two marvelous game plans. Lombardi changed some blocking assignments and used crossing backs to confuse the Cowboys' defense. Never one to waste motion, he threw out his best play, the power sweep, because Cowboy pursuit

killed end runs. Bart Starr says of the Packer thinking, "It was a marvelous game plan. We were down to only six passes, with variations, and eight runs. Of course, a game plan is nothing without execution, but this was a great plan." Of his own plan, Dallas quarterback Meredith says, "By the time of the game we were brainwashed. We knew we could run and move on the Packers. Even when we got 14 points behind early, there was

no reason to go away from our planning."

And this Cowboy comeback was one of the great stories of the game. The Cowboys spotted the impenetrable Packer defense a two-touchdown lead and then caught them. The Packers opened the game sending halfback Elijah Pitts on an off-tackle play with the backs crossing and Pitts rolled 32 yards. Soon Starr hit Pitts with a swing pass and the halfback ran down two Cowboys for

Green Bay Packers 34
Dallas Cowboys 27

a 17-yard touchdown and 7-0. On the following kickoff, the ball was batted out of Renfro's hands and Packer rookie Jim Grabowski scooped it up for the 14-0 touchdown. Only four and a half minutes had passed.

The Cowboys had a great chance to fold or panic. Instead, they ran off-tackle. In a 13-yard play drive of runs and quick passes, they moved to a score, blasting Reeves through a wide hole. They took the ball away immediately and drove right back. On the Packer 23, Don Perkins got a hole at right tackle, slashed through two Packers and skipped to the tying score. It was 14-14 in the first quarter.

The rest of the game lived up to those first fifteen minutes. The Cowboys' defense took away the Packer running, and Packer receivers were just barely getting open. But just barely was enough for Bart Starr this day. Over and over he slid in the third down pass. Throwing deep to Carroll Dale and short to anybody eligible, he moved the Packers to three more touchdowns on passes to Dale, Max McGee and Boyd Dowler. He wound up with an imposing 304 yards throwing.

The Dowler touchdown (see Diagram 1) is an example of the way an offense must manipulate a modern defense in order to score. Starr wanted to throw to his split end on a pattern over the center. To do this he had to clear linebackers Jordan and Howley out of the way. His tool was fullback Jim Taylor. Starr faked Taylor on a draw play, which pulled Jordan

up close. Then Taylor ran to his right, into Howley's territory, and Howley ran up knowing that Starr loved to throw to his fullback. Both linebackers were close to the line and the areas they could cover (gray tones) were split. Starr had a clear alley to throw to Dowler. The touchdown put Green Bay ahead, 34-20, since the last kick was blocked.

This was important because Meredith had the Cowboys moving, too. Using a more balanced attack than Green Bay, he lined up two field goals and then, down 34-20 in the fourth quarter, he passed to Frank

Clarke for a 68-yard touchdown. This play was another example of offensive maneuvering. To throw to tight end Clarke deep over the center, Meredith had to get free safety Willie Wood out of the way. For this purpose, he had split end Bob Hayes. The Packers were so worried about the 9.1 Hayes that they put two men on him anytime he went deep. So Meredith sent Hayes deep to the outside and Wood ran over to help out. Also, Meredith sent halfback Dan Reeves in motion before the play started. The Packer linebackers, including Dave Robinson, moved

1. *Taylor sets up Starr's decisive pass to Dowler.*

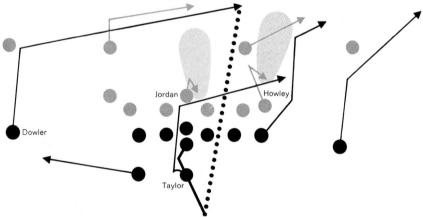

2. *Cowboy planning springs Clarke for long TD.*

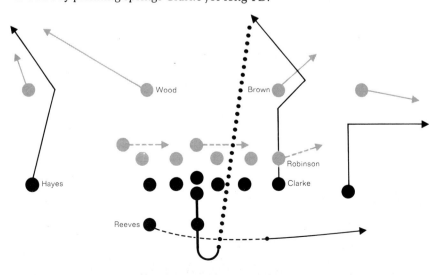

with Reeves and gave Clarke a free-running start. When safety Tom Brown slipped, this maneuvering left Clarke 20 yards open.

With a feeling of sudden death in the air, the Packers squibbed a punt and the Cowboys started on their final drive to frustration from the Packer 47. Clarke broke open again but was interfered with and the Cowboys had the ball on the two, first down. They made one yard at tackle, but disaster struck on second down. A lineman went in motion, and it was second down from the six. It took two downs to get back to the two.

Now, on fourth down, the two teams went out in style, strength to strength. Meredith called the strongest goal line play, a rollout, right at the Packers' strongest man, Dave Robinson. "I figured a rollout gave me two chances to score, running or throwing," says Meredith. "I called it to the right because that was the close sideline and I thought they wouldn't expect it. Robinson is supposed to go for the off-tackle fake, but instead he made a strong move to the outside and shut me off." Robinson was responsible for the off-tackle play first, then the rollout. "I could

tell from Hayes' first move it was no off-tackle play," Robinson remembers. "But I thought I'd blown it. I'm not supposed to let the passer get the ball off. I only had his left arm and I was sick to my stomach when he flipped it out there."

Softly, with no steam on it, the ball settled into the arms of Green Bay safety Tom Brown in the end zone. The Packers had a 34-27 championship.

And Mel Renfro said it for everybody after the game. "Oh, boy, was it a great one. I feel fortunate just playing in a game like this."

Lombardi enjoys classic win.

Mike Gaechter punishes Boyd Dowler for scoring Packer's winning TD.

10

New York Jets   0   7   6   3   16
Baltimore Colts   0   0   0   7   7
Orange Bowl, Miami
January 12, 1969

Jets hit powerful Mackey low.
Namath beat blitz backing away.
MVP Morrall had hard day.

The third Super Bowl put the two halves of pro football together. For the first three years of the merger between the National Football League and the American Football League, it was widely assumed that the AFL was the weaker group, young and inexperienced. Because of this, the Super Bowl was viewed as a mismatch without the drama of a true world championship game.

Most of the football world expected another rout when the Baltimore Colts met the New York Jets at the conclusion of the 1968 season. Baltimore was favored by about three touchdowns. But, in a strange game, a cautious and controlled Jet team steadied out a 16-7 win. As illusions shattered, two things became clear—pro football entered its second half-century in balance and the Super Bowl would be thereafter the biggest single sports event of every year.

The Jets' win was a coordinated team effort, but one man rode it to immortality. This was Joe Namath, the 24-year-old quarterback who became the most famous example of a new style athlete.

Namath had already upset many people by refusing to let celebrity status flatten him into a one-dimensional man. Like many of his generation, he tried to build an existence honest with itself despite the demands of the surrounding society. He lived his own life as he was able to create it and he said what he believed as nearly as he could phrase it. This made him hard to take, but easy to believe—he knocked himself as hard as anyone else. The result was often publicly shocking and, figuring popularity and notoriety

together, Namath's fame spread wider than that of the usual sports star. His reputation was decidedly mixed, but many of the new group of fans who related to football through him, although they don't know anybody else in the game, might agree with one California blonde. "He's so groovy," she said in front of the TV Super Bowl. "He knows."

And his attitude was not lost on his teammates. "The guy is so downright honest," tackle Dave Herman said in the Super Bowl locker room. "He said we were going to win for sure. We won. He didn't lie. He never does."

But football games aren't decided by one man, whatever his veracity. Maybe a hundred men had a direct part in this game, and half of them were Baltimore Colts. In 1968, the Colts had an awesome season, winning fifteen times and losing only once. The NFL championship, which they won 34-0 over the Cleveland Browns, was the fourth shutout of the year for an amazing defense. John Unitas missed the season with a painful elbow, but the offense moved and scored behind a surprise Most Valuable Player performance from Earl Morrall at quarterback.

Head coach Don Shula brought his team into Miami with a basic game plan emphasizing the running game early. On defense he stayed with

Snell gained most of his 121 yards on slant left behind tackle Hill.

New York Jets 16
Baltimore Colts 7

shifting zone defenses buttressed by the terror weapon, the eight-man maximum blitz. This blitz was a key to the 1968 Colt defense, since any competent quarterback can find the holes in a zone if he remains cool. The maximum blitz keeps it hot.

New York Jet coach Weeb Ewbank also devised an uncomplicated plan emphasizing straight runs and the simplest type of hook and flare passes. For the Jets this was an oddity. At times during the season the Jets looked like they were using ten receivers and three balls at once. This was usually effective but in two nightmare ball games Namath had dispatched a total of ten interceptions. "For the Super Bowl," says Ewbank, "we stressed the importance of execution on each play throughout the game. Since we had a guard out of position playing tackle on the right side, we intended to run a fullback slant back to the left. As for the Colt blitz, I said before the game that I hoped they would use it. We were ready for it."

As the game was played, the confrontation with the Colt blitz was decisive. But it would not have been if Baltimore had translated first-half momentum into points. In the first thirty minutes, the Colts (1) came out on a storming ground drive that carried to the Jet 20, (2) forced a fumble on the Jet 12, (3) followed a 58-yard run by halfback Tom Matte to the Jet 16 and (4) completely fooled New York's defense with a sweep-

Snell bursts past Dennis Gaumbatz to Jet touchdown.

1. The Jet weakside slant.

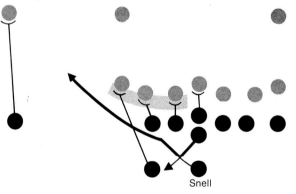

2. Namath and Sauer beat the blitz.

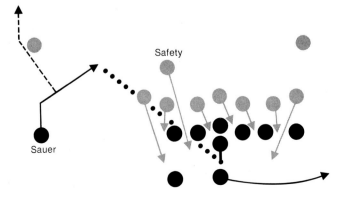

In pain, Unitas threw awkwardly.

lateral-pass. For all this they got no points; a combination of Colt errors and Jet aggressiveness turned opportunity to ashes.

As the Colts struggled, Joe Namath led a cohesive, if cautious Jet offense. Early in the game he found that fullback Matt Snell could batter out yardage on that weak-side slant behind guard Bob Talamini, tackle Winston Hill and halfback Emerson Boozer (see Diagram 1). As Snell churned toward his final total of 121 yards, it seemed as if the Colts could not believe that Namath would go on calling this simplest of all running plays. When he had to throw, he usually went to left end George Sauer. "It was just standard stuff, game-plan stuff," Namath says. "Their zone was rotating to our right usually and I felt that I could work the ball to Sauer. I wasn't throwing that well, but he was making some great catches."

Since the Colt offense was providing no pressure, only three things could disrupt the Jets' carefully built big-game calm: fumbles, interceptions and the Baltimore blitz. The Jets escaped the first two and beat the third. Namath, not talking strategy for the record, told friends in the off-season, "The way we read the blitz was the key (see Diagram 2). After a couple of years together, Sauer and I have an automatic play going. Any time that safety comes up and blitzes, Sauer breaks inside. It isn't called in the huddle. The time I hit him deep to the outside we had agreed that on the next Colt blitz he would fake in and then fly." As Ewbank says, "It is just a sight thing. With two great athletes, it works."

The Jets only had seven points at the half, scored when Snell veered a slant wide for four yards at the conclusion of an 80-yard drive, but that made it 7-0. And they had their confidence, if they could keep it, which is why Ewbank points to the first scrimmage play of the second half as the turning point. Tom Matte, the gut-running Colt halfback who had a 116-yard day, drove for nine yards but lost the ball. The Jets covered it, cashed a Jim Turner field goal and set the tone for the second half.

By the end of the third quarter, the Colts were driven to the desperation move. John Unitas came out to play clutch quarterback after a year in which he had passed but 23 times. The Jets were not out of reach, and the game could have become a romantic gem—the upstart proves his worth but the master pulls it out. Reality was against it. Unitas could not always keep his passes down, and his synchronization with receivers was just off. He drove to one touchdown and threatened twice more, but it was not enough. From the time he appeared, the game was between him and his aching arm. The arm won.

Namath, the new model athlete, nursed his team to one more field goal and the Jets went out with a 16-7 win, the win which unified professional football. And if in the future the United States is forced to go off the gold standard, tickets to the Super Bowl will nicely suffice.

Regalia

Pro football has paralleled the nation's evolution. The game was spawned in the dusty gloam of midwestern industrial towns and has evolved to the synthetic fields and monumental stadiums of an urban, technological culture. The skills developed by the men in woolen jerseys, leather helmets and canvas pants have passed on to the plastic-sheltered men of the TV age. And in the evolution of their apparel can be seen a description of their game.

For pro football players hit each other for a living. The challenge of the game lies in man's primal desire to excel with his body, to use it as a tool to conquer the forces of nature and the strengths of other men. The final test is physical power and the crucible is full-speed collision.

"We all know it's rough when we go out there," growls Don Paul, a former all-pro middle guard for the Rams. "But we're all taped, uniformed and prepared equally. When a man comes through the line let him expect the worst." Over the years

A helmet World War I period

bigger, faster men have assaulted each other at an ever-increasing intensity of impact.

In 1962, at the Pro Bowl game in Los Angeles, Dr. Stephen Ried of Northwestern University used Detroit's middle linebacker, Joe Schmidt, to conduct a series of radio-telemetric tests. Outfitting Joe's helmet with a pressure-detector and a wireless transmitter, Ried sat at the sideline and recorded the linebacker's onfield activity. When the results were analyzed, it was discovered that Schmidt's helmet had dealt with 5,780 Gs (5,780 times the force of gravity) and his head with 400 Gs. An airplane pilot will normally black out at 20 Gs. Dr. Ried determined that players like Schmidt receive 900 blows of similar intensity over the season.

Jersey from early 1900s

Under this type of punishment, a football player cannot afford to take the field in any haphazard arrangement of padding. His uniform and protective equipment must be as perfectly engineered and constructed as technical facility will allow. Due to this necessity, football equipment has continuously changed, following closely the development of new fibers, synthetics and plastics, and utilizing advanced production techniques and expensive research and experimentation. With major manufacturers like Rawlings, Wilson, Riddell, Spalding, McGregor and Nekoosa competing against one another in the classic American style for a market worth millions, equipment has evolved with the game, producing the most perfectly protected athletes in sports.

A football uniform has six basic parts, some protective and some decorative. The shoes, helmet and padding ready a man for battle while the jersey, pants and socks identify him with his team. Both the protective and the decorative aspects have altered drastically over the years.

In the development of protective equipment, one major complication has been that an article designed to prevent one type of injury may be an unforeseen source of another type of injury.

Shoes are one example. Football shoes obviously have to give the players traction or they will be slipping and sliding like something out of the Keystone Kops. But if the foot can't slide when the leg takes a severe blow, something has to give. Too often, it has been the knee.

The football shoe began in the last quarter of the 19th century as a modified baseball shoe. They were high topped and early football players removed the metal heel and sole plates which were too dangerous in a contact sport. By 1881, strips of leather were being sewn across the soles to give traction and, in the 1890s, the first true football shoe with permanent cleats appeared.

Made of four pieces of sole leather glued together and nailed to the sole and heel, these cleats were rectangular ridges about an inch long. About 1915, a one-piece fibre cleat in the same shape came into use. And in 1921, the interchangeable cone-shaped cleat was introduced, although not widely used until the Thirties.

1920s shoes with leather cleats

These cleats, five-eighths of an inch long, screwed onto the sole of the shoe and could be quickly changed if a cleat wore down. A one-inch cleat was available for muddy or wet fields. Since then, cleats have merely changed in materials, going from hard rubber through aluminum, which was soon outlawed as too dangerous, and finally to nylon steel-tipped cleats, the most widely used type today.

Since the late Fifties, there has been much concern over the shoe as

Head harness from the early 1900s

the chief cause for knee injuries. An analysis of game films by the Detroit Lions showed one-third of their player injuries were related to the problem of cleats catching in the turf.

Many teams have begun using shorter cleats on the heel of the shoe. Some players with chronic knee problems use a soccer shoe, which has many short cleats. There has also been an experiment with a flat nylon disc attached to the heel of the shoe which raises the heel up to the level of the front cleats, but does not catch in the grass. Another shoe has a nylon bar under the heel which supplies traction while the player goes forward or backward, but will slip if the leg is hit from the side.

Of course, if cleats are catching the grass, another solution is to change the grass. There are several types of artificial turf now available and although experiments are not yet conclusive, it is theorized that this

Typical 1920s shoes

kind of field will lessen the injury problem. Shoes for the artificial grass do not have regular cleats but rather a series of wedge-like protrusions which are molded as part of the sole and heel. Linemen wear shoes with rippled soles on artificial turf, eliminating the cleat altogether. Although traction on such a field is good, it is hoped that the shoes will not catch completely, as they do when cleats get tangled in the grass.

Another challenge to modern technology and science is the helmet, a piece of equipment that also works two ways. It was designed for protection but it is often used as a weapon.

In the early years of football, a full head of hair was considered adequate protection and most players played bare headed. Although a number of funny looking leather contraptions called head harnesses were available in the early 1900s, they supplied the approximate protection of a straw boater and were ignored by football's masculine types.

By 1920, the year the American Professional Football Association was formed, the "harnesses" began taking on the appearance of today's

Shoulder pads of the 1920s

familiar helmets. Although these early leather prototypes featured adjustable suspension cushions, forehead sweat bands and padded chin pieces, they weren't much use in a head-on collision. Hardy athletes found the hot, heavy head gear unappealing and continued taking their chances with uncovered skulls. As late as 1937, some pros were still playing regularly without helmets.

Not surprisingly, coaches were some of the leading idea men in the construction of better and more desirable helmets. But they were limited by the materials available. Well into the Thirties, leather remained the predominant material for helmets, but there were many innovations in ventilation and fibre cushioning. Bands of leather were used to reinforce the crowns, making helmets stronger and helping them retain their shape.

It was in 1937 that leather was first replaced by a one-piece fiber crown. This helmet featured sponge rubber padding on the inside and was much sturdier and lighter than conventional models. Just before the war, there were a number of these fibre and leather helmets incorporating various kinds of suspension and padding that won acceptance on different teams around the nation.

The plastic helmet came out of World War II, like the transistor radio

has come out of the space race. These helmets were designed after the ones worn by aviators during the war and were developed by the John T. Riddell Company. There were problems with the new plastic models, just as there are with most new products. The first helmets sometimes split on impact and the front edge of the helmet cut up the forehead and nose if jammed down on the face. By the early Fifties, after years of research and the expenditure of a good deal of money, the plastic hat became the dominant type of head gear. The helmet fit down low on the back of the neck, protecting the base of the skull better than ever before. The internal web suspension system held the shell high and away from the top of the skull and was designed to absorb and distribute severe impacts while allowing greater vision and ventilation.

The original plastic helmets were somewhat square in shape, but over

Aviator style helmet from early '20s

the years they have been refined into a virtual teardrop, a shape which will divert a blow from any direction. Modern helmets also feature a combination of foam padding and the web suspension system. In 1966, the U.S. Testing Laboratory found that this combination offered over 100% greater protection than either the suspension or padded systems by themselves.

At about the same time players began to wear plastic helmets, they also went behind bars. Although primitive nose guards had been worn since the early part of the century and face masks had been around since the Thirties, such facial protection was an affront to most players. Old pros reckoned their worth by the number of teeth they had lost or the nose fractures they had run into.

The post-war pros, considering these unappealing badges of courage, chose not to sacrifice their good looks to the violence of the game. By mid-century, many were wearing face masks of various styles. One was a clear lucite band which curved across the front of the nose and mouth. This device gained limited use, since it sometimes splintered on impact and it fogged up from heavy breathing. Finally, a one or two bar mask became standard for backs and ends and a birdcage version made of plastic covered tubular steel that protected the entire face, was adapted

by linemen. In 1954, a league ruling made face masks compulsory for all players.

The masks were good to the teeth, but unfortunately they also made great handles for tacklers to grab ball carriers by, a type of tackle that does the neck absolutely no favors. In 1962, a rule made it an infraction to grab the mask, costing the offender 15 yards as penalty.

A basic problem created by the combination of the plastic helmet and effective face mask was that ballplayers no longer had to worry about their heads when making a block or tackle. A new style of play developed, featuring reckless head-first charges. Collisions became more intense, and the hard helmets delivered to bodies and limbs

Canvas pants worn in '20s

punishment undreamed of when the game first started.

A new type hydraulic helmet may have some effect on this trend. First introduced in 1968, the helmet is lined with a series of connected plastic sacs half filled with alcohol. When the helmet is hit on one side, the fluid on that side is forced through tubes to the sacs on the other side, a hydraulic shock absorbing principle similar to the brain-skull relationship in natural physiology. A second feature is interior air cells.

This helmet is still in the experimental stages and the models tested so far have been uncomfortably hot and heavy. However, it seems to be the direction of the future and some people feel that the system is so effective that it will not be necessary to have the hard plastic shell on the outside of the helmet. If this proves true, it will take away the bone-cracking weapon which blockers and tacklers are currently wearing in the name of protection.

Shoes and helmets are easily visible, but hiding under the brightly

Detroit Lions helmet of the '30s

designed exterior uniform, the various body pads have also undergone major changes in pro football's first fifty years. The molded plastic, vinyl cushioned and riveted pads of today are light years removed from the old sewn leather and felt pads now exhibited in Pro Football's Hall of Fame.

These pads are not only stronger, more comfortable and lighter to wear, they are much safer. There are over 100 different types of pads for shoulders, hips, ribs, thighs, shins and elbows. Equipment manufacturers continually experiment with new ideas, realizing that the perfect pad is one that offers maximum mobility and comfort while insuring ultimate protection.

The choice of pads, as well as shoes and helmet, is left up to each ballplayer. Linebackers typically choose much heavier pads, for instance, than backs or receivers. Depending on their job and the kind of collisions

Giants helmet of the '30s

they get into, individuals choose to protect specific parts of their anatomy, such as the shins and forearms of the linemen which are heavily taped and padded.

The exact model and brand of equipment selected is largely determined by personal experience. Often pros continue to wear the same kind of gear they began with in high school or college and it is often difficult to get a player to try a newly developed piece of equipment. If a man has lasted for ten years safely protected, he is not likely to feel he should change the equipment he is using.

If players are allowed to select their own protective gear, they have little to say about the designs of their club's uniforms. Most young players, coming into the pros as rookies, slip into their new team jersey with the reverence of a kid experiencing a dream come true.

Uniform designs and colors have become important identifying marks of the game and the traditions that build up around the individual uniforms become increasingly valuable to the clubs. They have also become increasingly costly. To field-equip a single player runs as

(continued on pg. 209)

Evolution of the Uniform
A Portfolio

The following twelve pages illustrate the manner in which football equipment has developed over the first fifty seasons of the professional game. The teams and individuals pictured represent a visual chronology of the physiological changes and technological improvements that have made football players the most physical and best protected athletes in sport.

DECATUR STALEYS, 1920
George Halas, Player-Coach

GREEN BAY PACKERS, 1921
Earl "Curly" Lambeau, Player-Coach

DULUTH ESKIMOS, 1926
Ernie Nevers, Player-Coach

NEW YORK GIANTS, 1934
Mel Hein, Center-Linebacker

CHICAGO BEARS, 1936
Bronko Nagurski, Tackle and Fullback

DETROIT LIONS, 1940
Byron "Whizzer" White, Halfback

LOS ANGELES RAMS, 1948
Bob Waterfield, Quarterback

CLEVELAND BROWNS, 1950
Marion Motley, Fullback

SAN FRANCISCO 49ers, 1954
Y. A. Tittle, *Quarterback*

BALTIMORE COLTS, 1957
Lenny Moore, Flanker

GREEN BAY PACKERS, 1961
Paul Hornung, Halfback

DALLAS COWBOYS, 1964
Bob Lilly, Defensive Tackle

high as $225. The high cost of outfitting a pro does not end with uniform and gear. Training devices, tape, medications, maintenance and replacement must also be averaged into the total expenses required of a 40-man squad. The yearly cost for each team exceeds $25,000.

In the Twenties, uniforms looked alike, except for color. There was no real influence toward individual design until the middle of the next decade, when uniforms began to flower with a profusion of stripes, inserts and designs in bold, bright colors.

A further revolution in uniform design took place in 1948 when a Los Angeles Rams' halfback, Fred Gehrke, painted yellow horns on his team's blue helmet. When plastic helmets were introduced, it was possible to bake colors right into the shell, which meant the designs

Typical '40s style hip pads

would no longer be knocked off on the field. With the plastic shells, all kinds of designs were possible and teams began applying monograms, symbols and stripes that were either baked in or applied by plastic decals. Decorated football helmets began to take on the dizzying hues and designs of Easter eggs. Over the years, the NFL helmets have become such popular and significant identification symbols that the teams have registered their designs to keep them from being copied.

Uniform styling in general seems to have stabilized after a history of rapid changes in taste. The funny little inserts, bold chest stripes or odd stripes down the sleeves of jerseys and the back of pants are, like the campy days that inspired them, gone forever.

Teams and players today prefer the more conservative decoration which has been in favor for nearly 20 years. In a sport heavy on masculinity, uniform frills are hard to sell.

Shoulder pads of the 1930s

But if uniform styling is given to regulation through public identification, it is obvious that the protective equipment will continue to evolve. Pro football's life source is the skillful player functioning despite murderous collisions. As long as skill is threatened through injury, even minimally, the sport will insist on improved efficiency from its protective gear.

This is a scientifically innovative country and football is a sport peculiarly adapted to the changes which modern technology provides. As long as that technology goes forward, so will football equipment.

"Big Daddy" Lipscomb's shoulder pads

1920 DECATUR STALEYS

In the first year of the American Professional Football Association, uniforms were functional. The leather helmet offered minimal protection and many players disdained its use. Jerseys and socks were wool. The ribbing on the Staleys' jersey was there "to aid in holding onto the ball." Pants were light canvas with a high padded waist band to protect the back and kidneys. Shoes had permanent rectangular cleats. The football was fat and difficult to pass. The Staleys were employees of the Staley Starch Co., Decatur, Illinois. George Halas, 22, was coach and player. In 1921 the company gave up sports as promotion, and Halas, with the franchise as a gift, moved the team to Chicago.

1921 GREEN BAY PACKERS

The man responsible for originating the Packers was an ex-Notre Dame player named Earl "Curly" Lambeau, a hard driving young entrepreneur who struggled mightily to sustain the team he formed in 1919. The Indian Packing Co., his employer, paid $500 for the privilege of purchasing jerseys and socks. The company was eventually purchased by the Acme Packing Co., which in September, 1921, paid $50 for the Green Bay franchise at the annual league meeting in Canton. The team's first official NFL uniform was a nostalgic forebearer of today's famous Packers and a reminder that professional and commercial were innocently intertwined words in the lusty years preceding full league development.

1936 CHICAGO BEARS

In the mid-'30s, the Bears featured some of pro football's greatest stars and were building a brawling, winning reputation. Chicago had always worn conservative uniforms, an indication that sartorial innovation was not paramount to George Halas' game plan. In 1936, however, Halas stunned the league with an early version of psychedelia. Never before had striping and color been so generously applied to jerseys, socks and helmets. The colorful uniform was short lived. The next season, only the blue pants remained. Most of the stripes had disappeared, too. The Bears were back in style and all set to don their image as the feared Monsters of the Midway.

1940 DETROIT LIONS

By 1940, many new fabrics were being used in uniforms with Nylon, Rayon and cotton the most popular. In Detroit, the Lions were under new ownership and featured Byron "Whizzer" White. In 1938, White had led Pittsburgh and the NFL in rushing, but left football to go to England on a Rhodes Scholarship. Detroit's new owner, Fred Mandel, purchased the Steelers' contract and upon White's return, made him a Lion. Wearing the team's distinctive Honolulu blue and silver, White responded with 514 yards to again win the rushing title. He played one more season before embarking on a law career that eventually led him to a seat on the United States Supreme Court.

1954 SAN FRANCISCO 49ERS

By the mid-'50s, the plastic helmet, with its web suspension, had become a league standard. Face masks were also popular as players learned they could play football and keep their front teeth, too. Y. A. Tittle wore a lucite model that was a favorite until the single or dual bar replaced it. The "handle" on the side of the helmet was a special brace, designed to protect Tittle's jaw, which had been broken before he wore a face mask. The drop shadow numerals were dropped for conventional ones in 1956. Although Tittle wore high top shoes, low cuts were becoming the most popular shoes. With the mandatory taping of ankles, the high cuts were no longer necessary.

1957 BALTIMORE COLTS

The year after Lenny Moore came to the Colts as a number one draft choice, the team was issued new uniforms. The decision was a harbinger, for in 1957 the Colts were a team destined for greatness. The nylon-durene jerseys featured the UCLA shoulder loop, a device popularized by Red Sanders' West Coast teams in the early '50s. The horseshoes on the helmet and TV numbers on the shoulders were in accordance to unwritten league standards. Moore's carefully taped shoes won him the nickname, Spats. The sweat band on his wrist was borrowed from tennis. The yellowish substance on the shoes is a resin many ball carriers dab on their fingers to get more tack on the ball.

1926 DULUTH ESKIMOS

In 1926, twenty-two cities boasted pro football teams. The Duluth Eskimos became one of the most famous of the little town teams, for owner Ole Hagsrud managed to sign the most important college player since Halas had made a pro of Red Grange. Stanford's Rose Bowl hero, Ernie Nevers, became the headliner for a 16-man barnstorming club that traveled 19,000 miles and played 29 games in 112 days. The Eskimos displayed not only a great football player, but the first individualized professional uniform. Duluth's black and white igloo decorated luggage, topcoats, jerseys and posters. In the Roarin' Twenties, little Duluth showed the country how to dress football players.

1934 NEW YORK GIANTS

In 1934, new rules made the football more aerodynamic, encouraging the passing game. Numerals were "in," necessary to identify players like all-star Mel Hein on the 20-man squad. The "glove" helmet was disappearing, replaced by reinforced leather hats that offered real protection. Cleats were $^5/_8$" long, hard rubber cones that screwed onto the shoes. There were 1" long ones for muddy fields. But the '34 Giants made history with tennis shoes, which made the difference in a title battle with the Bears on an icy December day in New York. Trailing 10-3 at the half, the Giants donned sneakers to sprint to a 30-13 second half victory and their first official NFL championship.

1948 LOS ANGELES RAMS

The Rams, only two years in Los Angeles after moving from Cleveland, were struggling for fans in 1948, but its uniform had a winner's dash to it. Fred Gehrke, a halfback, took his leather helmet and painted horns on it. The design was an immediate sensation, creating a wave of imitations. The yellow jersey with the blue Northwestern stripes (in honor of the school that made the design famous) and the white nylon-lastex-rayon pants were properly flashy for players with the ability of Bob Waterfield. The socks ruled mandatory in 1946 were the only plain element. Like many quarterbacks, Waterfield shunned excess protection, cutting down his shoulder pads to insure maximum throwing movement.

1950 CLEVELAND BROWNS

When Paul Brown created the Cleveland Browns for the AAFC in 1946, his sense of organizational detail was to influence all of football. One of his most overlooked accomplishments was the uniform he designed for his team. Design and taste were so flawless that in 23 years there have been only two changes. The Browns' first uniform featured drop shadow numerals, which were gone by 1950, the team's first year in the NFL. The white leather helmet gave way to an orange plastic one in 1952. Until 1952, when a ruling affected jersey numbering, a player could wear any number he pleased. That is why FB Marion Motley is wearing 76, a number he eventually passed on to another famous teammate, Lou Groza.

1961 GREEN BAY PACKERS

By 1961, Vince Lombardi had established the Packer dynasty that was to dominate pro football in the '60s. The team's uniform became a national symbol of excellence. The "G" that appeared on the helmet profile became the most famous monogram in football. Paul Hornung, perhaps the team's most famous player, was a versatile athlete — a fine runner, blocker, passer and place kicker, as his square-toed right shoe attested. The shoe black under his eyes aided receiving by diminishing the glare of the sun. The roll bar around his neck kept his head from popping back in whiplash fashion. Hornung wore it to relieve pressure from a pinched nerve that hastened his retirement, in 1967.

1964 DALLAS COWBOYS

The Dallas Cowboys celebrated their sixth season in the NFL by ordering new uniforms. The jersey was nylon-coylon with satin numerals. The TV numerals, usually found on the sleeves, were on top of the shoulders. The pants were a silver-blue metallic knit of Polyurethane material. Bob Lilly displays the accoutrements of the modern lineman. His shoes are low cut, light weight Kangaroo leather with nylon steel-tipped cleats. His Cy-Co-Lac helmet features the lineman's tubular steel and plastic "bird cage" mask and his heavy-duty shoulder pads are molded from waterproof, impact-resistant plastic. Lilly, at 260 lbs., carries an additional 30 lbs. of equipment valued at $210.50.

A Continuum

1902 Philadelphia Athletics
1905 Massillon Tigers
1905 Canton Bulldogs

1892 In the year that James J. (Gentleman Jim) Corbett takes the heavyweight championship away from John L. Sullivan by knocking him out in the 21st round in New Orleans, the first known seeds of professional football are planted in Pittsburgh. The famed Pudge Heffelfinger of Yale, named to three successive All-American teams by Walter Camp, collects $500 to play in a game between two Pittsburgh athletic clubs. He brings three more players with him from Chicago, each of whom gets "twice railroad fare." Heffelfinger and his friends are probably the only mercenaries in the game, but they prove worthy of their pay. A guard, Heffelfinger smashes through the opponents' line, jars the ball loose, grabs it and lumbers for a touchdown in a 6-0 game.

1895 Hardly anyone notices, but the first professional football game takes place in Latrobe, Pennsylvania, on August 31 of this year. The Latrobe team, sponsored by the YMCA, hires a quarterback, John Braillier of Indiana Normal, for $10 and expenses and beats Jeanette, Pa., 12-0. Other members of the team are on some sort of a profit sharing basis — probably a split of a collection taken among spectators.

It's the talk of Latrobe, but the rest of the world is more concerned with the cleanup of Tammany Hall and appointment of Teddy Roosevelt as New York police commissioner; Halma winning the Kentucky Derby; and the adoption of the infield fly rule by organized baseball.

1896 Possibly encouraged by the singular success of Latrobe, additional professional football teams begin to pop up in the East. The more successful include the Duquesnes of Pittsburgh, the Olympics of McKeesport, Pennsylvania, and the Orange A.C. of Newark, New Jersey. Still, the boys in the pool hall and the American public in general are unconcerned. They talk about the discovery of gold in the Klondike and the election of William McKinley of Ohio as president.

1898 While everyone is busy remembering the Maine and Admiral Dewey is visiting Manila Bay, professional football's oldest continuing operation is founded on Chicago's South Side. That would be the St. Louis Cardinals, nee the Chicago Cardinals, nee the Chicago Normals, nee the Morgan Athletic Club. The team operates out of Chicago for 62 years before switching to St. Louis in 1960.

1902 Professional football seems to have gotten at least a toehold by now, although sides are still mainly "company teams" and spectator interest is limited.

Connie Mack organizes the Philadelphia Athletics football team with Rube Waddell on the squad and beats the Pittsburgh team with Christy Mathewson at fullback, 12-6, claiming the professional football championship. The Athletics also engage in the first night football

game, at Elmira, N.Y., beating the Kanaweola A.C., 39-0. The first professional indoor game is also held and Syracuse, with Glenn (Pop) Warner at guard, beats the Philadelphia Nationals, 6-0, in the original Madison Square Garden.

1905 Charles (Cy) Rigler organizes the Massillon (Ohio) Tigers with Charlie Moran and 10 unknowns in the lineup.

Not to be outdone, neighboring Canton forms the Bulldogs and signs Willie Heston, the immortal Michigan back. The Tigers and Bulldogs have at each other in pro football's first major rivalry.

Heston is to get $600 and expenses per game. Unfortunately for the Canton organizers, it turns out to be a short season for Heston. He breaks his leg on the first play of

his only professional game. Nevertheless, Heston's signing lends stature to the professional game. He had been the leader of the great Michigan point-a-minute team which went 56 games without defeat. News of his joining the Bulldogs lets some Americans know for the first time that there really is such a thing as professional football.

1906 It isn't quite as earth-shaking as what happens in San Francisco this year, but Eddie Wood, an end for the Canton Bulldogs, becomes the first man ever to catch a forward pass in a professional football game.

In intercollegiate football the pass is made legal and the flying wedge illegal in an effort to make the game safer after President Roosevelt threatens to abolish it because of a high mortality rate.

1915 While some people are concerned about women's suffrage and the sinking of the Lusitania, the football filberts of Canton are buzzing about the addition to the Bulldog team of Jim Thorpe and Pete Calac, stars of the Carlisle Indian Institute team which won the mythical national championship. "Bring on Massillon!" is the cry.

This is also a year of the itinerate athlete. The six Nesser brothers and

other players for the Columbus Panhandles are still shaking their heads at season's end. They find themselves playing Knute Rockne six different times — on six different teams.

1919 Professional football starts a revival following World War I and many teams are formed in the East and Midwest. One of these is the Green Bay Packers organized by George Calhoun and Earl (Curly) Lambeau. They talk Curly's employers at the Indian Packing Co. into putting up $500 for uniforms and equipment and letting the team use its field for practices. The Packers win 10 games and lose only one that first season, but news of their success doesn't get as far south as Milwaukee.

Professional football is still considered an activity of "town" and "company" teams. Sports fans are more concerned about which baseball players were returning from Europe with General

Pershing's American Expeditionary Force and the fact that Sir Barton becomes the first horse ever to win the Kentucky Derby, the Preakness and Belmont Stakes in one year. Erudite sportswriters promptly call Sir Barton a "triple crown winner."

1920 The Huppmobile Agency in Canton Ohio, enters history as the meeting place of the founders of the American Professional Football

1920 Dayton Triangles
The Famous Nesser Brothers
1925 Pottsville Maroons

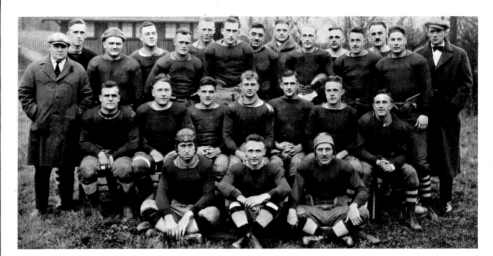

Association. The meeting is called by Frank Nied and A. F. Ranney of the Akron Steels, and Ralph Hays graciously offers the running boards of his machines as a meeting grounds and provides free beer. The founding fathers, including the driving young George Halas, choose football's best-known player, Jim Thorpe, as president, and elect Stan Cofall vice-president and Ranney secretary. Eleven teams come up with the $100 membership fee: Canton Bulldogs, Cleveland Indians, Dayton Triangles, Akron Professionals, Massillon Tigers, Rochester (N.Y.), Rock Island (Illinois), Muncie (Ind.), Decatur Staleys (Halas' team), Chicago Cardinals, and Hammond (Indiana).

Pro football's first player deal takes place when Buffalo buys Bob Nash from Akron for $300.

All doesn't go well this first year, however, because of poorly arranged schedules, team withdrawals and additions, and the association folds at the end of the season. It isn't a very good year all around, as a matter of fact. Prohibition goes into effect.

OFFICIAL PHOTO
POTTSVILLE MAROON FOOTBALL TEAM - 1925
NATIONAL LEAGUE CHAMPIONS - 1925. DEFEATED THE CHICAGO CARDINALS, AT CHICAGO DECEMBER 6, 1925 - 21 to 7.
WORLD CHAMPIONS - 1925. DEFEATED THE "FOUR HORSEMEN AND SEVEN MULES" OF NOTRE DAME, AT SHIBE PARK, PHILADELPHIA, PA.
DECEMBER 12, 1925 - 9 to 7. THE FIRST "ALL STAR" GAME PLAYED IN THIS COUNTRY.
OFFICIAL OUTFITTERS: ZACKO'S SPORTING GOODS, POTTSVILLE, PA.

1921 Joseph F. Carr of Columbus, Ohio, rallies the somewhat demoralized club owners and, meeting in a Canton hotel room, they install leadership which is to last for two decades. It is probably not the best year to start such a bold movement. There is severe unemployment and the government reports 20,000 business failures.

The franchise fee is dropped to $50 and 13 teams play in this first "organized" season. The Chicago Staleys, having moved in from Decatur, win the first championship, adding a special post-season game with the Buffalo All-Americans to beat them out of the title.

Among those coming up with $50 for a franchise this year is J. E. Clair of the Acme Packing Co., Green Bay, Wis.

1922 Seven years of prosperity begin for the United States, but everything isn't all that rosy with professional football. College coaches and alumni, who have fought the sport all along, continue to rap the game. Professional football gets its first recorded eight column headline in the Chicago Herald and Examiner: "Stagg Says Conference Will Break Professional Football Menace".

There are 18 teams in the league, however, and Canton wins the title followed by Halas' newly named Chicago Bears. The league also takes on a new name – the National Football League – despite the fact that all of the teams are located in the East and Midwest.

The Green Bay franchise is recalled from J. E. Clair when the Packers are discovered using high school players under assumed names (not really unusual in these days). Curly Lambeau rounds up new backers and gets the franchise back.

1923 There are 20 teams in the NFL in 1923, but none can beat the Canton Bulldogs who grab their second championship.

Player-coach George Halas of the Bears grabs a fumble and runs 98 yards for a touchdown, setting a record that stood for 49 years. He later said the fact that Jim Thorpe v chasing him made it all possible.

1924 The Frankford Yellow Jackets of Philadelphia are awarded a franchise and promptly win 11 games in league play, more than any other team. They finish third behind Cleveland and the Bears on percentage, though.

Sports editors still generally ignore pro football. The big news this year is Gene Tunney's 15-round KO of Georges Carpentier of France at the Polo Grounds.

1925 This is the year Harold (Red) Grange, the famed "Galloping Ghost" from the University of Illinois, calls the attention of the nation's sports fans to professional football. Grange quits school after his final college game in November and signs with the Chicago Bears. His deal, negotiated by C. C. (Cash and Carry) Pyle, a small-town movie theater man, is for half of the gate receipts. It proves to be a good deal for Grange, the Bears and the sport. Crowds reach 70,000 in New York and Los Angeles as the Bears play 18 exhibition games across the country, including eight in one 12-day stretch.

In this same year Tim Mara and Will Gibson are awarded a franchise for New York for $500 or $2,500 – the exact figure being a matter of some dispute. Mara

admits he knows nothing about football, but says, "I figure an exclusive franchise for anything in New York is worth $500." (Or $2,500 or whatever.)

This is also the year that the Pottsville Maroons roll up the best record in the National Football League, then, to celebrate the championship, schedule an exhibition game against the Notre Dame All-Stars at Philadelphia's Shibe Park, despite admonishments not to by the League office.

The Frankford Yellow Jackets protest the invasion of their territorial rights. League president

Joe Carr agrees and awards the championship to the Chicago Cardinals after they add two pickup games to their schedule to compile a better percentage record than the Maroons.

The people of Pottsville do not take this lightly. Forty-five years later they are still sending representatives to NFL meetings arguing their case.

One of football's headache's is the football. The ball in use at this point is fat and heavy, a bladder stuck in a leather casing. Worse, it has no lining and the more it gets beaten around in a game, the fatter

it gets. Ernie Nevers recalls punting a ball one time that exploded on contact and George Halas, once fielding a kickoff, found only a fragmented slab of leather to be run back. 1925 is the year the lined ball is introduced and from now on the ball at least holds its specified shape.

1926 Red Grange is in the news again this year. C. C. Pyle wants an NFL franchise, but is refused. Pyle, therefore, takes Grange and forms a new circuit, the American Football League. The whole thing doesn't ruffle too many people save Tim Mara who has the New York Giant franchise and is bucking Grange and the New York Yankees at the gate.

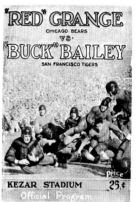

Joe Carr, perhaps making a peace bid to the college coaches, pushes through legislation which forbids any professional team from signing a ball player before his class graduates.

Ole Haugsrud of the Duluth Eskimos helps sink the rival league by signing Stanford fullback Ernie Nevers. Duluth immediately becomes a travelling team, playing in 29 cities in 112 days.

Nevers proves his worth by playing all but 27 minutes in the impossible 29-game schedule. He

has appendicitis before one game, but wins it anyway by throwing a TD pass in the last minutes. In another game he kicks five field goals for a 15-0 win. In another game he completes 17 passes in a row to defeat Pottsville.

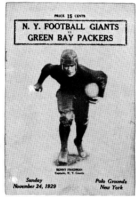

Despite such heroics, football still isn't really big business. The government, however, estimates the bootleg liquor trade at $3,600,000,000 for the year.

1927 The American League falls in on C. C. Pyle and Grange's Yankees go into the NFL. In a game against the Bears, Grange catches his cleats in the turf and ruins his knee. "After that," he says, "I was just another halfback."

The New York Giants, with a pair of monster tackles, Steve Owen and Cal Hubbard, win their first championship decided late in the year in a brutal game with the Bears, 14-7.

Even so, the big news in Gotham is Babe Ruth's 60 home runs and Gene Tunney retaining his heavyweight crown in the famous "long count" battle with Jack Dempsey. It is also the year that Al Jolson makes the first talking motion picture, "The Jazz Singer," and Charles A. Lindbergh decides

to try a solo flight from New York to Paris.

1929 Things are terrible everywhere but Green Bay. The stock market collapses but the Packer line holds firm and Green Bay wins its first NFL championship by a handful of percentage points over the New York Giants. Coached by Curly Lambeau, the Packers are led by backs Verne Lewellen and Johnny Blood and linemen Cal Hubbard (obtained from the Giants) and "Iron Mike" Michalske. This is the day of the 60-minute player and squads have a maximum of 18 players.

This is also the year that Ernie Nevers sets one of football's safest records. He scores all 40 points as the Chicago Cardinals defeat their bitter crosstown rivals, the Bears, 40-6.

1930 Green Bay adds hometown tailback Arnie Herber to the squad and the Packers win their second championship with Herber passing to Johnny Blood and Verne Lewellen.

In Chicago, George Halas and Dutch Sternaman, owners of the Bears, relieve themselves as head coaches and hire Ralph Jones, a former assistant to Bob Zuppke at Illinois. Jones is a very inventive man who, with Halas and Clark Shaughnessy, is to have a major role in refurbishing the T-formation. He also signs Minnesota's All-America fullback and tackle, Bronko Nagurski.

1931 The nation-wide depression deepens and there's still no legal way for a man to get a drink, but all is not gloomy. For one thing, Walt Disney introduces Mickey Mouse to the world; the Empire State Building is completed; Al Capone is caught and sent to jail; and Curly Lambeau's Green Bay Packers win their third straight NFL championship.

1932 Franklin Delano Roosevelt is elected president and the Olympic Games are held in Los Angeles, but the big news to Green Bay fans this year is how the Chicago Bears ace the Packers out of their fourth straight title.

The Packers end the season with a 10-3-1 record and Chicago has seven wins, one loss and SIX ties. Since ties are not counted, the Bears win it on percentage points. There

is also some dispute regarding the Bears' final game of the season against Portsmouth which decides the championship.

Because of minus 30 weather, the game is moved indoors to Chicago Stadium and played on turf left by a traveling circus. The field is 20 yards too short, 10 too narrow, and altogether too aromatic. The teams agree to bring the ball in from the sideline 10 yards when necessary to avoid the stadium wall. The move seems to open the game up and is adopted as a rule later. Portsmouth coach Potsy Clark,

the 9-0 loser, also claims that the Bears win it on an illegal pass from Nagurski to Grange. At this time the passer has to be five yards behind the line of scrimmage and Clark is sure Nagurski didn't get back there after faking a plunge.

1933 At the same time that FDR is launching his "New Deal," pro football starts one of its own. George Preston Marshall, who joined the league as a part-owner of the Boston franchise the year before, and Papa Bear Halas get together at the NFL meeting in February and shove through some vital changes to improve the game.

1932 championship game, indoors at Chicago Stadium
1936 Boston Redskins
1934 New York Giants

They vote (1) that the ball can be thrown forward one time per play from any spot behind the line; (2) that the goal posts will be moved to the goal lines; (3) that the ball will be placed 10 yards in from the sidelines anytime it is downed within five yards of the boundary; and (4) the league will be divided into two divisions with the winners meeting for the championship at the end of the regular season. The latter is Marshall's idea and few have been more vital to pro football.

The net result is movement,

scoring and excitement. And fewer ties. By the end of the Thirties, pro football is secure, if not sensationally successful, and much of the credit goes to these rules changes.

The Bears and the New York Giants meet in Chicago in the first championship game before 17,866 fans. The Bears win a tight one, 23-21, and the victorious players each get $210.34. The Giants' share is $140.22 each.

Several new owners join the league this year including Art Rooney and A. McCool in Pittsburgh; Bert Bell and Lud Wray in Philadelphia; Chris Cagle and Shipwreck Kelly in Brooklyn; and Charles Bidwill who sells his interest in the Bears and buys the Chicago Cardinals. The league

membership fee, by the way, is now up to $10,000.

1934 Radio station owner Dick Richards purchases the Portsmouth franchise and moves it to Detroit where the pro sport has failed three or four times. Richards, who has the radio station and a good team going for him, makes the game click in the Motor City.

This is also the year that the annual Chicago All-Star Game gets

its start with the collegiates playing the champion Chicago Bears to a 0-0 tie. The game is sponsored for charity by the Chicago Tribune.

The Bears then roll through a 13-0 regular season record with Bronko Nagurski and rookie tailback Beattie Feathers chewing up the yardage. Feathers is the first pro back to gain more than 1,000 yards in a season (and he misses three games, at that).

When the Bears meet the New York Giants on an icy field at the Polo Grounds, they are heavily favored to annex their second straight playoff victory. They lead at halftime, 10-3, but when the second half starts nine of the Giants are wearing sneakers. With better traction, the Giants go on to win, 30-13. It is a bigger upset than the one pulled by Max Baer this same year when he KO's Primo Carnera for the heavyweight championship.

Another full inch is taken off the girth of the football and the inflating pressure is reduced. The ball now is 21 1/4 - 21 1/2 inches around and is inflated to a pressure of 12 1/2 - 13 1/2 pounds. Since 1925, the ball has slimmed down from an object with the

approximate aerodynamic qualities of a fire hydrant to a streamlined missile, making the modern passing game possible. These 1934 specifications have remained unchanged.

1935 This is the year that a tall, skinny end from Alabama, Don Hutson, joins the Green Bay Packers. In Wisconsin, the years 1935-1945 are known as "the Hutson Era." On his first play as a pro, he takes a pass from Arnie Herber and goes 83 yards to score. The touchdown defeats the Bears, 7-0. Herber completes 17 passes for seven touchdowns to the rookie end this season and the Packers finish second in the Western Division to the Detroit Lions.

With Raymond (Buddy) Parker scoring the last Detroit touchdown, the Lions win the NFL championship by downing New York, 26-7, in only their second year of operation. The player limit by now is up to 24.

The first night major league baseball game (Cincinnatti vs. Philadelphia) is held this year, 33 years after the first night football game. It is also the year that the WPA, the China Clipper and the roller derby come into existence.

1936 The Herber-to-Hutson combination clicks well enough for the Packers to swamp the Western Division like

Roosevelt swamps Landon. Green Bay also beats Boston, 21-6, in the NFL championship game played in New York (moved there by Boston owner George P. Marshall who is piqued at the lack of support given his team by the Boston fans.)

This is also the year of the first NFL draft. Philadelphia takes University of Chicago halfback Jay Berwanger (the first Heisman Trophy winner) as the first selection of the first round. Unfortunately for the Eagles, Berwanger elects not to play professional ball.

It isn't a completely bad year for Eagle owner Bert Bell, however. He acquires complete ownership of the Philadelphia club by giving his partner (and coach) Lud Wray $4,000. The player limit increases to 25 men this year.

1937 Professional football's master showman, George Preston Marshall, moves the Boston franchise to Washington, D.C., where the Redskins start a great decade of six divisional titles and two NFL championships.

Spencer Tracy ("Captains Courageous") and Luise Rainer ("The Good Earth") win the Academy Awards this year, but Marshall steals the show by introducing spectacular halftime shows and publicity gimmicks to professional football. He signs Sammy Baugh of TCU and introduces him to the Washington press outfitted in a 10-gallon hat

and cowboy boots, neither of which Baugh has ever worn before.

In his first season, "Slingin' Sammy" leads the NFL in passing and Cliff Battles is the top rusher as the Redskins sweep through the Eastern Division, then upset the Bears for the league championship. 28-21.

It's almost enough to knock Joe Louis, who has become the youngest-ever heavyweight champ at 23 by knocking out James J. Braddock, off the sports pages.

Almost unnoticed in the year's activity is the fact that Homer Marshman is granted a franchise for Cleveland. General manager Buzz Wetzel names the team "Rams" so that it will fit in headlines. Unfortunately, the headlines read: "Rams Lose 10, Win One."

1938 The panic in Green Bay when Don Hutson turns up injured for the championship game against Eastern

titlist New York is second only to that felt in New Jersey this year when Orson Welles broadcasts his famous hoax invasion from Mars.

The Green Bay panic turns out to be real, though, and Hutson limps on to the Polo Grounds for only a few plays. The Giants please 48,120 New York fans by winning the title, 23-17.

Byron (Whizzer) White, later to become a Supreme Court justice, is the NFL's leading rusher for the Pittsburgh Pirates, gaining 567 yards.

This is also the year that Hugh L. (Shorty) Ray begins the work which will aid football's evolution into the modern game. Long interested in streamlining and organizing football rules, Ray is hired by the NFL in a part-time advisory capacity. His function is to work with officials and to make studies of the game with an eye toward improving the rules.

1939 Hitler's invasion of Czechoslovakia and Poland and the start of World War II seem far from Milwaukee where Curly Lambeau moves the NFL championship game between his Packers and the New York Giants. Europe might have been safer for the Giants, though. They

Giants' Tuffy Leemans carries against the Brooklyn Dodgers
1938 Washington Redskins
1941 Chicago Bears

are bombed, 27-0, by a team which has been described as Lambeau's strongest. Fans are charged $4.40 per ticket, a new high for pro football, but it doesn't affect attendance. The stadium is sold out in two days.

Joe F. Carr, the league president for 19 years, dies in Columbus. His drive and optimism have been rewarded with a sport which is solid when he leaves it. Carl L. Storck, league secretary since 1921, is named president.

1940 Never mind Bob Feller's opening day no-hitter for Cleveland against the White Sox; forget Cornelius Warmerdam being the first man to pole vault 15 ft.; don't even mention Wilbur Shaw winning his third Indianapolis 500—the sports story of this year is the 73-0 shellacking

given the Washington Redskins by the Chicago Bears in the NFL championship game.

It's a story that still isn't believed by many and a game which introduces revolutionary changes in the T-formation by Bear coach George Halas, Ralph Jones (the

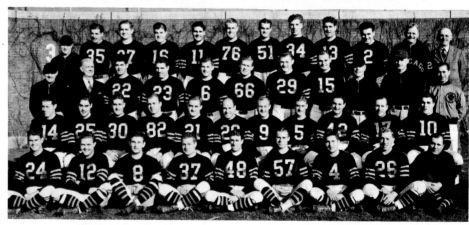

Soldier Field to see the Chicago juggernaut roll over the College All-Stars, 37-13, in the annual August game.

It takes a sneak attack on Pearl

former Bear coach) and Clark Shaughnessy, the Stanford coach who had formed a close association with Halas while coaching at the University of Chicago.

The Bears use quick openers counter to the flow of play and, with Sid Luckman directing the attack, 10 Bears score touchdowns. To make the story all the more incredible, the Redskins had beaten Chicago, 7-3, three weeks earlier and were favored in the game. This game, and Stanford's Rose Bowl

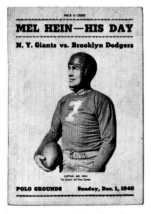

victory over Nebraska three weeks later, swings college and high school teams all over the country to the quick-opening T-formation.

Fred L. Mandel, Jr., purchases the Detroit franchise from Dick Richards and Alexis Thompson purchases the Pittsburgh franchise from Art Rooney who buys a half interest in the Philadelphia Eagles.

At 150 pounds, rookie Davey O'Brien of the Eagles is not too big so he figures he better get rid of the ball before the big boys get to him. He does, 60 times in one game against Washington, completing 33 passes.

1941 The magic of the Bears' 1940 championship T-party over the Redskins carries over to the next season and 98,203 fans storm

Harbor to arrest the game's rise to the top of the sports world. On that fateful Dec. 7, there are 43,425 fans at Wrigley Field to see the Bears win a 33-14 divisional playoff game against the Packers. News of the Japanese attack reaches the press box at halftime. One week later, with the Bears playing the Giants for the NFL championship and the war a week older, only 13,341 hard core fans show up to see Chicago take its fifth championship, 39-7.

During this same year Elmer Layden, one of the legendary Four Horsemen from Notre Dame, is elected league president and the Philadelphia club and franchise switches cities with the Pittsburgh club and franchise. Daniel F. Reeves and Fred Levy acquire the Cleveland franchise.

League attendance passes the million mark for the third straight year.

1942 The league survives despite the war and the dissemination of its

players and coaches. In the Western Division, Chicago coach George Halas is called up in mid-season for Navy duty as are many of his players. Hunk Anderson, Luke

Johnsos and Paddy Driscoll take over and the remnants of a great Bear team compile an 11-0 record.

In the Eastern Division the Redskins lose only one game and come into the title contest with only one thought: to avenge the 73-0 humiliation suffered two seasons before. They do it, 14-6, as Sammy Baugh passes to Wilbur Moore for one touchdown and Andy Farkas runs for another.

On the record front, Don Hutson catches 74 passes for the Packers,

17 of them for touchdowns. His batterymate, Cecil Isbell, becomes the first man in NFL history to pass for more than 2,000 yards.

1943 The lack of manpower plagues the league, but does not kill it. Lt. Dan Reeves and Major Fred Levy, being in no position to run a team, ask (and receive) permission to temporarily halt operations of the Cleveland Rams. Philadelphia and

Pittsburgh, in similar straits, combine forces and play as the Phil-Pitt Steagles.

Players not caught up in the service are distributed around the league and free substitution is voted in for the duration of the war.

In the West, Bronko Nagurski comes out of a six-year retirement and leads Chicago to the divisional title along with Sid Luckman (who passes for seven touchdowns in one game against the New York Giants).

In the East, the champion Redskins have to beat the Giants, 28-0, in a divisional playoff, then lose their NFL title to the 35-year old Nagurski and the Bears, 41-21. It is the Bronk's last game.

1944 The war continues to utilize most of the able bodied, but there are enough players to keep the NFL in business. Many of the players are in service, but made available on weekends just for the games. Others are working in essential industries but are able to play on Sundays and attend limited practices in off hours.

Curly Lambeau wins his sixth and last championship as Green Bay defeats the Giants, 14-7.

The Boston Yanks, owned by Ted Collins, play their first season. Pittsburgh changes wartime partners and plays as Card-Pitt. The Cleveland Rams resume functioning and finish with a 4-6 record in the West.

1945 Hostilities in Europe end in May and in the Far East in August. Of men who had played in NFL games, 638 served in World War II, 355 as commissioned officers. Sixty-six were decorated and 21 lost their lives.

Rookie quarterback Bob Waterfield of UCLA joins the Cleveland Rams and, confusing opponents with his adeptness on the bootleg play, leads them to the Western Division title. Washington beats out Philadelphia for the Eastern title and the two teams meet at Cleveland for the NFL championship on a day so cold that the instruments of the famed Redskin band freeze. Waterfield leads the Rams, who had never had a season over the .500 mark before, to the title. Redskin quarterback Sammy Baugh, however, provides the Rams with their margin of victory. Trying to pass out of his own end zone, he hits the goal post with the ball—an automatic safety in these days. The rule is changed the next season.

Attendance is back up over the million mark. There is pressure to expand the league, but the old guard is wary. More than 40 franchises have folded since the original formation of the NFL in 1920, twelve of them in one season after a premature attempt at expansion. The answer is no.

1946 Dan Reeves, recognizing the vast potential in Southern California, petitions the league to be allowed to move his champion Cleveland Rams to Los Angeles. He is turned down by the other owners at first, but they relent when Reeves points

out that he lost $50,000 with a championship club in Cleveland and vows he will sell his franchise and get out of football. In their first game in Los Angeles, a rematch with the Washington Redskins, the Rams draw 95,000 fans.

Elmer Layden resigns as league commissioner and Bert Bell, one of the Pittsburgh owners, is given the job and a three-year contract. Bell, who handled every phase of club operation at Philadelphia and Pittsburgh from hawking tickets to coaching the team, knows the

problems and has the personality to obtain the necessary cooperation from a dozen independent owners.

Bell is greeted by a new rival league, the All-American Football Conference, with teams in Buffalo, Brooklyn, Los Angeles, Miami, Chicago, New York, San Francisco,

and Cleveland. This precipitates a wage war between the leagues for players and few graduating college players can afford to pass up pro ball.

Both leagues do fairly well in overall attendance—about 1.7 million each—but certain franchises run into trouble. In the AAFC, Miami folds up and is replaced by Baltimore. In the NFL, the New York Giants have to battle two of the new league's teams for spectators, playing dates and players.

Pro football breaks the color line as Kenny Washington becomes the first Negro to sign with a major league athletic team since the

Twenties. Washington and Woody Strode play for the Rams this year. Marion Motley and Bill Willis play for the Cleveland Browns.

The Giants find more trouble when it is revealed that one of their players is offered a bribe before the championship game with the Bears. The player does not take the bribe, but he does not report it, either. He is suspended by commissioner Bell at once. Another player who was not involved, but knew of the offer, is allowed to play in the game (won by the Bears, 24-14) but is suspended immediately thereafter.

1947 The Chicago Cardinals, the oldest club in pro football in point of continuous operation, win their first NFL championship since 1925 with the "Million Dollar Backfield" of Paul Christman (Missouri), Pat Harder (Wisconsin), Charlie Trippi (Georgia) and Elmer Angsman (Notre Dame). Christman passes for more than 2,000 yards and 17 touchdowns during the season, then leads the Cards past Steve Van Buren and the Philadelphia Eagles, 28-21, in the championship game.

In the "other league," mastermind Paul Brown has guided the Cleveland Browns to their second straight championship with

quarterback Otto Graham doing the aerial work and fullback Marion Motley handling the ground attack.

Both leagues draw well—about 1.8 million each—but it's not enough. Only Cleveland makes money in the AAFC and the NFL teams aren't getting rich either. The rules makers put a fifth official, the Back Judge, on the field. And since tie games have the approximate result of a brisk stroll on a treadmill the NFL decides that any playoff championship will go into sudden death overtime if the first 60-minutes result in a tie. A new coin flip for the kickoff will be held and the first team to score will win.

1948 This is the year of the upset. Truman beats Dewey, Marcel Cerdan takes Tony Zale's middleweight title away, and a California schoolboy, Bob Mathias, wins the Olympic decathlon gold medal in London. It is a year for the chalk players in pro football, however.

In the NFL, the champion

1947 Chicago Cardinals
Steve Van Buren scores winning TD in 1948 title game
Lou Saban (66) backs up Browns Motley, Golella.

Chicago Cardinals rip through the Western Division with an 11-1 record. In the East the Philadelphia Eagles also repeat to set up a rematch of the '47 title game. This one is played in Philly's Shibe Park

in a blinding snow storm. Incredibly, 36,309 fans show up to watch the Eagles prevail, 7-0, after recovering a fumble on the Cardinals' 17 yard line. Steve Van Buren gets the touchdown.

In the AAFC, Cleveland continues its dominance by winning 15 straight. A notable addition to the AAFC Baltimore team is Y. A. Tittle, who completes

Steve Van Buren races by rain-soaked Rams in 14-0 championship game, 1949
Cleveland Browns celebrate first NFL championship, 1950

55% of his passes for 2,522 yards and 16 TDs.

Both leagues drop a bit in attendance and the Baltimore franchise merges with the New York Yanks. D. Lyle Fife heads a group which buys the Detroit Lions from Fred L. Mandel, Jr.

1949 Congress passes a law raising the minimum wage from 40 to 75 cents an hour, evidently not enough to boost attendance at Sunday football games. Each league takes another drop at the gate and, following the season, commissioner Bell and AAFC representative J. Arthur Friedlund announce a merger of the two leagues.

Four AAFC franchises are dissolved and their players scattered among the survivors. The new league retains the name of National Football League and Bell remains as its commissioner. Carryover teams from the AAFC are the Cleveland Browns, the San Francisco Forty Niners and the Baltimore Colts.

On the playing field, Steve Van Buren, Bosh Pritchard, Tommy Thompson and the rest of the awesome Philadelphia Eagles roll through the Eastern Division, then, in a driving rain, overpower a racehorse Ram team which had just won six straight, 14-0, for the NFL championship.

Cleveland wins another AAFC title; beating San Francisco, 21-7, in the championship game.

This is also the year that Clark Shaughnessy, now the coach in Los Angeles, introduces the flanker or "third end" to football. Already blessed with two good receivers in Tom Fears and Bob Shaw, Shaughnessy sends halfback Elroy (Crazylegs) Hirsch out wide. Twenty years later, every team in pro football will use the formation.

The influence of Shorty Ray as rules maker is being felt. Among Ray's more unexpected discoveries, from his detailed chart and stop-watch observations, is that the faster a football game is played, the longer it takes. That is, the quicker plays are run off, the more chances there are to stop the clock, and the longer the game lasts. Ray has worked hard with officials to expedite their handling of the game and the NFL is now running off many more plays per game. Ray has also instigated many rules changes so that pro football and college football now have 150 major differences in rules where they were nearly identical a decade ago. Most of these changes have opened up the game so that the pros are now averaging over five TDs per game, up from 2.7 in 1936. Ray's final major battle is for free substitution and this year the NFL votes to try it on a one-year basis, thus moving pro football into the era of specialization, 60-minute action and announcer confusion.

1950 The football war is over and the Korean War begins.

The expanded league is re-aligned into the American

Conference (sort of eastern) including the Chicago Cardinals, the Cleveland Browns, the New York Giants, the Philadelphia Eagles, the Pittsburgh Steelers and the Washington Redskins; and the National Conference (sort of western) including the Baltimore Colts, the Chicago Bears, the Detroit Lions, the Green Bay Packers, the Los Angeles Rams, the New York

Yanks and the San Francisco 49ers.

Cleveland goes on to tie New York for the Conference title, then downs the Giants, 8-3, in a playoff. On the coast, the Los Angeles Rams defeat the Bears, 24-14, in a playoff to win the National Conference and a trip to Cleveland. The championship game is played in freezing weather before 29,751 hearties who watch the two spectacular teams trade touchdowns all afternoon. With 28 seconds left, Lou Groza kicks a 16-yard field goal and the upstart Browns win the NFL champion-ship, 30-28, in their first year in the league.

This is also the year that everyone's All-America halfback Doak Walker of SMU, joins the

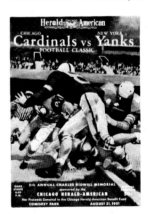

Detroit Lions as a rookie, leads the NFL in scoring with 128 points and silences critics who said he was too small for pro ball. Dan Reeves, owner of the Rams, shows everybody how not to use television to promote football. Reeves puts every game on the tube, home and

away, and in a touching display of
loyalty to home and hearth, the
good citizens of Los Angeles stay in
their living rooms every Sunday.
Ram records show 205,109 total
attendance in 1949. This year they
lose 100,000 of those. Next year
with a sensible home blackout of
TV, 234,110 return to the stadium.
The home game black-out, a rather
obvious idea, spreads rapidly in pro
football, helping to make football
the sport of the electronic era.

1951 Citation becomes the first million
dollar winning horse in history,
sending his Calumet Farm owners
scurrying for their adding machine.
Los Angeles fans need a bank of
them to keep up with the high-
scoring Rams. With Bob Waterfield

and Norm Van Brocklin sharing the
quarterbacking, Tom Fears and
Elroy Hirsch doing the receiving,
and running backs like Dan Towler,
Tank Younger, Dick Hoerner,
Vitamin T. Smith and Glenn Davis,
the Rams rewrite the record book.
They gain 5,506 yards during the
season (735 in one outburst against
the New York Yanks). Hirsch leads
the league in receptions (17 for
TDs) and Waterfield is the NFL's
top passer. It's enough to make
opponents cry like singer Johnny
Ray, who is also pretty hot
stuff this year.

The Cleveland Browns don't
scare easily, though. They waltz
through an 11-1 season in the East
and calmly walk into the eye of the

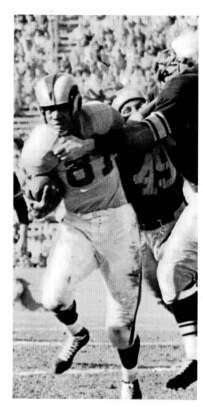

Ram hurricane before 59,475 Los
Angeles fans gathered for the
championship game. The record
crowd sees a hair-raiser, decided
in favor of the Rams, 24-17,
on a fourth quarter, picture-
perfect 73-yard pass from
Van Brocklin to Fears.

Sammy Baugh plays his last
season, a record sixteenth. Only
kicker Lou Groza and defensive end
Doug Atkins will last longer. Baugh,
whose stinging side-arm delivery
created the first precision passing
attack, retires with a page full of
passing and punting records. He has
led the NFL as a passer more seasons
than anyone with six, has the second

232

highest (to Bart Starr) lifetime completion percentage, 56.5%, and an astounding one-season high of 70%. His 45-yard average is still the lifetime standard for punters.

The fondest hopes of interior linemen are cruelly dashed by the rules committee as they outlaw a forward pass to center, guards or tackles.

Baltimore folds up. The league pays Abraham Watner $50,000 for the franchise and players.

1952 "I Like Ike" and the Academy likes Gary Cooper in "High Noon," but not enough New Yorkers like the Yanks. The franchise is moved to Dallas to operate as the Texans. Despite a transfusion given by the Rams, who trade 11 men to the Texans for Army Lt. Les Richter (who won't even be available for two more years), the team doesn't do any better in the new surroundings. Dallas folds before the season is completed and finishes its schedule on the road.

Back in Los Angeles, the Rams manage to get along well enough without the traded 11 players to get into a playoff for the National Conference with the Detroit Lions. Rookie defensive back Dick (Night Train) Lane snaps up 14 opposition passes, a season's record.

The resurging Lions whip the Rams, 31-21, in a fog shrouded game in Detroit, then win their first

NFL title in 17 years by beating the Browns, 17-7. Bobby Layne, Doak Walker and Pat Harder do most of the damage for the winners. This is the start of a great era for the Lions, now coached by Buddy Parker (who played on Detroit's last championship team in 1935.) Parker takes advantage of free substitution to build the first defensive unit capable of selling tickets on its own. Linebacker Joe Schmidt (who is to coach the Lions later) and safety Jack Christiansen lead the specialists and the Detroit fans flock to the ticket windows.

1953 Otto Graham of the Browns is the league's top passer; Pete Pihos of the Eagles is the top receiver; and Joe Perry of the Forty Niners is the leading rusher. But the best team is still the Detroit entry.

They prove it by storming through the Western Conference and then picking off the Browns again, 17-16, for the championship.

Doak Walker scores 11 points and Bobby Layne passes 33 yards to end Jim Doran for the winning score in the fourth quarter to delight 54,577 fans in Briggs Stadium. It's a suitable reward for the Motor City fans who support the Lions with an average attendance of 52,591.

Speaking of support, the Baltimore fans want their NFL franchise back so bad that they buy 15,000 season tickets for a non-existent team. The league promptly awards them the floating Dallas franchise. Baltimore fans turn out 28,000 strong per game and the team responds with a 3-9 season, beating the dreaded Chicago Bears twice. Carroll Rosenbloom, who had played for commissioner Bert Bell at the University of Pennsylvania in 1927, is the new franchise's owner.

The Federal government sues the NFL for a violation of anti-trust

Bobby Layne directs Detroit Lions
Alex Webster scores against Cleveland
Y. A. Tittle throws for San Francisco

laws, basically because, under the home game blackout, the clubs do not allow games to be televised into their territory while they are playing at home. U. S. District Court Justice Allan K. Grim lays down a complicated line—the gist being that the league can go on with the blackouts. This court decision is the groundwork for pro football's emergence as the game of the American mid-century.

1954 Roger Bannister of England breaks the four-minute barrier in the mile run with a 3:59.4 clocking and the Cleveland Browns break the strange mastery the Detroit Lions seem to

have held over them. The Browns win their fifth straight conference title since joining the NFL (ninth straight if you count the old All-America Conference) and then paste the defending champion Lions, 56-10. Otto Graham does most of the avenging, scoring three touchdowns himself and passing for three more (two to Ray Renfro).

In Baltimore, Weeb Ewbank is hired as coach and told that the faithful fans there would like a championship, please. Ewbank promises no miracles, says it will take five years.

Commissioner Bert Bell is given a new 12-year contract.

Starting this year, all players will have to wear face masks. It will no longer be possible to judge a football player by the number of missing teeth.

1955 Los Angeles and New York get caught in a tie at the end of an exhibition game and have to play it out as a test of the sudden-death system. The Rams win, 23-17.

Dr. Jonas Salk comes up with a vaccine which will prevent polio, but nobody can figure out a way to stop Paul Brown's Cleveland machine. Otto Graham, playing his last season, is the League's top passer again. The Brownies capture another conference title with relative ease, then drub the Rams, 38-14, before 85,693 silent fans in the Los Angeles Coliseum.

Meanwhile, that noble venture in Baltimore is beginning to pay off. The Colts win five games and rookie fullback Alan (The Horse) Ameche from Wisconsin leads the league in rushing.

1956 It's the year of the big breakthrough. The USA loses it's first Olympic Games since 1936 (to the Russians) and the Browns lose their first divisional championship since formation of the team in 1946 (to the Giants). With Otto Graham gone, Cleveland founders to fourth place in the Eastern Conference.

The Baltimore build-up continues. Seeking backup material for quarterback George Shaw, the Colts make an 80-cent phone call to

Giants Conerly, Gifford, Rote
Joe Perry

sandlot player Johnny Unitas and he joins the club.

Green Bay's Al Carmichael carries the ball farther than it has ever been advanced on one NFL play, 106 yards to a touchdown with a Chicago Bear kickoff.

A big rebuilding job at New York is completed by coach Jim Lee Howell (ably assisted by Vince Lombardi and Tom Landry, among

others) and the Giants win their first NFL title since 1938 by whipping the Chicago Bears, 47-7, before 56,836 partisans in Yankee Stadium. Big guns for the Giants are quarterback Charlie Conerly (who passes for TDs to Kyle Rote and Frank Gifford) and runners Mel Triplett and Alex Webster (both of whom score).

The game is played on an icy field and the Giants wear sneakers, just as they did in the famous "tennis shoe game" of 1934—and with the same result. By now the players' shares in the championship are $3,779 for winners and $2,485 for losers.

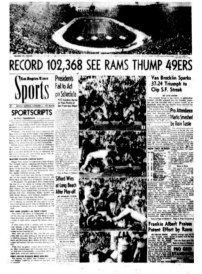

A record crowd, Nov. 10, 1957

1957 If you are a San Franciscan, this is your "almost" year—or the year that should have been.

The Russians steal a few headlines by launching Sputnik I, but even it is not as spectacular as the "Alley Oop" passes from Y. A. Tittle to R. C. Owens or the running of Hugh McElhenny and Joe Perry. Coached by Frankie Albert, the

Tobin Rote

Vince Lombardi

John Unitas
Bert Bell

colorful San Franciscans play before huge crowds everywhere, including 102,368 who jam the Los Angeles Coliseum for their game with the arch-rival Rams.

Emotions reach a peak when Tony Morabito, the club owner, collapses and dies during a game with the Bears. Trailing 7-17 at the time, the 49ers fight back and win their finest victory of all time, 21-17, on a fourth quarter pass from Tittle to end Billy Wilson.

San Francisco ties for the Western Conference title with

Detroit and plays the Lions for the right to meet Cleveland for the NFL championship. Cheered on by a full house, the 49ers lead 27-3 in the third quarter. The gutty Lions, however, dramatically reverse the tide of the game and come away with a 31-27 victory.

The championship game with Cleveland is almost anticlimactic, but the Lions get revenge for their lop-sided 1954 loss by thumping the Browns, 59-14. Tobin Rote fills in for injured Bobby Layne and throws four TD passes and scores

one himself as the Lions pick up their fourth NFL title.

1958 Alaska is admitted to the Union, the Dodgers and Giants move west and Baltimore joins the exclusive list of football's world champions. With Johnny Unitas coolly directing the attack, the Colts complete their five-year plan. They win their conference title, then meet the New York Giants (who have to survive a playoff with the Browns for the Eastern title) at Yankee Stadium.

Three days after Christmas the Colts and Giants tense through eight minutes of sudden-death overtime to a 23-17 Colt championship. The game sells the nation, and just as important, the New York TV men, on football as the sports spectacle of the electronic generation.

1959 This is the year of the arrival of the Roman gladiator. Charlton Heston arrives by chariot in the picture of the year, "Ben Hur," and wins an Oscar as best actor. Vincent T. Lombardi uses more conventional

transportation to get to Green Bay, Wisconsin, and wins the devotion of Packer fans by taking a team with a dismal 1-10-1 record (its worst in 40 years) to 7-5.

That's not a championship, but Green Bay fans have had 10 years of losing on the field and bickering among a 13-man committee supposedly running the club. "Let's get one thing straight," Lombardi announces upon arrival. "I'm in complete command around here."

Meanwhile the Baltimore Colts continue to win and to give their fans the willies with close calls. In the championship game against the Giants, they trail, 7-9, at the end of

three periods, then explode in the fourth to down the New Yorkers, 31-16.

While watching the teams he came up with, Philadelphia and Pittsburgh, play the game he shepherded to prominence, Bert Bell suffers a fatal heart attack at the age of 65. Austin H. Gunsel, league treasurer, is appointed temporary NFL president.

In mid-season the American Football League is formed and franchises are announced for Boston, Buffalo, Los Angeles, Denver, New York, Houston, Dallas, and Oakland. World War II flying ace Joe Foss is named commissioner. Both sides brace for the inevitable war for players.

60 In late January the NFL owners gather in Miami for a long and bitter conclave trying to select a new commissioner to succeed the late Bert Bell. It will be closer than the Kennedy-Nixon election later this year. After four days and 22 ballots, the owners select 33-year-old Pete Rozelle, a young man who has risen in the Los Angeles Rams organization from publicity writer to general manager. Rozelle is, admittedly, a compromise candidate, selected because he seems to be able to get along with almost anybody. He proves to be a master organizer and shrewd negotiator.

Not without some thought of the rival league, the NFL awards a new franchise to Clint Murchison, Jr., of

Dallas. The Cowboys play every team in the league, but list in the Western Conference. Next season the Twin Cities, Minneapolis-St. Paul, will get a franchise, and the protocol problem is solved by calling the team the Minnesota Vikings.

The Cardinals leave Chicago after 62 years and move the franchise to St. Louis.

Vince Lombardi continues his building program at Green Bay and the Packers win the Western Conference title. In the championship match, the Philadelphia Eagles come from behind twice to beat the Pack, 17-13. The Eagle scores come on a 35-yard pass from Norm Van Brocklin to Tommy McDonald and a five-yard run by Ted Dean.

In the rival AFL, the Houston Oilers beat the Los Angeles Chargers, 24-16, for the championship. Attendance in the new league averages only 16,500 a game, but a TV contract with ABC nets each club $200,000.

In the second to last game of the year, John Unitas neglects to throw

a touchdown pass for the first time since 1956. The string is 47 consecutive games, a record of the unbreakable type.

Paul Hornung lights up scoreboards with 176 points in one season. He scores 15 touchdowns with one of the game's best goal line noses and gets the rest on 15 field goals and 41 extra points.

1961 Cmdr. Alan Shepard becomes the first American sent into outer space, but he doesn't get any higher than the football faithfuls in Green Bay who get their first NFL championship in 17 years. Halfback Paul Hornung, on leave from the Army, scores 19 points in the first title game ever played in Green Bay and the Packers rout the New York Giants, 37-0, before 39,029 frenzied fans. In the AFL, the Los Angeles Chargers have become the San Diego Chargers. The change of

venue doesn't help the championship game. The Houston Oilers beat 'em, 10-3.

The Dallas Cowboys are switched into the Eastern Conference and the new Minnesota Vikings campaign in the Western. Battling for spectators with the AFL's Dallas Texans, the Cowboys display some wide-open football and win four games, one against the vaunted New York Giants. The city is still as divided as Berlin, but the addition of native Texan Bob Lilly, an All-America at TCU, helps solidify the Cowboys with the proud Texas fans.

Cleveland, which hasn't won its conference since Otto Graham retired, gets a new group of owners. Chairman of the board is Art Modell, a young New York television executive.

Detroit slides by Cleveland, 17-16, in the first Playoff Bowl, a game between the NFL's two second-place teams played in Miami in January. The game is controversial—the Loser's Bowl, it is called—but in the Sixties it is consistently in the Top Ten sports shows of the year in TV ratings and the proceeds of the live gate and TV are given to the Bert Bell NFL Player Benefit Plan covering group medical, life insurance and retirement benefits.

Commissioner Pete Rozelle, who has already shown the NFL club owners that he is not content to be a hand-shaker, earns further respect by nursing an important bill through congress. Having already convinced the owners that the league will have more bargaining power with the networks if he can present all NFL teams in one TV package, Rozelle goes to Washington to get a special law passed which will exempt football from possible monopoly charges. He makes his point that competition in football takes place on the field. In order to have equal competition, you must have equal funding. He convinces Representative Emanuel Celler of New York who introduces the bill; both branches of congress pass it; and President Kennedy who signs it into law. It is a monumental step for the league.

Canton, Ohio, gets back into the

big time when it is chosen as the site for pro football's Hall of Fame. Dick McCann leaves the Redskins to take the demanding job of director and performs with dedication and love. The Hall is soon an attractive tourist stop replete with historical data, photos and artifacts from the sport's colorful past.

1962 Jim Taylor rushes for 1,474 yards and breaks the string of rushing titles held by Cleveland's Jim Brown at five.

With Bart Starr directing the attack, Taylor scores a record 19 touchdowns rushing and the Pack storms through the League. Only a Thanksgiving Day upset by the Detroit Lions keeps Green Bay from a perfect record. In the championship game against the Giants, Taylor scores once and Jerry Kramer kicks three field goals and the Packers win, 16-7, before 64,892 freezing fans at Yankee Stadium.

Commissioner Pete Rozelle, who has just been given a new five-year contract, sells the television rights for NFL games to CBS for an impressive $9.2 million.

The American Football League charges the NFL with monopoly and conspiracy, claiming impropriety in the areas of league expansion, television coverage and player signing. The case goes two and a half years in court before U.S. District Judge Roszel Thomsen dismisses it.

The Bert Bell NFL Player Benefit Plan is extended to cover retirement benefits. Any player who lasts five years in the league, starting no earlier than 1959, will begin receiv-

ing benefits at age 65. Minimum life insurance benefits are raised from $5000 to $10,000.

Cleveland Browns' owner Art Modell introduces a new conception: five continuous hours of live football entertainment in one stadium. He begins a policy of scheduling one pre-season double-header each year. Four teams are involved on each date and the fans respond with capacity houses.

The NFL sets a pre-season attendance record by drawing over a million people for 35 games.

Commissioner Rozelle negotiates with the warring owners of the Los Angeles Rams. He asks each of the two factions to produce a sealed bid for purchase of the ball team and to agree to sell if its bid is unsuccessful. Dan Reeves, who brought the team west from Cleveland, is the successful bidder and assumes complete control of the franchise.

1963 President Kennedy and Premier Khrushchev install "hot line" telephones in the White House and the Kremlin. Commissioner Pete Rozelle burns up a few wires himself when he finds out that Paul Hornung of the Packers and Alex Karras of the Lions have been betting on football games. True, the amounts have been small and they have been betting for their own teams, not against, but the commissioner feels that, like Caesar's wife, NFL players must be above suspicion. Rozelle suspends the two players indefinitely. Five other Lions are fined $2,000 apiece for betting on games in which they did not play.

Despite the loss of Hornung, Green Bay loses only two games, but both are to the rejuvenated

Chicago Bears who give George Halas his sixth and last world championship. Linebackers Larry Morris, Bill George and Joe

Fortunato and safeties Roosevelt Taylor and Richie Petitbon lead the Bear defense which allows opponents an average of only 10 points a game. In the championship game against the Giants, the Bears intercept five of Y.A. Tittle's passes, turn two of them into scores, and win, 14-10.

In the AFL Tobin Rote leads the San Diego Chargers to a 51-10 rout of the Boston Patriots in the championship game.

The legal war between the AFL and NFL finally ends when the U.S. Fourth Circuit Court of Appeals refuses to overturn the decision made last year by Justice Roszel Thomsen. The case has been in the courts for three and a half years.

After arduous labor against heavy odds, Dick McCann and his staff preside over the opening of Pro Football's Hall of Fame. The proceedings are highlighted by the induction of 17 charter members into the Hall. These members are: Sammy Baugh, quarterback, Washington Redskins (1937-52); Bert Bell, NFL commissioner (1946-59); Joe Carr, NFL president (1921-39); Earl (Dutch) Clark, quarterback

Portsmouth Spartans and Detroit Lions (1931-38); Harold (Red) Grange, halfback, Chicago Bears (1925-37); George Halas, player, coach, founder, Chicago Bears (1920-   ); Mel Hein, center, New York Giants (1931-45); Wilbur (Pete) Henry, tackle, Canton Bulldogs, Akron Indians, New York Giants, Pottsville Maroons, Pittsburgh Steelers (1920-30); Robert (Cal) Hubbard, tackle and end, New York Giants, Green Bay Packers, and Pittsburgh Steelers (1927-36); Don Hutson, Green Bay Packers (1935-45); Earl (Curly) Lambeau, founder, player, coach, Green Bay Packers

(1919-49); Tim Mara, founder, New York Giants (1925-59); George Preston Marshall, founder, Washington Redskins (1932-64); John (Blood) McNally, halfback, Milwaukee Badgers. Duluth Eskimos, Pottsville Maroons, Green Bay Packers, Pittsburgh Steelers, (1925-39); Bronko Nagurski, fullback and tackle, Chicago Bears (1930-37, 1943); Ernie Nevers, fullback, Duluth Eskimos and Chicago Cardinals (1926-37); Jim Thorpe, halfback, Canton Bulldogs, Oorang Indians, Cleveland Indians, Toledo Maroons, Rock Island Independents, New York Giants (1915-25).

Commissioner Rozelle grants broadcast rights for the NFL championship game to NBC for $926,000, nearly half of which — $450,000 — goes into the Player Benefit Plan.

Cleveland's Jim Brown establishes new limits with 1,863 yards in a single season's running. This is more than a mile, over 400 yards better than anyone else has ever done. It is one of football's astounding records.

64 The Beatles cash in on "I Want To Hold Your Hand" and in Cleveland Blanton Collier's one year regrouping of the Browns, after taking over from Paul Brown, pays off big, too. With Jim Brown running and Frank Ryan passing the Browns win their first divisional title

since 1957. Everyone cringes at the thought of what the awesome Baltimore Colts will do to the Browns in the championship game. After a scoreless first half Ryan fires three touchdown passes to Gary Collins and Lou Groza boots two field goals and the Browns humiliate the highest scoring team in the league, 27-0.

CBS is awarded a $14.1 million contract to air all NFL regular

season games in 1964 and 1965. The AFL negotiates a healthy contract, too, signing all of its games for the years 1965-69 to NBC for $36 million. "People have now stopped asking me if we are going to make it," smiles AFL commissioner Joe Foss.

Money makes news in America and New York Jets' owner Sonny Werblin makes news for the AFL by saying that he is paying Alabama quarterback Joe Namath $400,000 for his signature and other services involving his right arm.

CBS buys the NFL championship game for 1964 and 1965 in a package deal, two for $1.8 million. Of this, $525,000 goes to the Player Benefit Plan and $317,000 more to pensions for coaches and other club personnel.

During this season, the NFL one-day paid attendance figure hits 369,718, which is 25,000 more than ever came into the stadium on any previous Sunday.

Bear end Johnny Morris catches 93 passes, breaking Tom Fears's respected record by nine.

This is also the year of the Tokyo Olympics and football fans who watch on television can't help but wonder if Bob Hayes, who sets a world record of 10-flat for 100

meters, can play football. "We'll see," says Cowboy coach Tom Landry who holds the draft rights on the world's fastest human.

After a year's suspension, Paul Hornung and Alex Karras are reinstated by commissioner Rozelle.

In its second year of operation, the Hall of Fame makes the following inductions: Jimmy Conzelman, halfback, coach, executive, Decatur, Rock Island, Milwaukee, Detroit, Providence, Chicago Cardinals (1920-48); Ed Healey, tackle, Rock Island and Chicago Bears (1920-27); Clarke Hinkle, fullback, Green Bay Packers (1932-41); William Roy (Link) Lyman, tackle, Canton Bulldogs, Cleveland, Chicago Bears (1922-34); August (Mike) Michalske, guard, New York Yankees and Green Bay Packers (1927-37); Arthur J. Rooney, founder, Pittsburgh Steelers (1933-); George Trafton, center, Chicago Bears (1920-32).

1965 In view of the battle for college players between the two professional leagues, the NFL declares: "No players will be signed to a contract or any form of document of intent, directly or through an agent, until after completion of all his team's football games, including

bowl contest, in which he is available to participate during his senior year. This will include collegiate football players who actually compete in seasons beyond the graduating date of their original class." Any team which violates this rule could lose all the players on its draft list. The pledge leads to a series of dramatic 'twixt-the-goalpost signings, as players leave the field following their final game.

Jimmy Clark of Scotland is the king of auto racing as he wins both the world driving championship for Grand Prix cars and the Indianapolis 500.

The NFL shows some world class speed also. A Chicago Bear rookie from Kansas, Gale Sayers, hits the League like a cyclone. He scores 22 touchdowns (14 rushing, six on pass receptions, and two on kick returns). Six of those TDs come in

one memorable game in the rain against the Forty Niners. This ties the NFL record set in 1929 by Ernie Nevers of the Chicago Cardinals and equaled in 1951 by Cleveland halfback-flanker Dub Jones.

The NFL ups the officiating crews one more time to six, adding the Line Judge. Big Brother is everywhere.

The league's latest TV contract with CBS is announced at $18.8 million per year for two years.

Atlanta's Rankin Smith is awarded an NFL franchise. The Falcons will open play in 1966, playing every team in the league, but ranked in the Eastern Conference. And just when people were beginning to think the Colts were taking over as kingpins in the Western Conference, Green Bay flexes its muscles again. First the two titans end up with identical 10-3-1 records, then they play an agonizing overtime playoff, Green Bay winning, 13-10 on a Don Chandler field goal, 13 minutes and 39 seconds after the regulation game has ended. The Colts are using halfback Tom Matte at quarterback because both Johnny Unitas and Gary Cuozzo are injured. Matte does a yeoman's job, mixing his plays well from a game plan strapped to his wrist. It might have been enough against anybody but the Packers.

After disposing of the gritty Colts, Green Bay entertains the defending champion Browns in the title game. The field is softened by a four inch

morning snow, but it doesn't faze Jim Taylor and Paul Hornung. They roll for 201 yards and Green Bay wins its third title in five years, 23-13

This is the last game for Cleveland's great fullback, Jim Brown, who retires from football in favor of an acting career. He takes 10 all-time rushing marks into retirement with him. In nine seasons with the Browns, he leads the League in rushing eight times and has a total of 12,312 yards gained, more than 4,000 yards better than his nearest challenger.

In the AFL, the Buffalo Bills defeat San Diego, 23-0, for the

league championship. The league's attendance hits 1.7 million, — not bad, even when compared to the NFL's 4.6 million.

Added to the Hall of Fame are: Guy Chamberlin, player-coach, Canton Bulldogs, Cleveland, Frankford Yellowjackets, Chicago Bears, and Chicago

Cardinals (1919-28); John (Paddy) Driscoll, player-coach, Chicago Cardinals and Chicago Bears, (1919-31, 1941-67); Daniel J. Fortmann, M.D., guard, Chicago Bears (1936-46); Otto Graham, quarterback, Cleveland Browns (1946-55); Sid Luckman, quarterback, Chicago Bears (1939-50); Steve Van Buren, halfback, Philadelphia Eagles (1944-52); Bob Waterfield, quarterback, Cleveland Rams and Los Angeles Rams (1945-52).

1966 All sorts of good news this year: Jim Ryun returns the world mile run record to the United States after a 32 year absence by zipping 3:51.3; NASA executes a successful unmanned "soft landing" on the moon; Medicare goes into effect; and the bitter professional football war ends. The truce comes only after a couple of major skirmishes early in the year. First the AFL replaces commissioner Joe Foss with Al Davis, the hard-charging leader of the Oakland Raiders. Before Davis is settled in his new New York office, the Giants welcome him to the city by announcing the signing of Peter Gogolak, a soccer style field goaler who has played out his option with the AFL Buffalo Bills. Both leagues have avoided opening this type of Pan-

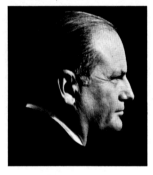

dora's Box and the AFL interprets the Gogolak signing as an escalation of the war. Soon announcements appear, official and unofficial, of the signing of many of the NFL super stars by the AFL. Peace talks, which have been dragging along (mostly between Tex Schramm of the Cowboys and Lamar Hunt of the Chiefs) suddenly get serious.

Before the 1966 season begins, peace is declared with the two leagues agreeing on a coalition government with Pete Rozelle as commissioner of all. The two

leagues will play separate schedules, but hold a common draft. They also agree to play a post-season game between the champions of each league. They call it the "AFL-NFL World Championship Game," but the public prefers "Super Bowl".

Anticipating the possibility of another question of legality on the merger, commissioner Rozelle goes to congress again seeking passage of a bill which will clear the way for the merger. Cooperative legislators attach the football bill as a rider on President Johnson's anti-inflation bill which is sure to pass. With such a formidable piece of legislation running interference, the desired bill becomes law. Key strategists in the manuever are Senator Everett Dirksen of Illinois and Representative Hale Boggs of Louisiana.

Back on the playing fields, a real showdown is shaping up. The champion Packers finish three games ahead of the Colts in the West and Dallas finally wins the Eastern title that everyone knew was coming. A crowd of 74,152 shows up at the Cotton Bowl for the title match. It turns out to be one of the NFL's greatest title games, pairing two outstanding offensive-defensive teams. Dallas is intercepted at the final gun and the Packers win a thrilling 34-27 championship.

What with one thing and another, Gale Sayers has the ball in his

possession while covering 2440 yards this year. This includes rushes, pass receptions and kick returns. It's a record.

The St. Louis Cardinals have a corner on fair catches. Johnny Roland ties Abe Woodson's record set last year by waving in 18. In 1965, Billy Gambrell caught 17 and in 1964 he caught 15. So Cardinals occupy the top four places on the

all-time fair catch list. Maybe they're on to something.

In the AFL, Len Dawson and Mike Garrett are the big guns for the Kansas City Chiefs as they win the Western title, then beat Eastern champ Buffalo, 31-7, for the league championship. AFL attendance jumps to 2.1 million and it's up to 5.3 million in the NFL.

John Mecom, Jr. heads a group awarded an NFL franchise for the city of New Orleans.

The following are admitted to the Hall of Fame: Bill Dudley, halfback, Pittsburgh Steelers, Detroit Lions and Washington Redskins (1942-53); Joe Guyon, halfback, Cleveland Indians, Oorang Indians, Rock Island Independents, Kansas City Cowboys and New York Giants (1921-27); Arnie Herber, quarterback, Green Bay Packers, New York Giants (1930-40, 1944-45); Walter Kiesling, player-coach, Duluth Eskimos, Pottsville Maroons, Boston Braves, Chicago Cardinals, Chicago Bears, Green Bay Packers, and Pittsburgh Steelers (1926-56); George McAfee, halfback, Chicago Bears (1940-41, 1945-50); Steve Owen, player-coach, Kansas City Cowboys and New York Giants (1924-53); Hugh (Shorty) Ray, NFL technical advisor and supervisor of officials (1938-56); Clyde (Bulldog) Turner, center-linebacker, Chicago Bears (1940-52).

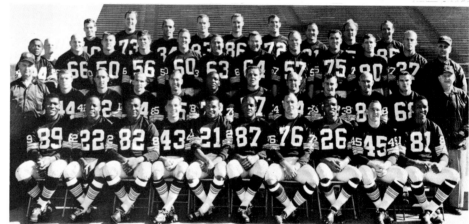

The mighty Green Bay Packers welcome Mike Garrett and the Kansas City Chiefs to the family in the first Super Bowl played in Los Angeles on January 15. The

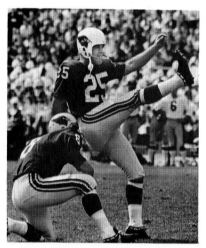

AFL champs are in the game only for the first half, trailing only 10-14 at intermission. Green Bay goes to a surprise blitzing tactic to wear down the Chiefs and claim a 35-10 victory. Each of the winners pockets $15,000.

Several inter-league games are arranged for the summer. The Denver Broncos deliver some sort of revenge for the AFL by beating the Detroit Lions in the first such encounter.

For league play, the NFL starts its "four-four system." That's four divisions, each with four teams, with divisional champions to meet for conference titles and conference champions to play for the NFL crown. In the playoffs, Dallas (Capitol Division) beats Cleveland (Century) for the Eastern Conference title, 52-14. Green Bay (Central) downs Los Angeles (Coastal) for the Western crown, 28-7.

All of that sets up a rematch of the NFL championship of a year ago, only this time they square off in 13-below weather in Green Bay. The Packers start off in identical fashion and lead, 14-0, on two scoring passes from Bart Starr to Boyd Dowler (eight and 46 yards, respectively) before the Cowboys can get their mittens adjusted. But Cowboy defensive end George Andrie runs a fumble recovery for a score and Danny Villanueva kicks a 21 yard field goal and Dallas is back in business, trailing by only four at

the half. It remains that way until the fourth quarter when Cowboy Dan Reeves connects with Lance Rentzel for 50 yards on a halfback option pass and it looks good for Dallas, 17-14. They reckon without Bart Starr, however. Cooler than the weather, he moves his team 68 yards in 12 plays and scores the winning TD from the one on third down with 13 seconds and no time outs left. The 21-17 victory gives Packer coach Vince Lombardi his third straight NFL championship and fifth in seven years.

Regular season attendance rises to 5,337,038 in 1966, which is 703,017 more than ever before.

The NFL votes in the tuning-fork goal post, with only one upright which Mike Ditka runs into anyway. It is also decided to decorate the sideline with a border three feet wide.

At the first AFL-NFL draft, commissioner Rozelle announces that no player will be drafted until he is actually through with his eligibility. Thus ends the policy of drafting "futures," players whose class has graduated but who have one more year to play because they have some way missed one year of competition.

Commissioner Rozelle announces that the second Super Bowl will be played in Miami.

NFL owners vote to give $1.2 million to the Player Benefit Fund every year for the next three years.

Cleveland Brown owner, Arthur B. Modell, is elected president of the NFL for one year.

NFL pre-season attendance now hits 2 million. Sixteen of those games were with AFL teams and drew 600,000.

In a testimony to (1) NFL defenses and (2) the specialization of modern football, Jim Bakken kicks seven field goals in nine attempts in one game for St. Louis, a record.

The following are inducted into the Hall of Fame: Chuck Bednarik, center and linebacker, Philadelphia Eagles (1949-62); Charles W. Bidwill, owner, Chicago Cardinals (1933-47); Paul E. Brown, coach, Cleveland Browns (1946-62); Bobby Layne, quarterback, Chicago Bears, New York Bulldogs, Detroit Lions, Pittsburgh Steelers (1948-62); Daniel F. Reeves, founder, Los Angeles Rams (1941-71); Ken Strong, halfback-placekicker, Staten Island Stapletons, New York Yankees and New York Giants (1929-39, 1944-47); Joe Stydahar, tackle, Chicago Bears (1936-42, 1945-46); Emlen Tunnell, defensive back, New York Giants and Green Bay Packers (1948-61).

1968 Lyndon Johnson calls it a career and so does Papa Bear. It is the first

year in 48 that George Halas doesn't stalk the Chicago sidelines as owner and coach of his beloved Bears. Since sitting in on the organizational meeting in Canton in 1920, Halas has been a driving force within the league and a football tactician who, unlike many, was not afraid to change his style to fit the material or keep up with modern trends. In his tenure at Chicago, Halas wins nine divisional titles and five world championships. He is best remembered for his Sunday afternoon patrols along the Wrigley Field sidelines exhorting to players and officials alike, semaphoring the next play to his quarterback, fighting for his Bears on the field and off. A hip injury now precludes this mobile involvement and Halas gives this as his reason for quitting. "I won't miss the detail work, the game analysis, the short list—but, the sidelines, the excitement, the decisions—that's what I love." That love drove Halas and Halas drove

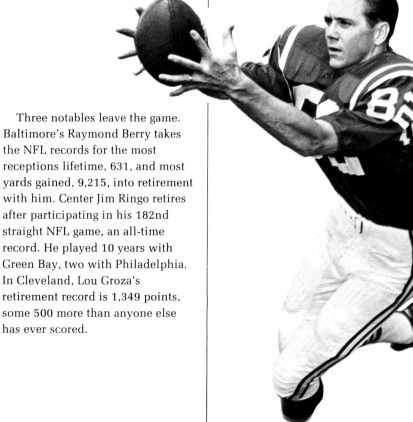

Three notables leave the game. Baltimore's Raymond Berry takes the NFL records for the most receptions lifetime, 631, and most yards gained, 9,215, into retirement with him. Center Jim Ringo retires after participating in his 182nd straight NFL game, an all-time record. He played 10 years with Green Bay, two with Philadelphia. In Cleveland, Lou Groza's retirement record is 1,349 points, some 500 more than anyone else has ever scored.

the league. It's sad to hear him say, "I knew it was time to retire when I realized I wasn't gaining on the referee."

It is also the year of the second Super Bowl, this time in Miami. The game is very similar to the first. Green Bay power wears Oakland down and the Packers roll 33-14. The live gate is $3 million and 60 million households have the game tuned in on television.

Vince Lombardi announces that he will no longer actively coach the Green Bay Packers, but merely oversee their operation as general manager.

Quarterback Earl Morrall, added to the Baltimore squad to fill in temporarily for the injured Johnny Unitas, performs spectacularly as he leads the Colts to the Coastal Division title with an amazing 13-1 record. The Colts beat Minnesota for the Western Conference title and Cleveland 34-0 for the NFL championship. A 13-year veteran in the league, Morrall had played with San Francisco, Pittsburgh, Detroit, and New York. At age 34, he is named the NFL's most valuable player.

1969 The AFL reaches symbolic parity with the NFL on one January afternoon in Miami. Joe Namath throws straight while backing away from the Baltimore Colts, Matt Snell makes 121 yards running right at them and the New York

Jets win the Super Bowl 16-7. John Unitas's arm is no longer strong enough to save the Colts and this has a wider significance.

Vince Lombardi leaves Green Bay and semiretirement to be-

come active coach, general manager, and part-owner of the Redskins.

It takes three separate convocations and a final 36-hour marathon meeting, but in May the professional football owners manage to devise a plan for league realignment. There have been sixteen teams in the NFL and ten in the AFL, but the terms of the 1966 merger agreement called for rearrangement of the teams by 1970. Rather than reshuffle the entire group, three NFL teams go over to the AFL to create a balance of thirteen each. Surprisingly, two of the three teams to move are the 1968 NFL conference champions, Baltimore and Cleveland. The third is Pittsburgh. Under the new alignment, all twenty-six teams

are in the National Football League, with a National Conference and an American Conference.

Each conference is broken into three divisions—East, Central, and West. The West and Central Divisions all have four members and the two Eastern divisions each have five. The Eastern Conference divisions are agreed to immediately, but it is not until December, by picking an alignment out of a hat, that the National Conference decides on its divisions.

Inducted into the Hall of Fame: Albert Glen (Turk) Edwards, tackle, Boston Braves, Boston Redskins, Washington Redskins

Roman Gabriel

After the longest game

(1932-40); Earle (Greasy) Neale, coach, Philadelphia Eagles, (1941-50); Leo Nomellini, tackle, San Francisco 49ers, (1950-63); Joe Perry, fullback, San Francisco 49ers, Baltimore Colts (1948-62); and Ernie Stautner, defensive tackle, Pittsburgh Steelers (1950-63).

Roman Gabriel wins the MVP award in the NFL and his Rams win their first eleven games, but they are beaten out of the Super Bowl race by the Minnesota Vikings in the Western Conference playoff. The Vikings themselves win twelve straight in the regular season, losing their first and last games. In the AFL, the Kansas City Chiefs take advantage of a one-year-only rule which allows second-place teams into the playoffs. They edge the Jets, then face their own divisional winners, the Oakland Raiders, and win in the championship game.

'70 In the Super Bowl, Kansas City upsets the favored Vikings 23-7.

Commissioner Pete Rozelle announces the first television agreement to include all three major networks. For four years, CBS will carry all Sunday National Conference games and NBC will carry all Sunday American Conference football games. The two networks will alternate years covering the Super Bowl. ABC contracts to carry 13 games in prime time on Monday evenings.

Elected to the Hall of Fame are Jack Christiansen, defensive back, Detroit Lions (1951-58); Tom Fears, end, Los Angeles Rams (1948-56); Hugh McElhenny, running back, San Francisco 49ers, New York Giants, and Detroit Lions

249

(1952-64); and Pete Pihos, end, Philadelphia Eagles (1947-55).

Eight teams battle in the playoffs with Baltimore defeating Oakland and Dallas stopping San Francisco in the conference championships.

1971 Baltimore edges Dallas in the viciously-played Super Bowl V, 16-13, on Jim O'Brien's field goal with eight seconds remaining to play.

The Boston Patriots change their name; they are now the New England Patriots.

A seven-man class enters the Hall of Fame: Jim Brown, running back, Cleveland Browns (1957-65); Bill Hewitt, end, Chicago Bears, Philadelphia Eagles, and Phil-Pitt Steagles (1932-39, 1943); Frank (Bruiser) Kinard, tackle, Brooklyn Dodgers and New York Yankees (1938-47); Vince Lombardi, coach, Green Bay Packers and Washington Redskins (1958-67, 1969); Andy Robustelli, defensive end, Los Angeles Rams and New York Giants (1951-64); Y. A. Tittle, quarterback, Baltimore Colts, San Francisco 49ers, and New York Giants (1948-64); and Norm Van Brocklin, quarterback, Los Angeles Rams and Philadelphia Eagles (1949-60).

A transfixed Christmas Day television audience watches the drama of the longest pro game ever unfold. Garo Yepremian's 37-yard field goal 7 minutes and 40 seconds into the sixth period wins it for Miami and inflicts an agonizing defeat on Kansas City in a divisional playoff game.

1972 Dismissed often as a team that could not win the big games, the

Dallas Cowboys take the grandest prize of all when they defeat the Miami Dolphins 24-3 in Super Bowl VI.

Inbounds markers, or hash-marks, are moved nearer the center of the playing field, to a point even with the goal post

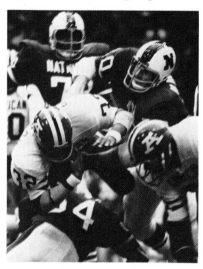

uprights; the intention is to do away with the "short side of the field" which, critics said, had given defenses unfair advantage. For the first time, ties count in standings—a half-game won, a half-game lost.

One of the strangest of trades occurs—a team for a team. Robert Irsay purchases the Los Angeles Rams and transfers ownership of the team to Carroll Rosenbloom in exchange for ownership of the Baltimore Colts.

The Hall of Fame inducts Lamar Hunt, president of the Kansas City Chiefs and founder of the American Football League; Gino Marchetti, defensive end, Dallas Texans and Baltimore Colts (1953-64, 1966); Ollie Matson, running back, Chicago Cardinals, Los Angeles Rams, Detroit Lions, and Philadelphia

Eagles (1952-66); and Clarence (Ace) Parker, quarterback, Brooklyn Dodgers, Boston Yanks, and New York Yankees (1937-41, 1945-46). The Miami Dolphins win the AFC title over Pittsburgh and the Washington Redskins win the NFC championship and their first title in 30 years when they defeat Dallas 26-3 to advance to the Super Bowl.

1973 Super Bowl VII, won by Miami 24-7 over Washington, is viewed in an estimated 27,670,000 homes, making it the most-watched tele-vised sports event ever.

The Pro Bowl is played outside Los Angeles for the first time in 22 years; the AFC defeats the NFC 33-28 at Texas Stadium in Irving, Texas, home of the Dallas Cowboys.

Continuing pressure moves the U. S. Congress to act on blackouts of games on television in league cities. Legislation is passed pro-hibiting local blackouts of games that have been sold out 72 hours before the kickoff.

Buffalo's O. J. Simpson concludes an incredible season in which be becomes the first man in NFL history to gain 2,000 yards rushing in one year. With 200 yards in his final game against the New York Jets, he finishes with a total of 2,003 yards.

Miami wins over Oakland for its third straight AFC championship, and Minnesota defeats Dallas to win the NFC title.

74 The Miami Dolphins become the only team other than the Green Bay Packers to win two Super Bowls, and win them consecutively, when they defeat Minnesota 24-7 in game VIII.

The NFL owners sign Pete Rozelle to a new 10-year contract as commissioner.

The city of Tampa, Florida, is awarded an NFL franchise to begin play in 1976.

The most sweeping rules changes in more than 40 years return the goal posts to the end lines; limit the dependence on field goals by ruling that after misses, the ball returns to the line of scrimmage or to the **20-yard line, whichever is farthest; institute sudden death to resolve tie games but limit the overtime to one 15-minute period for preseason and regular season games; assist pass catchers and kick returners by restricting harassment of receivers and holding the kicking team at the line until a kick is made; prohibit blocks below the waist by wide receivers moving toward the ball within three yards of the line of scrimmage; and reduce the penalty for offensive holding, illegal**

use of hands, and tripping from 15 to 10 yards.

Seattle becomes the league's twenty-eighth team, joining Tampa as one of two new franchises to begin play in 1976.

The new kick rule is modified, allowing two members of the kicking team to move downfield before the ball is kicked.

NFL owners approve 47-man active rosters for the 1974 season.

Clarence Davis squeezes between three Dolphins defenders with 26 seconds left to catch Ken Stabler's pass, giving Oakland 28-26 win over Miami in the first round of the AFC playoffs. Pittsburgh defeats Buffalo 32-14 in the other AFC elimination. Minnesota defeats St. Louis 30-14 and Los Angeles tops Washington 19-10 in NFC playoffs.

Pittsburgh whips Oakland 24-13 and Minnesota defeats Los Angeles 14-10 in the conference championship games, the winners advancing to Super Bowl IX.

1975 Franco Harris sets game records with 34 carries and 158 yards gained as Pittsburgh beats Minnesota 16-6 in Super Bowl IX at Tulane Stadium in New Orleans. Pittsburgh's first NFL championship since entering the

league in 1933 is witnessed by a live audience of 80,997 persons, and the NBC telecast is viewed by approximately 71 million persons, largest television audience ever for any program.

Los Angeles's James Harris throws two touchdown passes to lead the NFC to a 17-10 win over the AFC in the 1975 AFC-NFC Pro Bowl before 26,484 persons in Miami's Orange Bowl. Harris is named player of the game.

Pasadena, California, site of the historic Rose Bowl, is named host city for Super Bowl XI January 9, 1977.

NFL owners adopt numerous rules changes. One measure mandates that after a fourth-down incomplete pass into the end zone on a play that originated inside the opposing team's 20-yard line, the ball will be returned to the line of scrimmage instead of to the 20.

The Hall of Fame inducts Roosevelt Brown, tackle, New York Giants, 1953-65; George Connor, tackle-defensive tackle-linebacker, Chicago Bears, 1948-55; Dante Lavelli, end, Cleveland Browns, 1946-56; and Lenny Moore, running back, Baltimore Colts, 1956-67.

For The Record

O. J. Simpson

Larry Brown

Rick Casares

Rushing, Season Leaders

	Yards	Atts.	TDs
1974 — Otis Armstrong, Denver	1407	263	9
1973 — O. J. Simpson, Buffalo	2003	332	12
1972 — O. J. Simpson, Buffalo	1251	292	6
1971 — Floyd Little, Denver	1133	284	6
1970 — Larry Brown, Washington	1125	237	5
1969 — Gale Sayers, Chicago	1032	236	8
1968 — Leroy Kelly, Cleveland	1239	248	16
1967 — Leroy Kelly, Cleveland	1205	235	11
1966 — Gale Sayers, Chicago	1231	229	8
1965 — Jim Brown, Cleveland	1544	289	17
1964 — Jim Brown, Cleveland	1446	280	7
1963 — Jim Brown, Cleveland	1863	291	12
1962 — Jim Taylor, Green Bay	1474	272	19
1961 — Jim Brown, Cleveland	1408	305	8
1960 — Jim Brown, Cleveland	1257	215	9
1959 — Jim Brown, Cleveland	1329	290	14
1958 — Jim Brown, Cleveland	1527	257	17
1957 — Jim Brown, Cleveland	942	202	9
1956 — Rick Casares, Chicago Bears	1126	234	12
1955 — Alan Ameche, Baltimore	961	213	9
1954 — Joe Perry, San Francisco	1049	173	8
1953 — Joe Perry, San Francisco	1018	192	10
1952 — Dan Towler, Los Angeles	894	156	10
1951 — Eddie Price, New York Giants	971	271	7
1950 — Marion Motley, Cleveland	810	140	3
1949 — Steve Van Buren, Philadelphia	1146	263	11
1948 — Steve Van Buren, Philadelphia	945	201	10
1947 — Steve Van Buren, Philadelphia	1008	217	13
1946 — Bill Dudley, Pittsburgh	604	146	3
1945 — Steve Van Buren, Philadelphia	832	143	15
1944 — Bill Paschal, New York	737	196	9
1943 — Bill Paschal, New York	572	147	10
1942 — Bill Dudley, Pittsburgh	696	162	6
1941 — Clarence Manders, Brooklyn	486	111	7
1940 — Byron (Whizzer) White, Detroit	514	146	5
1939 — Bill Osmanski, Chicago Bears	699	121	7
1938 — Byron (Whizzer) White, Pittsburgh	567	152	4
1937 — Cliff Battles, Washington	874	216	6
1936 — Alphonse (Tuffy) Leemans, New York	830	206	2
1935 — Doug Russell, Chicago Cardinals	499	140	0
1934 — Beattie Feathers, Chicago Bears	1004	101	9
1933 — Cliff Battles, Boston	737	146	4
1932 — Bob Campiglio, Stapleton	504	104	2

All-Time Career Leader

	Years	Yards	Atts.	TDs
Jim Brown	9	12,312	2359	106

Passing, Season Leaders

	Att.	Comp.	Yards	TDs	Int.
1974 — Ken Anderson, Cincinnati	328	213	2667	18	10
1973 — Roger Staubach, Dallas	286	179	2428	23	15
1972 — Norm Snead, New York Giants	325	196	2307	17	12
1971 — Roger Staubach, Dallas	211	126	1882	15	4
1970 — John Brodie, San Francisco	378	223	2941	24	10
1969 — Sonny Jurgensen, Washington	442	274	3102	22	0
1968 — Earl Morrall, Baltimore	317	182	2909	26	17
1967 — Sonny Jurgensen, Washington	508	288	3747	31	16
1966 — Bart Starr, Green Bay	251	156	2257	14	3
1965 — Rudy Bukich, Chicago Bears	312	176	2641	20	9
1964 — Bart Starr, Green Bay	272	163	2144	15	4
1963 — Y. A. Tittle, New York	367	221	3145	36	14
1962 — Bart Starr, Green Bay	285	178	2438	12	9
1961 — Milt Plum, Cleveland	302	177	2416	18	10
1960 — Milt Plum, Cleveland	250	151	2297	21	5
1959 — Charlie Conerly, New York	194	113	1706	14	4
1958 — Eddie LeBaron, Washington	145	79	1365	11	10
1957 — Tommy O'Connell, Cleveland	110	63	1229	9	8
1956 — Ed Brown, Chicago Bears	168	96	1667	11	12
1955 — Otto Graham, Cleveland	185	98	1721	15	8
1954 — Norm Van Brocklin, Los Angeles	260	139	2637	13	21
1953 — Otto Graham, Cleveland	258	167	2722	11	9
1952 — Norm Van Brocklin, Los Angeles	205	113	1736	14	17
1951 — Bob Waterfield, Los Angeles	176	88	1566	13	10
1950 — Norm Van Brocklin, Los Angeles	233	127	2061	18	14
1949 — Sammy Baugh, Washington	255	145	1903	18	14
1948 — Tommy Thompson, Philadelphia	246	141	1965	25	11
1947 — Sammy Baugh, Washington	354	210	2938	25	15
1946 — Bob Waterfield, Los Angeles	251	127	1747	18	17
1945 — Sammy Baugh, Washington	182	128	1669	11	4
1944 — Frank Filchock, Washington	147	84	1139	13	9
1943 — Sammy Baugh, Washington	239	133	1754	23	19
1942 — Cecil Isbell, Green Bay	268	146	2021	24	14
1941 — Cecil Isbell, Green Bay	206	117	1479	15	11
1940 — Sammy Baugh, Washington	177	111	1367	12	10
1939 — Parker Hall, Cleveland Rams	208	106	1227	9	13
1938 — Ed Danowski, New York	129	70	848	8	8
1937 — Sammy Baugh, Washington	171	81	1127	7	14
1936 — Arnie Herber, Green Bay	173	77	1239	9	13
1935 — Ed Danowski, New York	113	57	795	9	9
1934 — Arnie Herber, Green Bay	115	42	799	8	12
1933 — Harry Newman, New York	132	53	963	8	17
1932 — Arnie Herber, Green Bay	101	37	639	9	9

All-Time Career Leader

	Years	Att.	Comp.	Yards	TDs	Int.
Sonny Jurgensen	18	4262	2433	32,224	255	189

Roger Staubach

Sonny Jurgensen

Bart Starr

Fred Biletnikoff

Raymond Berry

Pete Pihos

Pass Receiving, Season Leaders

	No.	Yards	TDs
1974 – Lydell Mitchell, Baltimore	72	544	2
1973 – Harold Carmichael, Philadelphia	67	1116	9
1972 – Harold Jackson, Philadelphia	62	1048	4
1971 – Fred Biletnikoff, Oakland	61	929	9
1970 – Dick Gordon, Chicago	71	1026	13
1969 – Dan Abramowicz, New Orleans	73	1015	7
1968 – Clifton McNeil, San Francisco	71	994	7
1967 – Charley Taylor, Washington	70	990	9
1966 – Charley Taylor, Washington	72	1119	12
1965 – Dave Parks, San Francisco	80	1344	12
1964 – Johnny Morris, Chicago	93	1200	10
1963 – Bobby Joe Conrad, St. Louis	73	967	10
1962 – Bobby Mitchell, Washington	72	1384	11
1961 – Jim Phillips, Los Angeles	78	1092	5
1960 – Raymond Berry, Baltimore	74	1298	10
1959 – Raymond Berry, Baltimore	66	959	14
1958 – Raymond Berry, Baltimore	56	794	9
Pete Retzlaff, Philadelphia	56	766	2
1957 – Billy Wilson, San Francisco	52	757	6
1956 – Billy Wilson, San Francisco	60	889	5
1955 – Pete Pihos, Philadelphia	62	864	7
1954 – Pete Pihos, Philadelphia	60	872	10
Billy Wilson, San Francisco	60	830	5
1953 – Pete Pihos, Philadelphia	63	1049	10
1952 – Mac Speedie, Cleveland	62	911	5
1951 – Elroy Hirsch, Los Angeles	66	1495	17
1950 – Tom Fears, Los Angeles	84	1116	7
1949 – Tom Fears, Los Angeles	77	1013	9
1948 – Tom Fears, Los Angeles	51	698	4
1947 – Jim Keane, Chicago Bears	64	910	10
1946 – Jim Benton, Los Angeles	63	981	6
1945 – Don Hutson, Green Bay	47	834	9
1944 – Don Hutson, Green Bay	58	866	9
1943 – Don Hutson, Green Bay	47	776	11
1942 – Don Hutson, Green Bay	74	1211	17
1941 – Don Hutson, Green Bay	58	738	10
1940 – Don Looney, Philadelphia	58	707	4
1939 – Don Hutson, Green Bay	34	846	6
1938 – Gaynell Tinsley, Chicago Cardinals	41	516	1
1937 – Don Hutson, Green Bay	41	552	7
1936 – Don Hutson, Green Bay	34	526	9
1935 – Tod Goodwin, New York	26	432	4
1934 – Joe Carter, Philadelphia	16	237	4
1933 – John Kelly, Brooklyn	21	219	3
1932 – Luke Johnsos, Chicago Bears	24	321	2

All-Time Career Leader

	Years	No.	Yards	TDs
Don Maynard	15	663	11,834	88

Interceptions, Season Leaders

Year	Player	No.	Yards
1974	Emmitt Thomas, Kansas City	12	214
1973	Dick Anderson, Miami	8	163
1973	Mike Wagner, Pittsburgh	8	134
1972	Bill Bradley, Philadelphia	9	73
1971	Bill Bradley, Philadelphia	11	248
1970	Johnny Robinson, Kansas City	10	155
1969	Mel Renfro, Dallas	10	118
1968	Willie Williams, New York Giants	10	103
1967	Lem Barney, Detroit	10	232
1967	Dave Whitsell, New Orleans	10	178
1966	Larry Wilson, St. Louis	10	180
1965	Bobby Boyd, Baltimore	9	78
1964	Paul Krause, Washington	12	140
1963	Dick Lynch, New York Giants	9	251
1963	Rosie Taylor, Chicago	9	172
1962	Willie Wood, Green Bay	9	132
1961	Dick Lynch, New York Giants	9	60
1960	Dave Baker, San Francisco	10	96
1960	Jerry Norton, St. Louis	10	96
1959	Dean Derby, Pittsburgh	7	127
1959	Milt Davis, Baltimore	7	119
1959	Don Shinnick, Baltimore	7	70
1958	Jim Patton, New York Giants	11	183
1957	Milt Davis, Baltimore	10	219
1957	Jack Christiansen, Detroit	10	137
1957	Jack Butler, Pittsburgh	10	85
1956	Lindon Crow, Chicago Cardinals	11	170
1955	Will Sherman, Los Angeles	11	101
1954	Dick (Night Train) Lane, Chicago Cardinals	10	181
1953	Jack Christiansen, Detroit	12	238
1952	Dick (Night Train) Lane, Los Angeles	14	298
1951	Otto Schnellbacher, New York Giants	11	194
1950	Orban (Spec) Sanders, New York Yankees	13	199
1949	Bob Nussbaumer, Chicago Cardinals	12	157
1948	Dan Sandifer, Washington	13	258
1947	Frank Reagan, New York Giants	10	203
1947	Frank Seno, Boston Yanks	10	100
1946	Bill Dudley, Pittsburgh	10	242
1945	Roy Zimmerman, Philadelphia	7	90
1944	Howard Livingston, New York Giants	9	172
1943	Sammy Baugh, Washington	11	112
1942	Clyde (Bulldog) Turner, Chicago Bears	8	96
1941	Marshall Goldberg, Chicago Cardinals	7	54
1941	Arthur Jones, Pittsburgh	7	35
1940	Clarence (Ace) Parker, Brooklyn	6	146
1940	Kent Ryan, Detroit	6	65
1940	Don Hutson, Green Bay	6	24

All-Time Career Leader

	Years	No.	Yards
Emlen Tunnell	14	79	1282

Mel Renfro

Lem Barney

Larry Wilson

Garo Yepremian

Fred Cox

Doak Walker

Scoring, Season Leaders

	TD	PAT	FG	Points
1974— Chester Marcol, Green Bay 0		19	25	94
1973—David Ray, Los Angeles 0		40	30	130
1972—Chester Marcol, Green Bay 0		29	33	128
1971—Garo Yepremian, Miami 0		33	28	117
1970—Fred Cox, Minnesota 0		35	30	125
1969—Fred Cox, Minnesota 0		43	26	121
1968—Leroy Kelly, Cleveland 20		0	0	120
1967—Jim Bakken, St. Louis 0		36	27	117
1966—Bruce Gossett, Los Angeles 0		29	28	113
1965—Gale Sayers, Chicago 22		0	0	132
1964—Lenny Moore, Baltimore 20		0	0	120
1963—Don Chandler, New York 0		52	18	106
1962—Jim Taylor, Green Bay 19		0	0	114
1961—Paul Hornung, Green Bay 10		41	15	146
1960—Paul Hornung, Green Bay 15		41	15	176
1959—Paul Hornung, Green Bay 7		31	7	94
1958—Jim Brown, Cleveland 18		0	0	108
1957—Sam Baker, Washington 1		29	14	77
Lou Groza, Cleveland 0		32	15	77
1956—Bobby Layne, Detroit 5		33	12	99
1955—Doak Walker, Detroit 7		27	9	96
1954—Bobby Walston, Philadelphia 11		36	4	114
1953—Gordy Soltau, San Francisco 6		48	10	114
1952—Gordy Soltau, San Francisco 7		34	6	94
1951—Elroy Hirsch, Los Angeles 17		0	0	102
1950—Doak Walker, Detroit 11		38	8	128
1949—Pat Harder, Chicago Cardinals 8		45	3	102
Gene Roberts, New York Giants 17		0	0	102
1948—Pat Harder, Chicago Cardinals 6		53	7	110
1947—Pat Harder, Chicago Cardinals 7		39	7	102
1946—Ted Fritsch, Green Bay 10		13	9	100
1945—Steve Van Buren, Philadelphia 18		2	0	110
1944—Don Hutson, Green Bay 9		31	0	85
1943—Don Hutson, Green Bay 12		36	3	117
1942—Don Hutson, Green Bay 17		33	1	138
1941—Don Hutson, Green Bay 12		20	1	95
1940—Don Hutson, Green Bay 7		15	0	57
1939—Andy Farkas, Washington 11		2	0	68
1938—Clarke Hinkle, Green Bay 7		7	3	58
1937—Jack Manders, Chicago Bears 5		15	8	69
1936—Earl (Dutch) Clark, Detroit 7		19	4	73
1935—Earl (Dutch) Clark, Detroit 6		16	1	55
1934—Jack Manders, Chicago Bears 3		31	10	79
1933—Ken Strong, New York Giants 6		13	5	64
Glenn Presnell, Portsmouth 6		10	6	64
1932—Earl (Dutch) Clark, Portsmouth 4		6	3	39

All-Time Career Leader

	Years	TDs	PAT	FG	Points
George Blanda 25	25	9	899	322	1,919